HUMAN RIGHTS, CULTURE AND CONTEXT

Anthropology, Culture and Society

Series Editors:
Dr Richard A. Wilson, University of Sussex
Professor Thomas Hylland Eriksen, University of Oslo

Women of a Lesser Cost:
Female Labour, Foreign Exchange and Philippine Development
SYLVIA CHANT AND CATHY McILWAINE

Ethnicity and Nationalism:
Anthropological Perspectives
THOMAS HYLLAND ERIKSEN

Small Places, Large Issues:
An Introduction to Social and Cultural Anthropology
THOMAS HYLLAND ERIKSEN

Anthropology, Development and the Post-modern Challenge
KATY GARDNER AND DAVID LEWIS

Power and its Disguises:
Anthropological Perspectives on Power
JOHN GLEDHILL

Anthropological Perspectives on Kinship
LADISLAV HOLY

Anthropology of the Self:
The Individual in Cultural Perspective
BRIAN MORRIS

New Directions in Economic Anthropology
SUSANA NAROTZKY

HUMAN RIGHTS, CULTURE AND CONTEXT

Anthropological Perspectives

EDITED BY RICHARD A. WILSON

Pluto Press

LONDON • STERLING, VIRGINIA

First published 1997 by Pluto Press
345 Archway Road, London N6 5AA
and 22883 Quicksilver Drive, Sterling, VA 20166-2012, USA

www.plutobooks.com

British Library Cataloguing in Publication Data
A catalogue record for this book is available from the British
Library

Library of Congress Cataloging in Publication Data
Applied for

ISBN   0 7453 1143 1 hardback
ISBN   0 7453 1142 3 paperback

Printed on demand by Lightning Source

CONTENTS

ACKNOWLEDGEMENTS

The formulation of this volume has benefited from ongoing conversations with Steve Baranyi, Stan Cohen, Patrick Costello, Marie-Bénédicte Dembour, Saul Dubow, Carolyn Hamilton, Shirley Brice Heath, Elsa van Huyssteen, Helene Kvale, Joanne Moores, Fiona Ross, Colin Samson and Jock Stirrat. Thanks especially to Michael Freeman, Bryan S. Turner and Tony Woodiwiss for their encouragement early on in this project. I would also like to thank the participants of seminars at the Human Rights Centre at the University of Essex, the social anthropology department at the University of Sussex, the Centre for Ethnic Studies, University of Warwick, and the departments of social anthropology and sociology at the University of the Witwatersrand.

At Pluto Press, thanks are due to Anne Beech and Roger van Zwanenberg for their support and encouragement.

CONTRIBUTORS

Talal Asad is Professor in Anthropology at Johns Hopkins University, having been at the Graduate Faculty of the New School for Social Research for the previous seven years. He has also taught in Britain, where he received his university education, and in the Middle East, where he was born. He is interested in post-Enlightenment conceptions of religion and secularism, and their applications to non-Western societies. He edited *Anthropology and the Colonial Encounter* (Ithaca Press, 1973) and his most recent book is entitled *Genealogies of Religion: Discipline and Reasons of Power in Christianity and Islam* (Johns Hopkins University Press, 1993).

Thomas Hylland Eriksen is Professor of the Department and Museum of Anthropology, Oslo University. He has undertaken field research in Mauritius (1986 and 1991–92) and Trinidad (1989) in the areas of social identity, ethnicity, nationalism, creolisation, cultural change and social theory. His publications include numerous books and articles in Norwegian and English, including *Ethnicity and Nationalism* (1993), *Small Places, Large Issues* (1995), *Det nye fiendebildet* (The New Image of the Enemy, 1995) and *Kampen om fortiden* (The Struggle Over the Past, 1996). He is co-editor of the Pluto Press Anthropology, Culture and Society series.

John Gledhill is Professor in Anthropology at the University of Manchester. He is the author of two monographs on Mexico, *Casi Nada: A Study of Agrarian Reform in the Homeland of Cardenismo* (University of Texas Press, 1991) and *Neoliberalism, Transnationalization and Rural Poverty: A Case Study of Michoacán, Mexico* (Westview Press, 1995). He has also published a more general book on political anthropology, *Power and Its Disguises: Anthropological Perspectives on Power* (Pluto Press, 1994) and is a Managing Editor of the journal *Critique of Anthropology*.

Sally Engle Merry is Professor of Anthropology and the Class of '49 Professor in Ethics at Wellesley College. She is the author of *Urban*

Danger: Life in a Neighborhood of Strangers (Temple, 1981), *Getting Justice and Getting Even: Legal Consciousness among Working-Class Americans* (University of Chicago Press, 1990), and co-editor of *The Possibility of Popular Justice: A Case Study of American Community Justice* (University of Michigan Press, 1993) with Neal Milner. She has published numerous articles on legal ideology, mediation, urban ethnic relations, legal pluralism and law and colonialism. She was President of the Law and Society Association from 1993 to 1995. She is writing a book on law and the cultural transformations of family, sexuality and violence against women during the American colonisation of Hawai'i.

Jennifer Schirmer is a Fellow of the Pacific Basin Research Center of Soka University of America currently engaged in research at the Program on Human Rights Policies at the Center for Business and Government of the J.F. Kennedy School of Government at Harvard University. She is also 1996–97 Peace Fellow at the Bunting Institute at Radcliffe College.

David Stoll is an anthropologist studying the peace process in Guatemala. His research has been supported by the Fundamentalism Project, the Harry Frank Guggenheim Foundation and the Woodrow Wilson International Center for Scholars. His books include *Is Latin America Turning Protestant?* (1990), *Between Two Armies in the Ixil Towns of Guatemala* (1993) and *Rethinking Protestantism in Latin America* (1993, co-edited with Virginia Burnett).

Richard A. Wilson is Lecturer in Social Anthropology at the University of Sussex, and co-editor of the Pluto Press Anthropology, Culture and Society series. He is the author of *Maya Resurgence in Guatemala: Q'eqchi' Experiences* (University of Oklahoma, 1995) and co-edited *Low Intensity Democracy: Political Power in the New World Order* (Pluto Press, 1993) with Barry Gills and Joel Rocamora. He has published numerous articles on political violence, ethnicity and civil war in Guatemala, and more recently on human rights, nation-building and constitutional reform in South Africa. He is presently working on an Economic and Social Research Council (UK)-funded project titled 'Legal Strategies and Normative Orders: Human Rights in the New South Africa'.

1 HUMAN RIGHTS, CULTURE AND CONTEXT: AN INTRODUCTION

Richard A. Wilson

The past few decades have witnessed the inexorable rise of the application of international human rights law as well as the extension of a wider public discourse on human rights, to the point where human rights could be seen as one of the most globalised political values of our times. The language of liberal human rights has moved in to fill the vacuum left by the demise of grand political narratives in the aftermath of the Cold War. Notwithstanding disputes over their conceptualisation and application, human rights are among the few utopian ideals left, and there is still a remarkable degree of consensus by governments on the principle at least that certain rights be protected under international law.

Anthropology has just begun to respond to this expansive transnational legal discourse. In 1988, the edited volume *Human Rights and Anthropology* (Downing and Kushner), demonstrated the overlap between anthropology and indigenous rights advocacy, and in 1994, the American Anthropological Association (AAA) convened on the theme of human rights. Increasingly, anthropologists began to ponder the relationship between anthropological debates about culture, identity and state violence and the activities of human rights organisations. However, the numbers of anthropologists actively researching transnational legal processes is relatively small, and of these the number specialising in human rights law is even fewer.[1]

Historically, anthropological perspectives on transnational processes have been hampered by two related factors: (1) a methodological emphasis on localism; and (2) a theoretical concern with 'culture'. Anthropology's prolonged love affair with local culture has meant that at various junctures, anthropologists have positioned themselves in critical opposition to universal values and transnational processes such as 'human rights'. The canonical post-Second World War

1

statement shaping the response of a generation was made by Melville Herskovits, the author of the AAA executive board's statement on human rights in 1947. The relativism of Herskovits and others in the Boasian tradition shone through their critique of what they perceived as the ethnocentric extension of absolutist Western values. Herskovits exhorted the emergent world order to respect cultural differences, and raised 'culture' to the level of a supreme ethical value. In this position, of radical cultural relativism, as Jack Donnelly (1989: 109) comments, 'culture is the sole source of the validity of a moral right or rule'. Particular cultural values, so it follows, should under no conditions be supplanted by universal moral values, for example, conceptions of human rights. In a key paragraph, the AAA statement read (1947: 543):

Even where political systems exist that deny citizens the right of participation in their government, or seek to conquer weaker peoples, *underlying cultural values* may be called on to bring the peoples of such states to a realization of the consequences of the acts of their governments, and thus enforce a brake upon discrimination and conquest. (my emphasis)

In his reference to 'underlying cultural values', Herskovits hoped to play anthropology's trump card in order to reassert the continued usefulness of the discipline. In so doing, he defined the role of anthropologists as advocates of indigenous peoples who would defend them from attempts by international agencies such as the UN to globalise a set of 'Western' moral values. He also sought to enshrine the unique capacity of the anthropologist to construct a holistic version of each society's inner cultural logic. Herskovits's position has been subjected to a number of critiques (Barnett 1948; Steward 1948; Washburn 1987), but its most serious flaw lies in a rather hopeful belief in the essential moral rectitude contained within 'culture'. Herskovits was saying that even if the political system is abusive, cultural values (as opposed to say, political values?) could be invoked to restore a balanced social order. Such rose-tinted optimism was particularly inappropriate so soon after the Second World War and the Nazi Holocaust, and left unexplained why 'underlying cultural values' in Germany during the Third Reich did not check Nazi hegemony. Clearly Herskovits was not willing to consider the possibility that certain values might actively promote cruel and inhumane practices, or, more specifically with regard to the constellation of 'cultural values' around anti-semitism in modern Europe, mass genocide.

Because of anthropologists' exalting of culture, and enduring fascination with the more unfamiliar and seemingly bizarre characteristics of the non-Western other (encountered in symbolism, ritual

and forms of representation generally), some human rights theorists have lambasted anthropology as the last bastion of cultural absolutism, and anthropologists as purveyors of exotica. For instance, Rhoda Howard (1993: 326–7) rhetorically charges that: 'Anthropological conclusions both about the substance of cultural values and about the integrative, unchanging nature of cultural norms are drawn from highly questionable data that reflect both the arrogance and the romanticism of Western observers.' This is all part of Howard's project to reject the position of 'romantic communitarianism' (shared by a rogue's gallery of anthropologists, communists and fascists) and reassert a liberal individualistic conception of human rights. Howard over-homogenises the variety of perspectives within anthropology and she operates with an anachronistic vision of how anthropologists deal with 'tradition'. Yet some aspects of her critique are warranted, in that more than any other discipline, anthropology has contributed to culturalist, constructivist and communitarian conceptions of society (though only marginally more so than Howard's own intellectual bolt-hole, sociology).

At present, discussions of the cross-cultural applicability of human rights still revolve around the universalism/relativism debate and the importance of culture (see Pannikar 1992; Renteln 1988, 1990; Washburn 1987). Two main issues here are: first, what concept of human ontology is to be used, and what rights naturally extend from that view of human nature; and, second, what significance should be given to the notion of 'culture' in the construction of a normative moral order, and to what degree does global diversity in systems of justice undermine any basis for the universality of human rights. The conundrum facing those seeking to integrate the variety of legal and normative codes, and especially those which appear to violate international human rights law, was succinctly summed up in a recent British newspaper headline which read 'Cruelty or Culture?'[2]

This volume seeks to go beyond the dualism of universalism/relativism by considering recent theoretical insights into 'culture', and making some empirical observations regarding the ongoing globalisation of human rights. Both universalism and relativism have something to recommend themselves to the ethnographer; universalism makes comparison possible, and yet relativism grants precedence to immediate contexts and engenders a sensitivity to diversity. Yet as with most absolutist dualisms, the universalist/relativist polarity is too totalising in its conceptualisation. The intellectual efforts of those seeking to develop a framework for understanding the social life of rights would be better directed not towards foreclosing their ontological status, but instead by exploring

their meaning and use. What is needed are more detailed studies of human rights according to the actions and intentions of social actors, within wider historical constraints of institutionalised power.

The Cultural Relativist Critique of Human Rights

The inability of philosophers and social and legal theorists to agree on the moral foundations of human rights is perhaps the most immediate factor in the relativists' favour. This fact greatly strengthens the hand of moral pluralists such as Steven Lukes (1991) who has challenged the efforts of writers such as Habermas, Kant and Rawls to establish an 'Archimedean point' which would provide universal rational foundations for generalisable norms and categories of justice. This has brought us to a situation where an open contempt for conceptions of human rights abounds within political and legal theory; from Bentham's famous statement that the idea of natural rights is 'nonsense upon stilts', to MacIntyre's (1981: 67) comment that: 'the truth is plain: there are no such rights and belief in them is one with belief in witches and unicorns'. In this introduction, I cannot do justice to the complexity of these debates within political philosophy, only examine the implications of some of them for an anthropological or sociological inquiry into human rights.

All approaches broadly within the cultural relativist tradition point towards the historically and culturally bounded nature of human rights discourses, and therefore to their socially constructed nature.[3] According to relativists, human rights are inseparable from the mentality of the Enlightenment, and as presently construed are the product of a particular society at a particular time: Europe in the aftermath of the Second World War. The *Universal Declaration of Human Rights* made in 1948 is therefore universal only in pretension, not in practice, since it is a charter of an idealist European political philosophy.

Many forms of relativism begin with a critique of universalists' conceptions of 'human nature'. Within the rationalist tradition, human rights presuppose a stable (and usually Hobbesian) conception of human nature which includes a unified subject with a knowable essence and basic needs. Having established the nature of a universal human ontology, objectivity can be claimed for value judgements about political, economic and legal arrangements. The construction of 'human nature' was put to direct political usage by those such as John Locke and Immanuel Kant to uphold their versions of the social contract and therefore to limit the absolute rights of monarchs.

A more recent and influential conception of human nature/rights is found in the work of the sociologist Bryan S. Turner (1993), which incorporates elements of relativism, with the aim of creating a more flexible and globally applicable conception of human rights. Turner rejects the rationalist and individualist elements in Kant's philosophy, since they do not allow for a moral community to be built·upon sympathy and emotive criteria. Turner argues that a conception of human ontology is a precondition for any notion of human rights and he invokes the 'philosophical anthropology'[4] of Arnold Gehlen and Helmut Plessner. According to this view, humans are characterised by their 'world-openness' and relative lack of instincts. In contrast to the Hobbesian version of history, social institutions are needed because humans are physically and ontologically frail and 'unfinished', not because they are aggressive and bent on domination. Social institutions and social arrangements are precarious, so social relations are characterised by risk and instability. Whereas human happiness is noted for its variety, human misery is relatively uniform, leading to a notion of human frailty as the universal feature of human existence.

For most anthropologists, the category of human nature is one of the more offensive ways of imposing the prejudices of 'Western culture'. In the AAA statement, much of Herskovits's argument rested on the principle that the individual's personality is shaped by his/her culture. The first proposition which Herskovits (AAA 1947: 541) deemed essential in any 'Bill of Human Rights' stated, 'The individual realizes his personality through his culture, hence respect for individual differences entails a respect for cultural differences.' Here, 'culture' and 'cultural differences' are deployed to deconstruct the universal rational individual of classical political economy upon which human rights discourses depend.

As part of a general anti-essentialism, relativists reject the notion of a unified subject with a knowable essence, whether it be frail or domineering.[5] There can be no essential characteristics of human nature or human rights, which exist outside of discourse, history, context or agency. A relativist critique of Bryan Turner's formulation of a 'frail' human nature would say that Turner is advancing an inherently paradoxical claim – that it is our lack of essence which is universally human. The concept of frailty may be open to a certain degree of relativisation since it constructs human nature in the weakest possible terms without abandoning the idea altogether, but it ultimately does not escape from problems which arise from attempts to classify through demarcated definitional boundaries based upon particular shared (manifest or latent) commonalities.

Existence must precede essence[6] for relativism to be possible, and the aspect of existence which most challenges any universal essence is 'culture'. If 'human nature' presupposes a conception of 'human being', then there is an immediate difficulty of translation in that some cultures may not have such a concept at all. American Indian languages such as those of the Navajo and Hopi construct humanness as belonging solely to those within the boundaries of the community, whose collective name means 'the people'. Outsiders are perceived to be non-human to a certain degree, particularly in origin myths. Even if there is a conception of 'human being' within a language and culture, universal notions of rights or duties may not be necessarily derived from it. Dignity may not be universally human at all, but may be distributed unevenly by a system of social stratification, as in the Hindu caste system.

Anthropological critiques of human nature, being based on the socially constructed nature of the 'person', inherently imply a rejection of the category 'individual' which is fundamental to human rights law.[7] Relativists point out that as it is presently constituted, international human rights law is fundamentally grounded in individual rights, and therefore remains unable to flexibly respond to a global diversity of legal systems. The UN is still uncomfortable with less individualist conceptions of rights in its application of human rights procedures. It operates with what Richard Falk (1992: 48) calls a 'normative blindness towards indigenous peoples', who may claim communal rights to land ownership or political self determination.

The critique of rights as an ideology of Western individualism and liberalism has a long pedigree. Marx (1977) noted long ago that eighteenth-century European notions of rights are predicated to a large degree on bourgeois categories of possessive individualism and the free market. According to some relativists, moral status belongs more to collective entities (such as a 'Culture' or 'Community') than to individuals. In their conception and application, then, human rights are an ethnocentric extension of European concepts of individualistic rights to societies with more communalistic political traditions. The implication here parallels that of the AAA statement on human rights: that outsiders should not interfere in moral issues which are internal to another culture, since this would usually lead to the arbitrary silencing of collectivist narratives by 'Western' individualist ones.

In arguing for an empirical basis for human rights, Alison Dundes Renteln (1985, 1988, 1990), accepts cultural relativist descriptions of the world as made up of different societies with divergent moral value

systems, but rejects the prescription of tolerance which conventionally results from such portrayals. This seemingly contradictory argument merits close attention.

Renteln (1988: 67) argues that 'Relativism is compatible with cross-cultural universals' and she has elaborated an approach which grounds its universalism empirically (Renteln 1990). Unlike the political philosophers entering into this debate, her theoretical discussion of the universalism/relativism issue is combined with a cross-cultural survey of moral values. She claims that human rights as such do not exist empirically, and that there is remarkable diversity in notions of justice and morality. For instance, neither freedom of speech nor freedom of religious practice seem particularly entrenched, and the death penalty is enforced in different contexts for an enormous range of different offences – from adultery to witchcraft to blasphemy. Renteln concludes that there is only one ubiquitous moral principle and that is, 'retribution tied to proportionality' – that the punishment is proportional to the gravity of the crime. One expression of this principle is *lex talionis*, or in the Old Testament, 'an eye for an eye, etc.'. Renteln's ultimate objective is to build human rights standards which have a legitimacy across the globe. These values would be grounded not in Western theories of natural rights, but on the empirically proven universality of a moral principle of reciprocal vengeance.

Renteln believes that the principle of negative reciprocity limits violence and encourages stability, but anyone remotely familiar with the history of over 25 years of revenge killings in Northern Ireland is aware that *lex talionis* can incite, escalate and perpetuate violence as much as restrain it. Furthermore, any logical move from prevalence to moral rightness is obviously problematic, and Renteln makes a naïve conflation of what is common and what is morally justifiable.[8] Renteln (1990) advocates ethnography, but her own study indulges in Frazerian sweeps of the globe, effacing the attitudes, perceptions and practices invoked in local struggles over rights. In her urge to present the global evidence for a single value which supposedly underpins human rights standards, Renteln elides the richness of ethnographic accounts. Perhaps more importantly, Renteln is caught on the horns of her own contradictory stance: that is, she is a relativist who asserts the ethnocentric nature of any value judgements, yet she wants to build a universal conception of human rights through an empirical survey of local forms of justice. Put bluntly, we could say that if there is enough local evidence to build a universalistic foundation for human rights, then there must be enough evidence to cause subsidence in claims of moral incommensurability.

The Limitations of Cultural Relativism

Relativism does have merits when thinking about the possible methods of a social inquiry into rights. For ethnographers of human rights, the most valuable critique of universalist perspectives is that they provide little or no framework for studying rights 'on the ground'. In defending conceptions of human nature, and arguing that universal rights must be designated through an overarching super-perspective, rationalist social philosophy and natural law lift the discussion of rights out of any particular context and raise it to the level of the categorical imperative. Practical reason is swept away by a formalistic analysis of a priori synthetic principles, and human actions are continually related to absolute maxims and 'natural' law. In particular, the influence of the neo-Kantian tradition in human rights theory has led to too great an emphasis on securing a priori foundations and continues to obstruct empirical attempts to understand rights.

Despite its methodological insights, cultural relativism suffers from a number of delusions and limitations. As many have noted, it undermines its own truth claims and it implies moral nihilism (Gellner 1982; Jarvie 1984). That is, relativism generates a meta-narrative with totalising claims at the same time as generating a self-undermining critique of the very possibility of meta-narratives and totalising claims.

Accusations of moral nihilism are perhaps easier for relativists to defend; Richard Rorty (1993) makes an impassioned plea for the continued value of doing human rights, yet he justifies such actions in the contingent present rather than by appealing to a-temporal universals. Yet one can only construct a very weak defence of actions by relying on emotions and courage alone, and eschewing all recourse to rational forms of argumentation. Rights without a meta-narrative are like a car without seat-belts; on hitting the first moral bump with ontological implications, the passengers' safety is jeopardised. Ironically, the emphasis on conventions by social constructionists such as Rorty means that their position ends up sharing many attributes with utilitarianism and legal positivism insofar as they too are founded upon convention and precedent, the open recognition of which would surely horrify most postmodernists.[9]

Yet the most serious contingent 'reality' is that relativism itself is an integral part of the meta-narrative of those governments who actively oppose the applications of international human rights to their polities. The tolerance of relativism here has a directly conservative political implication – the maintenance of highly

inegalitarian and repressive political systems. An undeniable truth is that many governments around the world continue to carry out abominable acts against 'their' populations, and relativism is the most useful available ideology which facilitates international acquiescence in state repression.

Cultural relativism provides an inaccurate set of descriptions of moral pluralism since it wields a misguided conception of culture. Relativist rights theorists such as Ronald Dworkin (1977) seem quite unaware of the recent discussions of 'culture' in the social sciences and humanities which have sought to de-reify this concept and so deprive it of its ontological security. Instead, the various relativisms totalise and reify 'culture', constructing it as internally uniform and hermetically bounded. 'Culture' is seen as shared and normative, not as cross-cut by social differences (age, caste, gender, etc.), or characterised as contested, fragmented, contextualised and emergent. Culture is referred to as an entity, not as a process; as a noun, not a verb.[10] For their doctrine to be coherent, cultural relativists seem to hold a nineteenth-century notion of culture as discrete and homogeneous, as the product of isolation, and as the basis of all difference and similarity between human beings. Their relativism is predicated upon bounded conceptions of linguistic and cultural systems, but it falls apart in contexts of hybridity, creolisation, intermixture and the overlapping of political traditions.

Just as earlier Boasian relativisms ignored global realities such as colonialism, attempts at undermining human rights by reference to 'culture' have ignored transnational juridical processes. Despite the charges of some governments of 'cultural imperialism' in the application of international law, human rights doctrine has been adopted by many people to whom it was once foreign. For instance, Mayan human rights organisations in Guatemala reproduce international human rights law faithfully, and only invoke *'la cultura'* to reinforce universal conceptions of needs.[11] Groups who now refer to themselves as 'indigenous peoples' are aware of human rights discourses, if only because they have experienced state violence and marginalisation from national political processes. Indigenous peoples in contexts as different as Panama, Canada and South Africa are engaging in close negotiations with their governments over their constitutional claims for linguistic and territorial rights and political sovereignty. It is simply not possible now to live anywhere without regular encounters with agents or institutions of the nation-state, as it was during the heyday of anthropological functionalism and cultural relativism in the early to mid-twentieth century.

A lack of participation in state institutions and an awareness of a lowly status position in national society is now as indicative of 'indigenous' status as it was of 'peasant' status when Wolf defined it in the 1950s. This is paralleled by an awareness on the part of many indigenous peoples of international institutions and of their greater possibilities for participation in them compared to national institutions. Increasingly, indigenous peoples actively seek representation at international fora, and attend such bodies with legal advisers in tow. Indeed, the whole concept of 'indigenous peoples' is now inseparable from human rights discourses which represent them as victims of abusive governments. It is no coincidence that the activities around the UN Year of Indigenous Peoples in 1993 came under the UN's human rights budget line, just as it is no coincidence that they represented less than 1 per cent of that budget.[12]

The Globalisation of Human Rights

Despite the more offensive demonstrations of ethnocentrism in the human rights field, certain aspects of the universalists' case need to be considered by anthropologists, at least as future possibilities. As was argued in the rationality debates of the 1960s and 1970s (see Gellner 1982), cultural relativists' arguments are increasingly undermined by the globalisation of cultural, economic and political processes and the increasingly convincing judgement that we are moving into a 'post- cultural' world. Those such as Fredrik Barth (1992) propose that the holistic model of society was always an illusion of nineteenth-century nationalism and Durkheimian sociology. The 'fantasy' that humanity is divided into nation-states with clear frontiers of language and culture seems finally to be giving way to notions of disorder and openness.

Due to communications and media, tourism, financial capital, consumer images, transport technologies, migration and so on, the world's societies are increasingly integrated into global networks (see Featherstone 1990; Hannerz 1992). Human rights organisations form one such network and Weissbrodt (1988: 1) is only mildly guilty of hyperbole when he writes that: 'International human rights is the world's first universal ideology.'[13] Some of the seemingly utopian speculations of eighteenth-century human rights theorists are now realised in the values and practices of human rights institutions. For instance, in 1795 (shortly before he became benignly senile), Immanuel Kant (1983: 119) wrote 'To Perpetual Peace: A Philosophical Sketch' in which he argued that:

Because a [narrower or wider] community widely prevails among the Earth's peoples, a transgression of rights in *one* place in the world is felt *everywhere*; consequently, the idea of cosmopolitan right is not fantastic or exaggerated, but rather an amendment to the unwritten code of national and international rights, necessary to the public rights of men in general. Only such an amendment allows us to flatter ourselves with the thought that we are making continual progress towards perpetual peace. (emphasis in original)

Traces of Kant's brand of universalism still colour the doctrines of human rights institutions,[14] the difference being that with developments in communications technology, it is a practical possibility for a transgression in one place to be felt nearly everywhere immediately. For instance, the development of the World Wide Web has meant that the networked dissemination of human rights information (and all other types) is more rapid and extensive than before. One recent demonstration of the 'human rights' potential of the Internet can be seen during the events in Chiapas in southern Mexico since January 1993. Information on each stage of the EZLN rebellion has been freely available over the Internet. During a one-week period in early 1995, Latin American Internet lists[15] received literally dozens of messages per day denouncing human rights abuses against Maya communities by the Mexican military. The communiqués of rebel leader 'Sub-Commandante Marcos' – reportedly written on his laptop PC linked to the Internet – were regularly posted on World Wide Web bulletin boards at the same time as they appeared in other media forms. In the same way that Vietnam was the first 'television war', Chiapas is the first 'cyberspace insurrection'. The nature of each confrontation has been altered according to their mode of representation to a global audience.

Due to the ascent of international and human rights law in the late twentieth century, nearly all the world's peoples live in a situation which Clifford Geertz (1983: 220) has described as a 'confusion of legal tongues'. For legal anthropologists, all societies are characterised by 'legal pluralism' – being subject to overlapping local, national and transnational legal codes. These normative orders are, as characterised by Sally Engle Merry (1992: 358), 'mutually constitutive' and hierarchised according to shifting power inequalities. The recognition of legal pluralism undermines any over-exoticising conceptions of 'traditional law' and one of the most significant findings of legal anthropology was that 'customary law' in colonial societies was not the legacy of a pre-colonial past, but the construction of an ongoing colonial context.

However, globalisation does not mean the same as westernisation, modernisation or standardisation. As Ulf Hannerz (1992) has argued,

we should not adopt a diffusionist view of globalisation since it does not just imply a process of homogenisation and integration, but involves a proliferation of diversity as well. A diversity of normative orders may still prevail, and may even be exacerbated by global processes, but they are no longer predicated upon isolation. Rather, a sense of difference is constructed out of relatedness, opposition and an awareness of plurality. Nor are moral differences as reliant on enclosed systems as before, but are more fragmented and susceptible to transnational flows of moral values, particularly through world religions. Just because a cultural form is global, it does not mean that everyone relates to it in the same way – its interpretation depends on local and individual value distinctions.

The universality of human rights (or otherwise) thus becomes a question of context, necessitating a situational analysis. It is possible to have contextualisation without relativisation, since one can keep open the possibility, and in the dying embers of the twentieth century, the likelihood, that contexts are interlinked through a variety of processes; from movements of financial capital, to global political discourses (neo-liberalism, human rights, etc.), to transnational legal practices such as international law, to interconnections of meaning and webs of significance which span huge distances and generate long-distance identities and intersubjectivities (for example, Indian 'Bollywood' films shown in the United Kingdom, or Latino rap music from Los Angeles played in San Salvador).

Local interpretations of human rights doctrine draw on personal biographies, community histories, and on expressions of power relations between interest groups. Their relationship to formal, legal versions has to be discovered, not assumed. Just because an Asian or African human rights organisation uses the language of human rights against its government, it should not be assumed that human rights are being invoked in an orthodox and positivist legal manner. This assumption ignores the degree to which human rights doctrine does get reworked and transformed in different contexts, whether that context is 'non-Western' or not. As Ellen Messer (1993: 223) has stated: 'the key to comparative analysis … may lie less in the particular "rights" and more in the social categories which are included or excluded from their protections. Contextualization, interpretation and negotiation are critical.'

The realisation that ethnography must give up its pretensions to a bounded holism, and instead embrace partiality and transnational relationships still leaves open the question of how to conceptualise the relationship between local and global discourses. Ulf Hannerz (1992) has offered some insights through his notion of a 'global

ecumene', or 'network of networks', a mosaic ramifying in all directions, a pattern of cross-cutting or overlapping connections which are pluralised and mutable. For Hannerz, a network consists of sets of relationships with degrees of both asymmetry and reciprocity. Meaning does not emerge from culturally bounded and set values, but instead flows through global interconnections. The ethnography of a network would look at the way people are drawn into a more globalised existence and become enmeshed in transnational linkages.

Within such a perspective, the task of anthropologists is to study the interconnectedness and interaction of legal processes operating on different levels. This might include a study of how human rights law frames and shapes localised normative orders and how they in turn resist and appropriate transnational law. It could also encompass how social actors develop distinct ways of using transnational law in national courts to construct a case as a 'human rights case', as with recent cases of indigenous peoples of the Americas deploying human rights law to press their land claims, and how local courts try to resist usurpation of their powers by international courts. Thus our study of human rights becomes an exploration of how rights-based normative discourses are produced, translated and materialised in a variety of contexts.

Recent analyses of interacting legal and normative orders have become too embroiled in discussions of whether or not human rights exist in the legal codes of 'traditional societies'. Renteln (1988: 538) argues that: 'To decide whether there is a concept of human rights in African or Islamic societies will obviously require extensive research drawing on not only legal but also cultural materials' in her search for 'homeomorphic equivalents' to orthodox conceptions of human rights.[16] This seems to be going about the question the wrong way around: instead of hunting for conceptual similarities in different moral traditions, it might be better to look at how concepts are implanted in contexts from which they did not necessarily originate. The approach of Renteln and Pannikar (1992) tends towards idealism – as if one could foresee the implications for social action through a comparison of the inner logic of concepts. Similarities may exist, but we can never know how they will articulate until the concepts are brought into a concrete relationship in a particular socio-historical context.

Here I am in agreement with Jack Donnelly's (1989) critique of those who seek to find parallels to human rights notions in non-Western traditions, and particularly Islamic *sharia* and Chinese 'traditional' law. Donnelly argues that what is being compared with human rights are notions of human dignity, or limitations on the arbitrary exercise of power. These are not rights in the strict sense since they are obligations

constituted between rulers and divine authority, not between rulers and ruled. They are therefore not human rights in the sense of being special entitlements to protection which derive from the mere fact of being human. Instead of projecting the conceptions of international human rights law onto all other formulations of legal categories, it might be more fruitful to examine how this plurality is related; how differences in institutional practices become systematised, and how moral values traverse contexts. Since the search for commonalities and shared attributes tends to essentialise both international and local codes, then all we can study are the conjunctural relationships between various juridical categories and processes.

Power and Agency in the Study of Human Rights

Thus far my argument has only served to locate the space of anthropological studies of human rights, but it has yet to formulate a theoretical framework for understanding the variegated expressions of human rights themselves. The difficulty of securing any eternal foundations for either human ontology or human rights means that we can afford to be agnostic about such cabalistic musings and seek instead to build strong theories of the operation of rights. The question of 'human nature' is a metaphysical one which cannot be answered on phenomenological grounds, and therefore we should bracket it and proceed with our contingent and historical investigations.

This emphasis on empiricism and synthetic explanations does not result from an anti-theoretical stance, since it is motivated by an analytical premise: that human rights are not a product of social relations, nor even indicative of them, but immanent in them, internal to their very expression. They are a particular form of power and governance interior to the social body and are embedded in matrices of value distinctions. In this perspective, rights are positioned at the concrete conjuncture of two fields of the social: agency and power.

My emphasis on agency in the anthropological study of legal processes owes a debt to Clifford Geertz (1983) who portrays law as a system of meanings, as a form of social imagination. For Geertz, legal reasoning is a distinct manner of imagining the real, and is one of the most significant ways in which people try to make sense of their world. Legal thought is constitutive of social realities rather than merely reflective of them, and it proceeds through relating general concepts to specific cases.[17] The advantage of this approach is that it takes seriously the process of how local legal expectations translate into legal actions, and how local knowledge interacts with the

specialised discourse of law. Geertz's hermeneutics has also shaped postmodernist conceptions of law, such as that of Santos (1987) who sees law as a system of signs which distorts reality in the same way a map does – through mechanisms of scale, projection, symbolisation. The empirical focus on specific social processes furnished by an interpretative approach serves as a palliative to the heady heights of Olympian macro-theorising. Kantian universalism, to mention but one rationalist intellectual current, obscures the untidiness of everyday life by accepting the compromise of categorical certainties. An existential ethnography of rights, on the other hand, shows humans replete with feelings, engaged in their brute material existence, and enmeshed in the complexities of their social world. It gives us a basis, for example, to document how agents' experiences of political violence are translated into human rights narratives. If human rights reports strip events free of actors' consciousnesses and social contexts, then part of anthropologists' brief is to restore the richness of subjectivities, and chart the complex fields of social relations, contradictory values and the emotional accompaniment to macro-structures that human rights accounts often exclude. This framework is not just a re-rehearsal of the localism and interpretivism of traditional brands of hermeneutics, since it also traces local connections to macro, global networks. This takes us beyond the polarised approaches of universalists or relativists, and transcends the legalistic and statist approaches common in the human rights field itself.

Interpretative readings also allow us to see rights not just as instrumental mechanisms but also as expressive of tensions around ethnic, nationalist and religious identities. Human rights are involved in defining the self in opposition to the other, and this is especially clear in some postcolonial regimes' opposition to human rights, for example, the Bangkok Declaration of Asian States, 1993. Some Asian regimes, many of them practising the Islamic legal code *sharia*, are saying: 'We are Muslims/Asian *because* we deal with criminals in this way.' Pakistan's law of blasphemy has provided recent examples of internal wrangling over nationalist and religious identities, for instance in the death penalty judgement on the 11-year-old boy Salamat Masih and his uncle, Manzoor. The decree was later repealed by Pakistan's High Court, but by then Manzoor was already dead, having been murdered by orthodox Sunni Muslims. Those prosecuted under the blasphemy law brought in by General Zia have primarily been Christians, Hindus, and members of smaller Islamic sects such as Shi'as, demonstrating the particular convergence between Islamic and nationalist identities which has characterised Pakistani politics since the execution of President Bhutto.

The main weakness of Geertz's cultural hermeneutics of law is that its insights are confined to the inner logic of signs in textual interpretations of key legal categories such as the Indic notion of '*dharma*', and the Malaysian notion of '*adat*'. Geertz (1983) makes a static reading of the structure of ideas attached to legal notions, and his interpretation elides local usage and the micro-social context. Geertz mentions that legal categories have been transformed under colonialism, but he does not thoroughly investigate the particularities of how, for instance, the Islamic notion of '*haqq*' has been transformed by decolonisation. Surprisingly, local knowledge is not present in his account which reifies macro-categories of 'Islamic justice' and 'Indic law'. This line of criticism of Geertz's method is a common one (cf. Asad 1983). It does not apply to all his works,[18] but is relevant to his portrayal of law, which is highly idealistic and takes an over-systematised view of culture and the imperatives of symbolic logic. In short, there is in Geertz's work an over-emphasis on law as a form of thought rather than as a form of the exercise of power.

The focus on law as a form of power is necessary as a palliative to relativism, which, in looking for explanations of rights by reference to a putative 'cultural logic' tries to draw an inherent connection between a system of signifiers and the application of certain rights. Instead, analysis could more profitably start the other way around, to paraphrase Eric Wolf (1980), by looking at how power inhabits meaning. Human rights are above all the result of historical political struggles between individuals and interest groups. Human rights doctrine is a political principle which orders and selects from a surplus of signifiers. This is not to say that representations and meanings do not matter in struggles over rights, since the ability to successfully carry out a struggle depends upon the ideational aspect which shapes the cohesiveness, direction and internal legitimacy of project.

Law is more than a form of thought or a system of signs, as in the formulations of cultural relativism, hermeneutics and post-modernism – it is also 'a form of violence endowed with the legitimacy of formally constituted authority' (Merry 1992: 360). An exaggerated concern with ideal categories and symbols can obscure the way in which law serves as a mode of social control and of enforcing power relations, particularly those linked to property rights. Legal categories are not just a benign cognitive product of 'social imagination', but are the operational concepts for institutions which are dedicated to the practice of violence, coercion and surveillance.

Human rights are the product of the rise of modern nation-states and a chequered history of nationalism, colonialism and postcolo-

nialism. Agrarian states did not have 'human rights', as the power of the ruler was constrained in a different manner, and violence was not exercised through the kind of institutions which constitute modern states. The emergence of apparatuses and technologies of mass violence along with a highly individualistic political-economy created the conditions in which human rights became both possible and necessary. Human rights are both a product of, and a response to, the rise of the modern nation-state. Thus our inquiry must also focus on how the technologies of state violence, as well as more disciplinary bureaucratised forms of coercion and control, frame the operation of both international and local expressions of human rights.[19]

A significant component of the sociological perspective on rights offered here draws from a Weberian tradition, which shares many features with more recent non-essentialist conceptions of rights.[20] In this view, civil, political, social and human, rights are all claims for powers by competing social groups, and such rights are continually transformed as the result of struggles over political, symbolic or economic resources within a state and transnational context. There are also echoes of Marx here: in 'The Jewish Question Revisited', Marx (1977) argued that rights are not natural, God-given or innate, as posited by French revolutionaries and liberal thinkers such as Adam Smith. Instead they are the creation of political struggles between social classes and serve as an indicator of the balance of power. Despite their shared view of rights as the result of historical social conflicts, the difference between Marx and Weber was that Marx had already decided who had won the struggle (the bourgeoisie) and foreclosed further discussion. Weber kept the question of rights open, maintaining the possibility that rights might transform beyond the mere propping up of a class structure of ownership and perhaps this formulation has proved more flexible and relevant over time.

Finally, researchers should be careful not to grant too much emphasis to rights, which are but one of many aspects of the exercise of power.[21] Power, in this more Foucauldian view, is not a right, or a possession to be alienated or transferred as in the Enlightenment tradition of political-economy. Rights seek to constrain the flow of power like bottlenecks, by framing power as fixed, confinable and normative, but power leaks out, and flows around rights. Applying this to our subject, we can say that human rights therefore depend on power relations in a given context for their implantation, and accordingly alter forms of governance and the exercise of power. All this brings us back to the argument for an ethnography of human rights which situates them within a 'multiplicity of force relations' and explores

not just how rights are founded or possessed, but how they transform in each complex strategic situation.

Contextualising Human Rights

Sally Engle Merry asserts that although human rights was originally a Western legal regime framed in the hegemonic categories of Western law, a close examination of the way it is used in an indigenous rights movement in Hawai'i reveals that this movement operates at three legal levels simultaneously: global human rights law, national law and local Kanaka Maoli law. This is the process of legal globalisation and vernacularisation: the deployment and refiguring of Western law in more plural terms, both global and local. Such transnational cultural appropriations are fundamentally creative and represent forms of resistance to global homogenisation. Legal vernacularisation is part of a process of the emergence of new national identities and Merry's study details the appropriation and reinterpretation of international law by the Hawaiian Sovereignty Movement at the People's International Tribunal of Native Hawaiians in 1993. The Tribunal was constituted as a criminal trial, with the US government indicted on nine charges, and drew upon the symbolic power of law to recommend the return of Kanaka Maoli land and water rights, and political sovereignty for the Kanaka Maoli people. The Tribunal provided a legally plural framework in which to express the claims of an emergent nationalism, in that it drew together claims based upon notions of descent, culture and tradition, but also used the language of sovereignty, citizenship and constitutionalism. Merry concludes that law is a site of contestation, where the hegemony of state law may be undermined by the pluralising of law and the redefining of the legal subject.

Thomas Hylland Eriksen documents multicultural debates and practices in Mauritius in order to explore some of the contradictions between multiculturalist ideas and individual human rights. He argues that the dual origin of nationalism in Enlightenment and Romantic thought created the contradiction between the right to be equal and the right to be different, which has since been exacerbated by the increasingly polyethnic character of states. Eriksen asserts that all modern societies are now 'multicultural', that 'multicultural politics' are universalistic in their operation, and that some versions of multiculturalism are compatible with human rights whereas others are not. Multiculturalism is universalistic in that differences between people are the result of closer relationships which engender comparability and similarity; that is, that the assertion of 'cultural

uniqueness' implies a shared subscription to a global political discourse. These points are illustrated in Mauritius by reference to conflicts around discrimination on the basis of religion in private schools and the application of state and customary law to divorce among Muslims. With regard to the place of customary Muslim family law in divorce, it became apparent that the disparity in perspective between younger and female, and older male Muslims belied any multiculturalist claim that 'cultures' (as bounded and unified) have a single set of discrete 'values'. Another multiculturalist paradox exists where collectivist notions of cultural identity conflict with the notions of personal autonomy inherent in human rights. In the present ideological climate of both neo-Romanticism and hybridity, one must also have the individual right not to have an ethnic identity. Eriksen cites the example of Mauritian socialist politicians who refused to register their ethnic identity (which entrenches parliamentary representation along ethnic lines) with the result that a white Mauritian of foreign birth was registered as a Hindu on the election rolls. For multiculturalism to coexist with individual human rights, Eriksen asserts that it must include a 'dialogic principle' in political communication, as well as being enmeshed in political and economic commonalities and shared meanings.

John Gledhill argues that socio-economic rights must be contextualised with reference to the forms of regulation and capitalist property relations in which liberal political institutions are embedded. Through an examination of the liberal writings of Locke, Mill and Hayek, Gledhill charts the rise of discourses of possessive individualism and the emergence of natural law principles and rights-based states, where individual rights transcend (and pre-date) society. Gledhill moves on to consider the assertions of John Rawls that political liberalism must embrace the 'difference principle' for an authentic pluralism to emerge. Gledhill's critique of Rawls operates on many levels; including the degree to which liberalism (especially in the post-welfare US) can create a consensus among a section of the body politic for the withdrawal of the state's responsibility to protect basic rights, and how disputes over rights may involve collective as well as individual actors. Gledhill contextualises this discussion in the negotiations between the Mexican government and the Zapatista Army of National Liberation (EZLN). The indigenous rights politics which informs EZLN doctrine calls for the creation of a 'multicultural society', the recognition of collective rights (including the management of mineral and forest resources) and political autonomy. Indigenous rights movements present a different vision of 'conceptions of the common good' and result in a clash between individualistic and non-

individualistic premises for rights, society and liberty. Gledhill argues against the attribution of distinctive rights on the basis of an 'indigenous identity' by indicating that both victimhood status and 'culture' are fixed when granted a legal status, and on the grounds that neo-liberal states grant space to 'identity politics' in order to regulate and normalise dissent. At the same time, indigenous politics in Mexico and elsewhere does significantly contest neo-liberalism and 'disciplinary-bureaucratic regimes' by seeking non-individualistic discourses of entitlement predicated upon a moral economy.

Talal Asad discusses modern conceptions of cruelty and torture in order to interrogate the ways in which the *Universal Declaration of Human Rights* encompasses a variety of different forms of behaviour such as the deployment of pain in religious practices and sadomasochism. The history of the concept of 'torture' is not only a history of the prohibition on certain cruel practices, but also constitutes a narrative about modern secularised formulations of humanness. The reference to 'cruel, inhuman or degrading treatment or punishment' in Article 5 of the Declaration is presently used to make universal moral and legal judgements about what constitutes pain and suffering. Attempts to eliminate pain and suffering stand in a contradictory relationship to other cherished values such as individual autonomy and the duties of the state. Since it is used to measure qualitatively different practices, the category of 'torture' within Western modernist discourse emerges as an unstable category. Asad is clear to point out that his scepticism is not towards the existence of cruelty, but towards the universalistic discourses within which it is couched. Asad charts the historical rise of a cross-cultural discourse on torture, beginning with Enlightenment reformers such as Beccaria, Voltaire and Bentham, and moving on to nineteenth-century debates about the replacing of painful punishment with legal incarceration. Within the context of colonialism, discourses upon torture became inextricably linked to a 'civilising' project and the lifting up of the non-European to the status of 'fully human'. Asad moves on to consider the contradictions when cross-cultural categories of 'pain' encounter consensual practices where people subject themselves to pain; either for purposes of pleasure/pain as in sadomasochism, or religious redemption and piety in the annual event of Shi'a Muslim self-flagellation at Muharram. Asad calls for more accounts of how cruelty is experienced in order that practices are not always and immediately characterised as a violation of rights, and so that we might create a fuller picture of the moral struggles taking place within a globalised language of rights.

Richard Wilson examines the genre of human rights reporting by reference to two cases of murder in Guatemala, those of the

anthropologist Myrna Mack Chang and the local politician Waldemar
Caal Rossi. Human rights reporting operates with a particular set of
legal criteria of truth, facticity and evidence, as well as with implicit
assumptions about the distinction between criminal and state violence,
and about the type of victim who is likely to be subjected to a human
rights violation. Specific events are codified according to a universal
template and represented within a realist and legalistic language. This
objectivist language and legal case method has a number of
implications. Local discussions around the murder of the political
leader Waldemar Rossi demonstrate how existing forms of human
rights reporting may fail to capture the multiplicity of narratives on
political violence, and therefore engage in a process of decontextualisation. Human rights accounts impose meaning and coherence
upon chaotic and indeterminate events in order to create discrete units
of information which are capable of being distributed and consumed
globally. The reporting of the murder of the anthropologist Myrna
Mack demonstrates the ways in which reports exclude subjectivity
– of authors, of victims and their surrounding social circumstances
– in order to cultivate an aura of authority, neutrality and legitimacy.
Wilson concludes by arguing for a greater variety of forms of writing
within human rights reporting, as well as reflecting upon how social
science forms of writing can be complementary or contradictory to
human rights accounts.

Jennifer Schirmer examines the operation and dissolution of the
Special Tribunals in Guatemala during 1982–83, which were
established by General Ríos Montt who had come to power through
a coup in March 1982. The *Tribunales de Fuero Especial* were special
courts which combined elements of emergency counter-insurgency
measures with more conventional elements of the country's legal
code. They operated in secret and were run by executive appointee
judges who had the power to impose the death penalty (leading to
the execution of 16 men by firing squad). Suspects who appeared before
the Tribunals were deprived of any semblance of meaningful legal
representation and due process, and a number had been 'disappeared'
for months on end and tortured. The Tribunals converted suspects
into subversive guerrillas, publicly pronounced guilty by army
ministers even before their 'trials'. The international human rights
community, including the Inter-American Court of Human Rights,
campaigned vigorously, and in the end successfully for the abolition
of the Tribunals. Yet for many local human rights lawyers, this
represented a further deterioration of the rule of law in the country.
After the disbanding of the Special Tribunals, 112 prisoners were extra-
judicially executed by the army on their release. Further, the transfer

of 400 sentences to the Supreme Court intermingled the traditional rule of law with the kinds of clandestine procedures which had limited the right to due process in the Tribunals. One Guatemalan lawyer stated that such co-mingling created 'legal lagoons' where legal practitioners were not sure which legal code (traditional or counter-insurgency) was operating. To the international community, the demands for the end of certain practices seemed to have been met, but instead, Tribunal practices which undermined the rule of law had just been instituted within the formal legal system. Schirmer considers wider questions of how the formulaic application of universal principles without a sense of the context of the operation of law may actually obstruct the development of 'sustainable rights'. Human rights strategies would be better informed by an analysis of contingent, historical forms of regulation and the actions and intentions of local actors, rather than by liberal ideals of justice and rights formulated in an a-temporal vacuum.

David Stoll considers the role of foreign human rights activists, or *internacionalistas*, in two local land disputes in the Ixil area of Guatemala. Internationalists arrived in Guatemala in some numbers in the early 1990s and directly confronted army hegemony so as to open up the space for human rights, by publicising human rights cases, exhuming clandestine cemeteries and acting as 'human shields' to protect refugees returning from Mexico to their communities. Yet internationalists also encountered long-standing and newly created peasant tensions, particularly those involving competition over land. The internationalists' assumptions that social conflicts are reducible to victim/victimiser dichotomies and the oppositional dualism of the army vs. 'the people' has had serious implications for how they insert themselves into local disputes. In the Ixil-speaking municipality of Chajul, internal refugees are claiming ownership of the fertile lands to which they fled during the counter-insurgency sweeps of the 1980s. Organised into the Communities of the Population in Resistance (CPRs), the refugees have received considerable support from foreign human rights activists, who have privileged CPR claims over those of other Ixils from Chajul, who farmed the area before the war and now want to return. A separate dispute at Los Cimientos between Ixils from Chajul and K'iche colonists goes back to the early 1900s, when errors by land surveyors led to a contradiction between customary/municipal and national definitions of land boundaries. As the war abated in the late 1980s, the dispute flared anew, with the army backing the Ixils of Chajul and the K'iche's garnering support from the human rights movement. Eventually, foreign activists helped the K'iche's reoccupy the land and take the dispute to the Inter-

American Commission on Human Rights in Washington, DC. The intervention of human rights in this local land dispute 'verticalised' the dispute and re-localised it in a global legal arena, and in so doing transformed its original local attributes.

Each chapter makes a distinct contribution to the understanding of a particular context, yet all confront the same overarching issue of the tension between global and local formulations of human rights. All chart aspects of the two intertwined processes of the legal vernacularisation of human rights law, and the projection of local political discourses and practices into the global political language of rights, and explore the linkages between struggles around human rights and other levels of the social and political. Each chapter discusses the problems of universalist conceptions of rights which can elide the complexity of local disputes. At the most general level, a number of contributors engage in a critique of liberal and legalistic conceptions of human rights (Asad, Eriksen, Gledhill, Schirmer, Wilson). In particular, it is argued that the abstract categories of liberal conceptions of justice and rights are unstable, and result in decontextualisation and a disregard for subjective agency (Asad, Wilson). The formulaic applications of international human rights principles can lead to unintended consequences and actually harm the cause of developing sustainable human rights in a locale (Schirmer, Stoll).

Human rights are involved in both social classification, the creation of legitimacy and the formal expression of power in legally plural contexts, and therefore are the focus of acute social struggles between interest groups (Merry, Eriksen, Gledhill, Stoll). In particular, rights are not only entitlements which result from principles of justice, but are involved in the construction of indigenous identities and claims for self-determination and sovereignty (Merry, Gledhill). In such contexts, the individualism common in liberal conceptions of rights confronts the collectivist visions of multiculturalism, setting up opposing conceptions of the 'common good' (Gledhill, Eriksen).

This volume puts forward the view that human rights are not founded in the eternal moral categories of social philosophy, but are the result of concrete social struggles. Rights are embedded in local normative orders and yet are caught within webs of power and meaning which extend beyond the local. By looking at how a transnational discourse and set of legal institutions are materialised, appropriated, resisted and transformed in a variety of contexts, this volume locates itself within a *comparative anthropology of rights*. This approach seeks to trace the asymmetrical interconnections between diverse contexts which are part of a global network, balancing an

awareness of both meanings and narratives with a sense of how a field
of action is structured by transnational discourses and practices.

Notes

1. See Sally Engle Merry (1992), Ellen Messer (1993).
2. *Guardian* 24 Feb. 1995, although the article actually referred to
   continued whaling in Norway, its discussion of animal rights
   parallels that of human rights.
3. See, for example, Ronald Dworkin (1977) and Jack Donnelly
   (1989: 113), who defends a weak form of cultural relativism,
   which he calls 'logically impeccable' though 'morally defective'.
4. Philosophical anthropology is an invention of philosophy, not
   anthropology, and could be characterised as a theologically
   inspired anthropology without the participant observation. It
   remains obscure to most social and cultural anthropologists.
   This mutual non-recognition is the result of philosophers being
   too-bold in their appropriation of 'anthropology' and anthropologists being too restrained in contributing to wider
   philosophical debates.
5. Ernesto Laclau and Chantal Mouffe (1985), in their application
   of Saussure's theory of the sign, argue that human rights do not
   exist outside of how discourse constructs them. Human rights
   are not special in this regard, and are as contingent as any other
   social category. Lying behind this radical social constructivism
   is the rather hopeful view that the renunciation of the 'totalitarian'
   rationality of the Enlightenment will lead to theories with a
   more radically democratising potential.
6. To repeat the classic slogan of existentialism (Sartre 1966: 26).
7. The widely read sociologist of human rights Rhoda Howard
   (1992) offers us one striking example of an over-generalising,
   decontextualised view of the individual with teleological echoes
   of the nineteenth century. She refers to 'social evolution' (1992:
   81) of the world's societies, and refers to indigenous peoples as
   'primitive societies' and (1992: 83) 'remnants of pre-capitalist
   societies'. In order to oppose conceptions of communal rights,
   Howard draws upon over-drawn and ill-informed oppositions
   between the modern, individualistic and egalitarian versus the
   pre-modern, collectivist and status-based.
8. Thanks to Michael Freeman for sharing his observations on
   Renteln (personal communication, 1994).

9. Though not Richard Rorty himself. During a lecture at Essex University in 1990, Rorty made a surprisingly dedicated defence of the continued value of utilitarianism for political thinking.
10. See Brian Street (1993) 'Culture as a Verb'.
11. As can be seen from a review of the public statements of Mayan organisations such as CONAVIGUA and CERJ over the past five years.
12. Julian Berger of the UN Working Group on Indigenous Populations (personal communication).
13. Perhaps eighteenth-century ideas of nationhood were really the first global ideology, but increasing systemic integration means that twentieth-century versions of human rights have disseminated more extensively and quickly. A related point would be that no one can now claim that nationalism as a political ideal is not applicable to non-Western contexts because it is originally a Western political sentiment.
14. One could also compare Kant's statement with that of Ian Linden, the General Secretary of the Catholic Institute of International Relations who wrote in the 1993 *CIIR Annual Review* of 'the rights and duties of citizens in *international civil society*'. It is no mistake that Christian organisations as well as human rights organisations are actively participating in the construction of a futuristic notion of an 'international civil society' based upon human rights, since both share a commitment to universalism and global intervention.
15. Such as Chiapas-L and latam-info@mailbase.ac.uk.
16. A notion drawn from R. Pannikar (1992).
17. In the Geertzian tradition, those such as Sally Engle Merry (1992) have deployed this method to research how white working-class Americans understand their legal system and their rights within it.
18. See Geertz's book *Negara* (1980).
19. At the same time, researchers should beware of reproducing the statist assumptions of liberal, social democratic and Marxist approaches to human rights (see Stammers 1995).
20. Recently restated by Bryan Turner in his 'Outline of Theory of Human Rights' (1993: 495)
21. See, in particular, Michel Foucault (1980) 'Two Lectures'.

References

American Anthropological Association. 1947. 'Statement on Human Rights'. *American Anthropologist* 49(4): 539–43.

An-Na'im, Abdullahi Ahmed. 1992. *Human Rights in Cross-cultural Perspectives: A Quest for Consensus*. Philadelphia: University of Pennsylvania Press.

Asad, Talal. 1983. 'Anthropological Conceptions of Religion: Reflections on Geertz', *Man* 18: 237–59.

Barnett, H.G. 1948. 'On Science and Human Rights', *American Anthropologist* 50: 352–5.

Barth, F. 1992. 'Towards a Greater Naturalism in Conceptualising Societies', in A. Kuper (ed.) *Conceptualising Society*. EASA Series. London: Routledge.

Donnelly, Jack. 1989. *Universal Human Rights in Theory and Practice*. Ithaca: Cornell University Press.

Downing, T. and G. Kushner (eds). 1988. *Human Rights and Anthropology*. Cambridge, MA: Cultural Survival Report 24.

Dworkin, Ronald. 1977. *Taking Rights Seriously*. London: Duckworth.

Falk, Richard. 1992. 'Cultural Foundations for the International Protection of Human Rights', in Abdullahi Ahmed An-Na'im (ed.) *Human Rights in Cross-cultural Perspectives: A Quest for Consensus*. Philadelphia: University of Pennsylvania Press.

Featherstone, Mike. (ed.) 1990. *Global Culture: Nationalism, Globalization and Modernity*. London: Sage.

Foucault, Michel. 1980. 'Two Lectures', in *Power/Knowledge: Selected Interviews and Other Writings 1972–1977 by Michel Foucault*, Colin Gordon (ed.). Brighton: Harvester Press.

Geertz, Clifford. 1980. *Negara: The Theater State in Nineteenth-century Bali*. Princeton, NJ: Princeton University Press.

—— 1983. 'Local Knowledge: Fact and Law in Comparative Perspective', in *Local Knowledge*. New York: Basic Books.

Gellner, Ernest. 1982. 'Relativism and Universals', in M. Hollis and S. Lukes (eds) *Rationality and Relativism*. Oxford: Blackwell.

Hannerz, Ulf. 1992. *Cultural Complexity: Studies in the Organization of Meaning*. New York: Columbia University Press.

Howard, Rhoda. 1992. 'Dignity, Community and Human Rights', in Abdullahi Ahmed An-Na'im (ed.) *Human Rights in Cross-Cultural Perspectives: A Quest for Consensus*. Philadelphia: University of Pennsylvania Press.

—— 1993. 'Cultural Absolutism and the Nostalgia for Community', *Human Rights Quarterly* 15(2): 315–38.

Jarvie, I.C. 1984. *Rationality and Relativism: In Search of a Philosophy and History of Anthropology*. London: Routledge.

Kant, Immanuel. 1983. *Perpetual Peace and Other Essays*, trans. Ted Humphrey. Indianapolis: Hackett.

Laclau, Ernesto and Chantal Mouffe. 1985. *Hegemony and Socialist Strategy: Towards a Radical Democratic Politics*. London: Verso.

Lukes, Steven. 1991. *Moral Conflict and Politics*. Oxford: Clarendon Press.
MacIntyre, A. 1981. *After Virtue: A Study in Moral Theory*. London: Duckworth.
Marx, Karl. 1977. 'The Jewish Question Revisited', in D. McLellan (ed.) *Karl Marx: Selected Writings*. Oxford: Oxford University Press.
Merry, Sally Engle. 1990. *Getting Justice and Getting Even: Legal Consciousness among Working-Class Americans*. Chicago: University of Chicago Press.
—— 1992. 'Anthropology, Law and Transnational Processes', *Annual Review of Anthropology* 21: 357–79.
Messer, Ellen. 1993. 'Anthropology and Human Rights', *Annual Review of Anthropology* 22: 221–49.
Pannikar, R. 1992. 'Is the Notion of Human Rights a Western Concept?' in P. Sack and J. Aleck (eds) *Law and Anthropology*. Aldershot: Dartmouth Publishing Co.
Renteln, Alison Dundes. 1985. 'The Unanswered Challenge of Relativism and the Consequences for Human Rights', *Human Rights Quarterly* 7: 514–40.
—— 1988. 'Relativism and the Search for Human Rights', *American Anthropologist* 90: 64.
—— 1990. *International Human Rights: Universalism versus Relativism*. London: Sage.
Rorty, Richard. 1993. 'Human Rights, Rationality and Sentimentality', in Stephen Shute and Susan Hurley (eds) *On Human Rights*. New York: Basic Books.
Santos, B. de Sousa. 1987. 'Law: A Map of Misreading: Toward a Postmodern Conception of Law', *Journal of Law and Society* 14: 279–302.
Sartre, Jean-Paul. 1966. *Existentialism and Humanism*. London: Methuen.
Stammers, Neil. 1995. 'A Critique of Social Approaches to Human Rights', *Human Rights Quarterly* 17: 488–508.
Steward, Julian. 1948. 'Comments on the Statement on Human Rights', *American Anthropologist* 50: 351–2.
Street, Brian. 1993. 'Culture as a Verb: Anthropological Aspects of Language and Cultural Process', in D. Graddol, L. Thompson and M. Byram (eds) *Language and Culture*. Clevedon: BAAL and Multilingual Matters.
Turner, Bryan S. 1993. 'Outline of a Theory of Human Rights', *Sociology* 27(3): 489–512.
Washburn, Wilcomb E. 1987. 'Cultural Relativism, Human Rights and the AAA', *American Anthropologist* 89: 939–43.
Weissbrodt, D. 1988. 'Human Rights: An Historical Perspective', in P. Davies (ed.) *Human Rights*. London: Routledge.
Wolf, Eric. 1980. 'Facing Power', *American Anthropologist* 92(3): 586–96.

2 LEGAL PLURALISM AND TRANSNATIONAL CULTURE: THE *KA HO'OKOLOKOLONUI KANAKA MAOLI* TRIBUNAL, HAWAI'I, 1993[1]

Sally Engle Merry

Anthropologists have historically resisted engagement with human rights movements because they feel that the concept of human rights is an artefact of Western cultural traditions raised to the status of global normativity. The parallels with imperialism have been too close for anthropological comfort. Recent controversies concerning practices such as female genital mutilation have uncomfortably juxtaposed feminism, with its universal claims to protection of women, to the basic premise of cultural relativism – tolerance for difference. My anthropology students say to me, 'Why didn't anthropologists criticise genital mutilation, or even talk much about it – perhaps they didn't know about it?' To which I can only reply, 'Of course they did, but they tried to understand it in the terms of that culture, an approach which made sense in an imperialist world. These anthropologists wanted to avoid ethnocentrism.'

The new global discourse of human rights re-poses this question for anthropology. The simple stance of tolerance has become increasingly arid in the face of feminist and human rights activists' demands for global attention to practices such as violence against women and political torture. Yet, anthropologists rightly recognise that human rights language is historically rooted in the Western legal tradition and grew out of its particular social conditions. The global spread of human rights discourse is similar in many ways to the imperialist introduction of legal orders from the West to the rest. Does this mean that anthropologists should continue to shun human rights discourse as a new phase of Western imperialism?

I argue that in the current era, such a rejection of human rights discourse as too 'Western' is a mistake. The present global situation is very different from that of the earlier era of imperialism. There are no longer cultures for whom the legal regimes of the West are totally alien or irrelevant. Even during the high colonialism of the early twentieth century when anthropologists writing the classic descriptions of indigenous legal systems in colonised areas treated them *as if* they were pristine, most groups had already been influenced by Western law. These accounts of isolated legal systems were artefacts of a particular era of anthropological theorising during which colonial influences were analytically subtracted. Even the partial isolation of the 1930s and 1940s is no longer found in the 1990s – the era of globalisation of AIDS, transnational capitalism and the Internet. Members of small, isolated communities increasingly speak in the global arena, whether they are Penang tribesmen or Kayapó from the Amazon.

And what they speak is law; a law which is a multi-layered amalgam of United Nations resolutions, national law, and local categories and customs. Human rights is obviously based on Western liberal-legalist ideas, but in the postcolonial world, it is no longer exclusively owned by the West. As various societies mobilise Western law in their demands for human rights, they reinterpret and transform Western law in accordance with their own local legal conceptions and with the resources provided by the global human rights system. They talk rights, reparations, and claims – the language of law – but construct a new law out of the fragments of the old.

There are two sides to this process. One is the incorporation of local understandings, the other is the addition of global legal discourses. To some extent, the law mobilised in indigenous rights movements is becoming vernacularised, analogous to the way languages become vernacularised over time. In postcolonial states, imperial languages are typically separated into various kinds of pidgins with distinctive accents, vocabularies, styles of speaking, and grammars. The English spoken in Nigeria is very different from that spoken in India, the continental United States, and Hawai'i, for example. In each region it has been shaped by local languages and speaking patterns. On the other hand, what is being vernacularised is an imperial system of law based on rights and procedure, just as the vernaculars listed above come from English.

Legal vernacularisation is linked to the emergence of new national identities much as the development of vernacular languages served as the basis for European nationalism. According to Anderson's analysis of the rise of European nationalism, just before the sixteenth

century, administrative vernaculars separated themselves out of the wider network of Latin-using Christendom (1991: 40–2). Gradually, and by serendipity, some local languages became the language of an entire state while others remained as regional languages. Print capitalism and the spread of Protestantism in the sixteenth century further entrenched these languages as those of government and of the nation. Vernaculars entrenched through book publishing and the emergence of reading publics laid the basis for a developing national consciousness in place of the broader network of communication between educated elites based on Latin (1991: 44). The emergence of vernaculars eroded the transnational power of Latin as a mode of communication linking all of Christendom.

As indigenous peoples mobilise human rights as the basis for conversations about justice, they typically vernacularise and globalise the law they use. The Hawaiian Sovereignty Movement, and in particular *Ka Ho'okolokolonui Kanaka Maoli* (the People's International Tribunal of the Native Hawaiians) held in Hawai'i in 1993, exemplify the creative reconstitution of law by an indigenous group. Other indigenous groups have followed similar strategies (see, for example, Asch 1984; Wilmsen 1989). These movements show that the emerging regime of global human rights is not simply the imposition of Western cultural forms and legalities. Instead, human rights is an open text, capable of appropriation and redefinition by groups who are players in the global legal arena.

The concept of culture has historically been a stumbling block to appreciating the extent to which transnational cultural systems such as human rights are vernacularised. As long as cultures are seen as integrated, cohesive, bounded, and more or less static, it is simple to perceive human rights as an intrusive, alien discourse. However, recognising that cultures are complex repertoires of systems of meanings extracted from myriad sources and reinterpreted through local understandings and interests provides a more fluid way of considering how human rights might be incorporated into local cultural practices and understandings. Cultures consist of a wide assortment of signs and meanings in discrete locales. Contemporary human rights movements clearly draw on Western concepts of law and legality.[2] Since 1945, the United Nations has served as a central source of human rights, through its covenants on economic, social, and cultural rights and on civil and political rights. The principles enunciated in the UN World Conference of Human Rights in June 1993 asserted the universality and indivisibility of human rights, the right to development and to self-determination, the role of civil society in contributing to the development of human rights, the

importance of more effective implementation of human rights at the international and the national level, and the need for human rights education in a systematic way and on a massive scale (Parmentier 1993: 3). Human rights discourse has gained greater importance than ever in the 1990s and the UN has emerged as a new factor in international relations, challenging state sovereignty by establishing conditions under which international intervention is legitimate (Messer 1993; Parmentier 1993).

Indigenous rights movements build on the human rights framework, which has cumulatively incorporated formulations of indigenous rights since the post-war period. Until the late 1950s the notion of indigenous rights was dominated by the International Labour Organisation and the image of the indigenous primitive who needs to be modernised (Tennant 1994). From the 1970s to the present, the discourse has increasingly been shaped by the UN and associated with an image of the noble primitive close to nature. Thus, the meaning of indigenous rights has changed over time. Terminology has also shifted from indigenous populations to peoples and indigenous peoples have gained greater voice in the process of articulating indigenous rights (Tennant 1994).

During the 1980s and 1990s, the UN has produced a stream of documents on indigenous peoples' self-determination and autonomy, primarily through the Working Group on Indigenous Populations, established in 1982. Over the last decade it has produced a Draft Declaration on the Rights of Indigenous Peoples which proclaims the right of indigenous peoples to self-determination and to the full enjoyment of all human rights recognised in the UN Charter and international human rights law (Trask 1993: 281). Indigenous groups have consistently sought to shape the language of the Draft Declaration and the policies of this Working Group through participation in its meetings, presentation of reports and a wide range of other kinds of political activity. Yet, despite the extent to which human rights discourse has proved fruitful for indigenous rights movements, it has also constrained their claims and the kinds of remedies they can seek.

The Hawaiian Sovereignty Movement

The Hawaiian Sovereignty Movement, a political movement by some of the descendants of the Polynesian Hawaiian people inhabiting the Hawaiian islands before Captain Cook arrived in 1778, draws on national and global law and, to a lesser extent, indigenous law to frame its demands and claims. There are many different factions among those who currently self-identify as Hawaiians and seek to improve the

economic, social, and political position of Native Hawaiians. These groups espouse an equal number of understandings of sovereignty and self-determination. The most radical factions are demanding political sovereignty for Native Hawaiians and attempting to construct a land base for this claim. International human rights law has become increasingly central to the claims of the more radical groups, transforming this movement since the 1970s and providing the framework for asserting claims and specifying redress (Trask 1993; Hasager and Friedman 1994). With this transition to the use of global indigenous rights has come a move from a 'local' constituency to a Native Hawaiian one emphasising blood and descent rather than long-term residence and the linguistic and social markers of 'local' culture.

The political movement demanding sovereignty grew out of a much larger and older renaissance of Hawaiian culture, language, arts, dance and music. The cultural movement is inclusive, drawing in a large proportion of the 'local', or long-term residents of the islands regardless of their 'blood' or ethnic heritage. The sovereignty movement, in contrast, tends to be exclusive, emphasising the claims of people deemed to be of Hawaiian descent. Given the nature of intermarriage practices over the last 200 years, however, such distinctions are hardly unambiguous. For many, Hawaiian identity is a matter of self-identification and social situation validated by some ancestral heritage. Many who did not claim Native Hawaiian identity in the past are now re-identifying as Hawaiians. Thus, the sovereignty movement is a political movement founded on a very complex politics of identity.

The claims for Hawaiian sovereignty grow out of the 1893 US invasion and 1898 annexation of the independent Hawaiian nation. During the late nineteenth century, increasingly powerful American and British sugar planters who controlled the Hawaiian Kingdom's economy sought duty-free access to the US market for their sugar. Although American and British legal and political systems had been introduced in the mid-nineteenth century, Hawai'i remained an independent constitutional monarchy until 1893. The US minister in Hawai'i at the time was eager to annex Hawai'i to the United States. In that year, a small group of sugar planters, many of whom were descendants of early missionary families from New England, conspired with the US minister to land US troops from a warship in Honolulu harbour and forced Queen Lili'uokalani to yield her government. She did so under strong protest, 'until such time as the Government of the United States shall, upon facts being presented to it, undo the action of its representatives and reinstate me in the authority which I claim as the Constitutional Sovereign of the Hawaiian Islands' (Public Law

103-150: 1993). The insurrectionist group of 13 white businessmen declared themselves a Provisional Government and offered Hawai'i to the US for annexation.

But the incoming US president, Grover Cleveland, balked at this seizure of an independent nation over the protest of its legitimate ruler. He sent a representative to Hawai'i to investigate the takeover. In a speech to Congress in 1893, Cleveland clearly condemned the action as carried out by force and without the consent of the Hawaiian government (Cleveland 1994). However, the election of William McKinley in 1896 and the imperialist fervour of the Spanish American War led to annexation, although the extent of opposition was sufficient to prevent passage of the annexation treaty by the required two-thirds majority of the Senate. The Senate Foreign Relations Committee circumvented this procedure by introducing a joint resolution of annexation which required only a majority vote (Fuchs 1961: 36; see Hasager et al 1994). In 1898 the United States annexed Hawai'i with the consent of the government of the Republic of Hawai'i – the name taken by the Provisional Government – but without the consent of the Queen or the Kanaka Maoli people.

On 23 November 1993, President Clinton signed Public Law 103-150 which was an apology to Native Hawaiians for the American diplomatic and military role in the 1893 overthrow and its consequences for them. This Law acknowledges that the indigenous Hawaiian people never directly relinquished their claims to their inherent sovereignty as a people or over their national lands either through their monarchy or through a plebiscite or referendum.

Hawai'i remained a Territory until 1959. In that year, a majority of the eligible inhabitants, of which the Native Hawaiians were now only a small fraction, voted for statehood. There was no alternative option available on the ballot, no choice for sovereignty offered. Some Native Hawaiians worked for statehood in the hope that a shift to more representative electoral politics would give them greater control than they had under the territorial system of appointment and limited voting franchise (Trask 1993: 119–22). During the 1960s, however, it became increasingly clear that the Native Hawaiians, now a small part of the total population of the state, were declining both in political power and in their overall social and economic conditions. By 1986 Native Hawaiians were only 20% of the population of the state (Blaisdell and Mokuau 1994: 53). Fully 96% of the population were of mixed ancestry (Blaisdell and Mokuau 1994: 53). They were at the bottom of all ethnic groups in Hawai'i in health, educational levels and representation in managerial and professional jobs and income, while at the top in

unemployment, non-participation in the labour force and proportion living in poverty (Blaisdell and Mokuau 1994: 55).

At the same time, Native Hawaiians experienced a rapid and profound transformation of their culture and language due to decades of pressure for American cultural assimilation, suppression of children speaking the Hawaiian language (banned in schools in the 1930s), and the widespread 'orientalising' of Hawaiian culture by tourism (Buck 1993). Beginning in the 1960s, rapid economic change, military expansion and the growth of tourism disrupted rural communities where indigenous language and practices such as taro farming and fishing were still prevalent (H.-K. Trask 1994: 20). These dwindling areas have become a key source of 'traditional' knowledge for the Hawaiian movement.

By the 1990s, the Hawaiian cultural renaissance was widespread, diverse and generally accepted, while the political movement, with its more radical demands for self-determination drew repeated attacks and opposition from conservative political groups. The cultural revitalisation movement endeavours to recover or recreate Hawaiian language, to revitalise Hawaiian music and dance (rescuing it from its commercialised manifestations), to rewrite Hawaiian history based on sources other than the early missionary accounts which constituted the basis for standard histories until recently (Kame'eleihiwa 1992; Kelly 1994), to re-establish technologies of taro farming, poi manufacture, fishing, ocean-going canoe building and navigation (Finney 1994), and to promote artistic and craft productions such as *lauhala* weaving, *lei*-making, carving, fabric-making and design, quilting, and many others. The movement includes an assertion of Native Hawaiian spirituality and connection to the land, the revaluing of Native Hawaiian healers and rights to gather medicinal plants, and a continuing emphasis on the importance of the family, the *'ohana*. Campaigns to protect sacred sites such as burial grounds and *heiau* (temples) draw on Native Hawaiian religious beliefs as well as legal claims.

Although the cultural florescence is not intimately connected with the political movement (Trask 1993), it reinforces the movement in its emphasis on a renewed pride in Hawaiian culture and identity. Hayden Burgess, or Poka Laenui, one of the early leaders of the sovereignty movement in Hawaii, traces the inspiration for the Hawaiian movement generally to the spread of decolonisation in the Pacific islands beginning with Fiji in 1970, the black power and American Indian movements for local cultural rejuvenation, and the impact of the Vietnam War (1992: 15). Music took on new vigour, *hula halau* or dance schools gained wider prestige and membership, canoe clubs became more popular, and interest in Hawaiian language and

healing with natural medicines expanded. Native Hawaiians became more familiar with their history and began to use their personal Native Hawaiian names in public.

The current political movement grew out of land struggles in the 1970s. The effort to stop military bombing on the island of Kaho'olawe was an explicit challenge to the military (Aluli and McGregor 1994). In evictions from Sand Island, Makua Beach and Waimanalo there were challenges to the jurisdiction of the courts to try Native Hawaiian citizens. The claim that lands ceded to the US government at the time of annexation were stolen was raised in a packed courtroom in the Makua Beach eviction case (Burgess 1992: 15). These lands had been taken from Queen Lili'uokalani by the Provisional Government in 1893 and were ceded to the US over protests and petitions by Kanaka Maoli people.

The legal system was always a central arena for political claims. By the early 1990s, protests included the refusal to pledge allegiance to the US flag in schools or to stand for the national anthem, to file tax returns, to pay income taxes, or to accept the jurisdiction of American courts when charged with criminal offences.

In 1978, the State of Hawaii created an Office of Hawaiian Affairs run by nine Trustees elected by Native Hawaiians (H.-K.Trask 1994: 23). Burgess points out that this may be a unique response to indigenous peoples' demands for self-determination because the Trustees are directly elected by the indigenous people and are, at least in theory, answerable only to Native Hawaiian constituents (1992: 16). But, because OHA was created by the state in order to provide an organisation with which the government can negotiate Native Hawaiian claims and because it is a state agency dependent on the state constitutional government, many activists challenge its ability to serve as a legitimate voice for Native Hawaiian interests and point out that it has often defended or promoted state policies which are to the detriment of Native Hawaiian people (for example, Trask 1993: 94–5).

Although the political side of the Hawaiian movement emerged out of community land struggles, during the 1970s it gradually shifted from 'local' people's rights against development by state, military and corporate interests to the assertion of indigenous Hawaiian rights (Trask 1993: 90). By the 1980s, a powerful movement drawing on the language of human rights and pronouncements of UN documents and Declarations on Human Rights was gaining increasing visibility. The movement that began as a call for restitution became a clear demand for Native sovereignty (Trask 1993: 93). Emerging UN initiatives concerning indigenous peoples encouraged the movement to adopt

the language of aboriginal rights. For example, in her recent book, *From a Native Daughter: Colonialism and Sovereignty in Hawai'i*, Haunani-Kay Trask, a prominent leader of the Sovereignty Movement, asserts that the Universal Declaration on the Rights of Indigenous Peoples should become the framework for discussions of the special status of indigenous peoples (1993: 41). The Kanaka Maoli Tribunal recommended that this UN declaration serve as the minimum standard for negotiations between the US and the Native Hawaiian peoples. The turn toward a global definition of the struggle has coincided with an increasing exclusivity in participation – a greater emphasis on Native Hawaiian ancestry.

A major initiative of the sovereignty movement was the creation of *Ka Lahui Hawai'i* in 1987, a sovereign Native Hawaiian nation-within-a-nation with a constitution, officers and citizens analogous to Native American nations (Trask 1993: 95–103). *Ka Lahui* claims to speak for Native Hawaiian people in negotiations with the federal government just as representatives of Indian nations do now (*Ka Lahui Hawai'i* 1990: 5). It seeks to establish a land base through the recovery of the so-called ceded lands, those taken from the Queen, and the Hawaiian Homelands. Non-Native Hawaiians are eligible to join *Ka Lahui* as honorary members.

The government of *Ka Lahui Hawai'i* is similar in some ways to that of the US, with a constitution and an executive, legislative and judiciary branch, but incorporates distinctively Native Hawaiian principles, language and structures such as a council of *Kupuna* (elders) and a council of *ali'i* (chiefs) whose jurisdiction covers culture and protocol (M. Trask 1994: 83–5). The constitution establishes a national *Pakaukau* (legislature) of representatives elected from *ahupua'a* (traditional land divisions) with law-making power, an independent judiciary and an elected executive (M. Trask 1994: 84; *Ka Lahui Hawai'i* 1990).

Rights enunciated in the constitution include protection against unreasonable searches and seizures, rights of an accused, habeas corpus, and customary rights such as free access to the mountains, caves, the sea, and sites of religious and cultural importance for personal, subsistence, religious and cultural purposes (*Ka Lahui* 1990: Section 5, 6, 7, 18). *Ka Lahui* is committed to self-determination for Native Hawaiian people and has enunciated Native rights to worship, fish, gather and undertake other commercial activities. Its land claims include the private trust lands of several major trusts (M. Trask 1994: 82). Citizenship, with the right to vote and hold office, is open to all Native Hawaiians while non-Hawaiians are welcomed as honorary citizens (*Ka Lahui* 1990: 4). *Ka Lahui* is founded on principles of peace,

disarmament and self-sufficiency (*Ka Lahui* 1990: 5). Thus, *Ka Lahui* represents a vernacularisation of the political and legal system of the United States which is appropriated and reinterpreted in terms of Native Hawaiian culture and politics. At the same time, it makes claims to nationhood in the international arena on the basis of a global discourse of nation: constitutions, laws and definitions of citizenship.

Ka Lahui has made repeated submissions to the UN Working Group on Indigenous Populations and has negotiated treaties with five Alaskan and American Indian Nations. One of its major objectives is educating Native citizens in land and water resource management, exploration of trust assets, legislative processes and historic sites, and working to understand the land base and trust assets and how the Western political system has disenfranchised them (1994: 83). By 1993, *Ka Lahui* had 16,000 Native citizens (M. Trask 1994: 82).

Although the Office of Hawaiian Affairs was not initially in favour of sovereignty, it came around to advocating sovereignty by 1988 as the movement strengthened (H.-K. Trask 1994: 26). *Ka Lahui* leaders worry that OHA serves as a false front for the sovereignty movement, agreeing to development projects that would not benefit the Native Hawaiian people (H.-K. Trask 1994: 23). In 1990, an agreement was reached between OHA and the governor's office to pay back rent from the income from some of the ceded lands of $100 million in 1991 and $8.5 million every year thereafter to OHA. These payments are to settle claims for the ceded lands and thus extinguish claims to the land itself (H.-K. Trask 1994: 28). The ceded lands are 1.4 million acres of Crown and Kingdom lands seized by the Provisional Government, transferred to the US at annexation and to the state in 1959 with the provision that the Native Hawaiian peoples were to be special beneficiaries of these lands. Clearly, there are substantial interests at stake in this political struggle.

The *Ka Ho'okolokolonui Kanaka Maoli*

During the summer of 1993, the centennial of the coup which removed the last Native Hawaiian monarch from the throne and replaced her with a Republic dominated by a small group of whites of US ancestry, one of the most radical pro-sovereignty groups under the leadership of Kekuni Blaisdell held a tribunal to try the United States for its takeover of the sovereign nation of Hawai'i and its acts of resource appropriation and cultural destruction to the Kanaka Maoli people. *Ka Ho'okolokolonui Kanaka Maoli* (the People's International Tribunal of the Native Hawaiians) was a 10-day trial which moved from island to island taking testimony from experts and ordinary people before

an international panel of nine judges (Hasager et al 1993). One hundred and thirty-five people testified. I talked to many of the leaders of this Tribunal, attended planning meetings, and listened to the tapes of the Tribunal and read the transcripts. My research assistant, Nancy Hayes, spent several months working closely with the Tribunal planners, attended and taped the entire Tribunal, and returned the following summer for several months of follow-up work on the impact of the Tribunal. My insights depend both on my own attendance at meetings, reading of the transcripts, and observations that she made.

Ka Ho'okolokolonui Kanaka Maoli claims as its ancestry about 50 tribunals of this kind over the past 30 years in which the citizens of a nation hold their government in judgement, inspired initially by a tribunal convened in 1966 by Bertrand Russell to examine the war crimes of the US during the Vietnam War. The Permanent People's Tribunal in Rome has organised up to 20 tribunals. In recent years, these tribunals have dealt with issues about indigenous peoples, particularly the International People's Tribunal on Indigenous Peoples and Oppressed Nations in San Francisco in 1992 (Interim Report, Kanaka Maoli Nation, Plaintiff v. United States of America, Defendant, 12–21 August 1993. 20 August 1993). The director of the San Francisco Tribunal was also the coordinator of the Kanaka Maoli Tribunal.

The Tribunal hoped to draw international attention to the situation of the Kanaka Maoli people. Its stated goals were to elicit and assemble a record of the wrongs committed by the US and its subsidiaries against the Kanaka Maoli people and to educate the Kanaka Maoli, the United States and the world about these wrongs (Blaisdell 1993: 2). One of the most important audiences for the Tribunal was the UN Working Group on Indigenous Peoples. According to Glenn Morris, one of the three prosecutors in the Tribunal, an important goal of the Tribunal was producing a document for submission to the Working Group. The initial statement of charges was submitted to the US President, the governor of Hawai'i, the Secretary General of the UN, and the chairperson/rapporteur of the UN Working Group on Indigenous Populations. A statement on behalf of the Kanaka Maoli was submitted to the fiftieth session of the Human Rights Commission in February 1994 and several members of the Tribunal organising committee went to Geneva in July 1994 to present testimony to the UN Working Group on Indigenous Populations.

The Tribunal took the form of a criminal trial, beginning with a complaint – a formal statement of nine charges against the United States by the Kanaka Maoli people. The complaint was drafted by the three prosecutor-advocates, Glenn Morris, Maivan Clech Lam and Jose

Morin, and edited by the Tribunal Komike (committee). These charges included interfering in the internal affairs of a sovereign people and nation, annexation of a sovereign people and their nation and territory without their free and informed consent, illegal appropriation of the lands, waters and natural resources of the Kanaka Maoli, economic colonisation and dispossession of the Kanaka Maoli, and acts of genocide and ethnocide against the Kanaka Maoli including the replacement of Kanaka Maoli institutions with Western ones and the suppression of the Kanaka Maoli language. Each charge cites the laws which have been violated. The laws included the laws of the Kanaka Maoli nation, international treaties from the nineteenth century, the US Constitution, and various UN declarations on human rights and the rights of indigenous peoples.

Among the several remedies sought in the complaint were the right to 'the reassertion and effective exercise of [the Kanaka Maoli] right to self-determination and sovereignty', the demand for negotiations between the Kanaka Maoli and the US to develop a 'just and evolving, as need be, relationship between the two parties', beginning from the premises of the rights enunciated in the Draft Declaration on the Rights of Indigenous Peoples as developed by the United Nations Working Group on Indigenous Populations. The complaint also demands the return of all Kanaka Maoli territory. Clearly, the statement of charges and the remedies sought are framed in the language of the law, but this is a plural law in which the law of the nation is nested between indigenous law and global human rights law of the United Nations.

The US, as defendant, was sent the complaint and invited to appear in the trial, but did not. Consequently, an empty chair sat beside the judges at each hearing labelled 'US Representative'. Prosecutor-advocates organised the taking of testimony. Hearings always opened with Kanaka Maoli ceremonies and prayers. Testifiers were both experts and 'taro-roots' (grassroots) people. Among the participants were representatives of other peoples colonised by the US in 1898, such as the Philippines, Guam, Puerto Rico and Samoa. The Tribunal began with the testimony of several historians who are re-examining Hawaiian history and challenging the conventional history of voluntary acquiescence to American control by emphasising the violence of early encounters, the coercive assimilation of the colonial process, and the economic exploitation and resource appropriation of American colonialism, including the occupation of lands for military purposes.

As the Tribunal moved to other islands, it heard testimony in places where Kanaka Maoli communities were contesting land rights.

On each island, local people testified about problems ranging from the encroachment of hotel and golf course development, inadequate housing provided by the state Department of Hawaiian Homelands, obstacles to asserting claims to family lands, the erection of fences and other forms of denial of access to traditional gathering and fishing areas, to the destruction of natural fishing and gathering environments, and the suppression and tourist commercialisation of Kanaka Maoli culture. The Tribunal was often held in places where people had experienced evictions and destruction of homes. One woman testified, 'I would like to see, in my lifetime, the Hawaiian people recognised by the world as a people, not as an attraction' (Mana'o 1993: 12).

The Tribunal concluded that the US was guilty of violating *na kanawai* (Kanaka Maoli law), elements of customary international law, and the US Declaration of Independence. The US engaged in interventions which violated its international treaties with the nation of Hawai'i, it supported a coup against the legitimate government of the country, and after annexation it forcibly degraded and dispossessed the Kanaka Maoli (Mana'o 1993: 6). US assertions of jurisdiction and property title in the Hawaiian Islands were held by the Tribunal judges to be legally invalid. Further, the judges concluded that the inherent right of the people to sovereignty has not been extinguished and that the Kanaka Maoli have been subjected to ongoing processes of physical and cultural genocide by the state and the US government (Mana'o 1993: 6). Ten years earlier, a Congressional Commission appointed by the Reagan administration to study the situation of the Kanaka Maoli people divided on these points. A majority report claimed that the US invasion and coup of 1893 was not unauthorised and that in 1959 Kanaka Maoli had not been incorporated into the US without the exercise of self-determination while a Kanaka Maoli minority wrote a separate dissenting report arguing that Kanaka Maoli had been subjected to an illegal takeover in 1893.[3]

The Tribunal recommended that the US and the world recognise the sovereignty and right to self-determination of Lahui Kanaka Maoli (the Kanaka Maoli nation) under several covenants of international law including the International Covenant on Civil and Political Rights and the International Covenant on Economic, Social and Cultural Rights. It recommended the return of all Kanaka Maoli lands including ceded lands, and associated water rights. The Tribunal recommended that in negotiations with Lahui Kanaka Maoli, the US should observe the provisions of the UN Declaration on the Rights of Indigenous Peoples as the minimal standard of negotiation (Mana'o 1993: 6).

Thus, the Tribunal appropriated Western legal forms and symbols in an effort to harness the power and legitimacy of conceptions of law held by the US government, the UN and the people of the United States. The Tribunal took on the form of a trial, of criminal legality, without the sanctions or the authority of a state. This was a process full of irony. As one of the organisers asked, how can we complain about the loss of Hawaiian culture in the language of Western law? The organisers were caught between the desire to use Hawaiian words and legal concepts, many of which would be unfamiliar even to Native Hawaiians, and their desire to produce a tribunal which could be understood by the national and international audience. The organisers sought to join the two legal cultures and argued that this conjunction was necessary in order to document the wrongs of the United States (Blaisdell 1993: 1). But little remains of the pre-contact legal system even among rural Native Hawaiians after nearly two centuries of legal incorporation and transformation. Both contemporary Native Hawaiians and the leaders of the Tribunal are deeply incorporated into the American legal system. The prosecutor and judges continually sought to redefine Western law even as they called on it, seeking to detach it from the nation-state context and link it to a more global notion of justice. Law acquired a fundamental pluralism. This move appears in the opening statement by the prosecutor, Glenn Morris, a Shawnee attorney at the University of Colorado at Denver and Director of the Denver chapter of AIM. He begins by linking this Tribunal to the struggles by Native Americans in the continental United States and Canada, then moves to redefining law:

it is our responsibility to tell the world that justice cannot be employed without also including an indigenous vision of what justice means. And so the proceedings for this Tribunal will not look necessarily like the proceedings from other kinds of tribunals that have been held that people might be accustomed to. Because we don't believe, and I will speak for myself now as part of the advocate team, that the legitimacy of law comes only from the Western model. We believe that as indigenous peoples we come from societies that had our own laws, that had our own understanding of the land and the sky and the ocean. And now it's time for the West to integrate those principles into their law. And it's time for the West to open up its ears and open up its jurisprudence to that wisdom. And so while this Tribunal will have some of the framework of Western law, it will also integrate much of the wisdom of Kanaka Maoli law and tradition and understanding ...

The nine judges themselves represented the community of international indigenous rights groups and scholars. They included US professors who have worked on indigenous rights and international law, Native American leaders from the US and Canada, a Korean

feminist theologian, an African-American law professor, a Maori attorney from Aoteoroa (New Zealand), a member of the Palestinian Rights Society, a human rights advocate at the UN who is a Cree from Canada, and a Japanese member of the Permanent People's Tribunal based in Rome. The verdict and recommendations, written by these judges at the close of the proceedings, clearly articulates their position on law (*Ka Ho'okolokolonui Kanaka Maoli, Interim Report*: 2–4):

'The Tribunal considers that it is applying the law as fully and as honestly as it knows how. It refuses, however, to define law in a formalistic or colonialist manner. It is guided by five mutually reinforcing conceptions of law from which it draws freely in developing its findings on the charges and its conclusions and recommendations for redress. These are:

1. Kanaka Maoli law: 'embracing sets of convictions about right action and righteousness on political, economic, and social relations'.
2. International law: 'The obligations of states and rights of peoples and their nations are outlined under international law, especially on matters of human rights, self-determination, sovereignty, democracy, and intervention in the internal affairs of foreign nations.' The document points out that international law has often served as an instrument to validate colonial rule, but that it is 'increasingly sensitive to the democratic claims of peoples and nations that insist on the accountability of states and their leaders'. The 1992 version of the Draft Universal Declaration on the Rights of Indigenous Peoples by the UN is referenced as an important source of authority.
3. The Constitution of the United States, the laws and judicial decisions of the United States and of the State of Hawaii: the judges challenge US law as the basis of valid legal relationships with the Kanaka Maoli and note the failure of the federal government to uphold its very limited efforts to acknowledge certain Kanaka Maoli rights, especially with reference to land and water.
4. The law of peoples as nations: 'By initiative of peoples and nations, the experience of international people's tribunals has itself become a source of law.' The text refers to the 1976 Algiers Declaration on the Rights and Duties of Peoples. The judges wish to strengthen this source of law.
5. The inherent law of humanity: 'In addition to other sources there exists a higher law based on the search for justice in the relation among persons and peoples and their nations; as well, there is a

law establishing the conditions for harmony between human activity and nature, drawing on ideas of stewardship that exist in many of the world's great cultural traditions, and that are especially embodied in the cultures of indigenous peoples.'

The verdict concludes:

Law is a great river that draws on these five sources as tributary rivers, and the Tribunal will apply law in this spirit. We have found indigenous Kanaka Maoli understanding of law to be an indispensable and powerful background for this verdict, and we believe that law experience and wisdom of indigenous peoples generally is helping the democratic movement of peoples and nations to develop a more useful and equitable sense of law than has been evolved by modern governments and states which sit in judgement of the world's peoples in such organs of world order as the UN Security Council and the Group-of-Seven.

Thus, the verdict and the Tribunal itself took the framework of Western law but localised and globalised the meaning of law itself. It is a plural law, with references to violations of Kanaka Maoli law, US law, and UN conventions and international law. It even incorporates the notion of natural law by drawing on the metaphor of the river.[4] The panel of judges represented an international social network engaged transnationally in constructing a more plural law including the developing law of indigenous rights. The UN was an inspiration as well as an important audience for the Tribunal committee. There is currently in process a major report by the judges which will be submitted to the UN Working Group.

Despite its powerful mobilisation of the language of indigenous rights and Kanaka Maoli law, the Tribunal received relatively little media attention on the mainland. The Tribunal, and indeed the many facets of the sovereignty movement, have never gripped the world the way the events in Chiapas, Mexico held global attention early in 1994. In the years after the Tribunal, the sovereignty movement in its various manifestations continues to strengthen on the islands, but has still made relatively little impact nationally or internationally. By and large, there is little awareness in the continental US of the historic invasion and takeover of the islands, the current plight of the Kanaka Maoli, or their demands for redress and sovereignty.

The Hawaiian movement has had greater difficulty linking itself to the international flow of information and opinion than the Kayapó or the Penang, for example, because it contradicts powerful cultural images already circulating internationally about the meanings of Hawai'i. Travel ads constantly define Hawai'i as a paradise opposite to the everyday world of industrial urban society. The images of

paradise are juxtaposed to the rational world of work, time discipline, and sexual control, creating a pungent combination of the exotic and the erotic. In this feminised imagined place, one is invited to step out of time into a world of sensuous pleasure, received by warm, welcoming Hawaiians (see H.-K. Trask 1993: 179–201). Anger and demands for redress are jarring reminders of a world tourists yearn to leave behind. Statements such as '*Haoles* go home' chill the welcome. These are not simply floating cultural images. They are created and disseminated through a powerful agency, the State of Hawaii Visitors Bureau, which pours vast amounts of resources into marketing the islands to tourists, increasingly seen as the only economic option for the islands. Since tourism depends heavily on the construction of the welcoming exotic/erotic Hawaiian, local political demands and indications of anger and discontent are deeply threatening. Visitors were urged by the Hawaii Visitors Bureau to stay away from the protest demonstrations marking the centennial of the 1893 coup by Kanaka Maoli, for example, even though these demonstrations occurred at the Iolani Palace (draped in black for the occasion), a central tourist attraction in Honolulu.

Conclusions

The Tribunal drew on the symbolic power of law to condemn the United States' treatment of Kanaka Maoli people by convicting the US government of a series of charges presented in terms of violations of law. But the laws violated were not simply those of the United States. Instead of working within the existing legal system, it seized the concept of justice and deployed it outside state law. Other parts of the sovereignty movement such as *Ka Lahui Hawai'i* also reflect the appropriation and re-deployment of law as a basis for imagining and creating a new national identity. Law is taken from its nation-state context and re-deployed as plural, as local and global as well as national. At the same time, it is blended with a 'natural' concept of law conflated with justice. Even as the signifiers are increasingly floating they are seen as more fixed.

This more plural law forms the basis for claims to sovereignty as well as for the emergence of new nationalisms. The Tribunal itself, as well as its expansive definition of law, provides a framework for a national identity and a stage on which to enact political sovereignty shaped by Hawaiian cultural practices and language. But, although Western legal forms offer a powerful language for Kanaka Maoli to make claims against the United States, they also channel and constrain the kinds of wrongs enunciated and the remedies demanded. Remedies

are sought in the language of 'sovereignty', whose shape is defined by categories such as 'citizenship' and a 'constitution'. This is not a situation of an authentic culture being distorted by outside influences, however, but a thoroughly modern set of cultural resources deployed for particular political interests.

Arguments between relativist and universalist perspectives on human rights depend on outdated notions of holistic and discrete cultures, as Richard Wilson (this volume) points out, rather than on the processes by which cultures are continually reformulated through local practices. The universalist/relativist debate distracts from understanding human rights in practice: from examining local political struggles which mobilise rights language in particular situations. In this example, we see the creative deployment of the language and symbolic power of rights and law in constantly shifting local circumstances in which the global, the national and the local are inextricably joined, both as resources and as constraints.

Since law is constituted by social practices and meanings, such movements have larger implications for law's symbolic identity. This Tribunal, as an instance of the wider practices of indigenous rights movements, is redefining law itself, promoting a legally plural notion of law in which state law is only one of many levels without privileged centrality. The concept of law is extracted from the nation-state arena and linked to local cultural orders and to international legal orders such as those enunciated by the UN. This development indicates the shifting importance of local, national, and global legal systems in the late twentieth century and the emergence of a new kind of legal pluralism in which the critical questions are how these systems intersect with one another. The claims of state law to be the ultimate authority are themselves challenged. The legal subject is no longer defined only by state law but also by local, transnational, and even natural law. The appropriated concept of law constitutes a space of resistance to the hegemony of nation-state law at the same time as it reinforces the centrality of law as a mode of protest.

Discourses of law are occupying an increasingly central space in debates about social justice. In other periods, debates about justice took place in terms of religious values or competing political systems, but in the late twentieth century, since the fall of the Berlin Wall and, to Western eyes, the ideological collapse of communism, Western legality is the dominant cultural form for these debates. The florescence of an international human rights language, with its 'four generations' of political and civil rights, socio-economic and cultural rights, development rights, and now indigenous rights, provides the global terrain for these contemporary debates (Messer 1993: 222–3).

Just as the English language has moved beyond the control of the metropole and is taking its own forms in Africa, India and the United States, so has Western law. Yet, just as local dialects are derived from the English or French of the colonisers, so local manifestations of legality are shaped by an imperial legacy. As the global becomes localised and the local becomes globalised, the plurality of law is reinvigorated. In law as in language, beneath the apparent uniformity of Western legality in human rights law, there is clearly vibrant and creative diversity. Rejecting human rights as a Western legal construct reflective of cultural imperialism ignores how much we all now live in a global world of legal pluralism.

Notes

1. This chapter was presented as a paper at the 1994 meeting of the American Anthropological Association. The research was generously supported by grants from the National Science Foundation and the National Endowment for the Humanities. Nancy Hayes contributed greatly to this project as my research assistant. I am grateful to Kekuni Blaisdell, Christine Harrington, Nalani Minton, Ann Marie Plane and Brian Tamanaha for thoughtful comments on the paper, although its final content remains my responsibility.
2. The use of rights language by political movements is of course not only a recent phenomenon. Ann Marie Plane pointed out to me that the women at Seneca Falls who enunciated the 1848 Declaration of Sentiments used the Declaration of Independence as a model for claiming 'inalienable' rights. Major political movements of the late eighteenth century such as the French Revolution and the American Revolution were similarly framed in a discourse of human rights.
3. The Native Hawaiians Study Commission, created by Congress, was asked to assess the American involvement in the takeover of Hawai'i and to ascertain whether American culpability existed as a consequence as well as advise on how to approach and to answer Native Hawaiian claims. The majority report argues that the United States has no legal or moral responsibility of culpability for the actions of American officials in 1893, nor is there any basis for claims by Native Hawaiians. The minority report, completed in 1983, disagrees with these conclusions (Kamali'i et al 1983: v).
4. I am grateful to Don Brenneis for this observation.

References

Aluli, Noa Emmett and Davianna Pomaika'i McGregor. 1994. 'The Healing of Kaho'olawe', pp. 197–210 in Ulla Hasager and Jonathan Friedman (eds) *Hawai'i: Return to Nationhood*. Copenhagen: IWGIA Document no. 75.

Anderson, Benedict. 1991. *Imagined Communities*. Revised edition. London: Verso.

Asch, Michael. 1984. *Home and Native Land: Aboriginal Rights and the Canadian Constitution*. Canada: Methuen.

Blaisdell, Kekuni. 1993. *'Na Kanawai a Me Ka Ho'okolokolonui Kanaka Maoli*: Kanaka Maoli Legal Traditions and the People's International Tribunal'. 10 August 1993, typescript.

Blaisdell, Kekuni and Noreen Mokuau. 1994. '*Kanaka Maoli*: Indigenous Hawaiians', pp. 49–68 in Ulla Hasager and Jonathan Friedman (eds) *Hawai'i: Return to Nationhood*. Copenhagen: IWGIA Document no. 75.

Buck, Elizabeth. 1993. *Paradise Remade: The Politics of Culture and History in Hawai'i*. Philadelphia: Temple University Press.

Burgess, Hayden F. (also known as Poka Leanui) 1992. *Collection of Papers on Hawaiian Sovereignty and Self-determination*. Wai'anae, HI: Institute for the Advancement of Hawaiian Affairs.

Cleveland, Grover. 1994. 'A Friendly State Being Robbed of Its Independence and Sovereignty (President's Message Relating to the Hawaiian Islands, 18 December 1893)', pp. 121–38 in Ulla Hasager and Jonathan Friedman (eds) *Hawai'i: Return to Nationhood*. Copenhagen: IWGIA Document no. 75.

Finney, Ben, et al. 1994. *Voyage of Rediscovery: A Cultural Odyssey through Polynesia*. Berkeley: University of California Press.

Fuchs, Lawrence. 1961. *Hawaii Pono: A Social History*. New York: Harcourt, Brace and World, Inc.

Hasager, Ulla, et al. 1994. *Ka Ho'okolokolonui Kanaka Maoli*, People's International Tribunal, Hawai'i 1993, Mana'o. Honolulu: Honolulu Publishing Co. 20 pp.

Hasager, Ulla and Jonathan Friedman (eds). 1994. *Hawai'i: Return to Nationhood*. Copenhagen: International Work Group for Indigenous Affairs, Document No. 75.

Ka Ho'okolokolonui Kanaka Maoli, People's International Tribunal, Hawai'i 1993. Interim Report: Kanaka Maoli Nation, Plaintiff v. United States of America, Defendant, 12–21 August 1993. Typescript.

Ka Lahui Hawai'i: The Sovereign Nation of Hawai'i. 1990. 'A Compilation of Legal Materials for Workshops on the Hawaiian Nation.' Hilo, HI.

Ka Ho'okolokolonui Kanaka Maoli: 1993 The People's International Tribunal Hawai'i Mana'o. Booklet, 1994. Kanaka Maole Tribunal Komike, 3333 Ka'ohinani Drive, Honolulu, HI (cited as Mana'o).

Kamali'i, K.,W. Beamer and H.R. Betts 1983. Report of the Native Hawaiians Study Commission Vol. II: Claims of Conscience. A Dissenting Study of the Culture, Needs and Concerns of Native Hawaiians. Submitted to the Committee on Energy and Natural Resources of the Unites States Senate, 23 June.

Kame'eleihiwa, Lilikala. 1992. *Native Land and Foreign Desires*. Honolulu: Bishop Museum Press.

Kelly, Marion. 1994. 'The Impact of Missionaries and Other Foreigners on Hawaiians and their Culture', pp. 91–106 in Ulla Hasager and Jonathan Friedman (eds) *Hawai'i: Return to Nationhood*. Copenhagen: IWGIA Document no. 75.

Messer, Ellen. 1993. 'Anthropology and Human Rights', *Annual Review of Anthropology* 22: 221–49.

Parmentier, Stephan. 1993. 'Opening Address: Human Rights for the 21st Century', Onati, Spain. *Newsletter of the Working Group on the Sociology of Human Rights* 1: 3.

Tennant, Chris. 1994. 'Indigenous Peoples, International Institutions, and the International Legal Literature from 1945–1993', *Human Rights Quarterly* 16: 1–57.

Trask, Haunani-Kay. 1993. *From a Native Daughter: Colonialism and Sovereignty in Hawai'i*. Monroe, ME: Common Courage Press.

—— 1994. '*Kupa'a Aina*: Native Hawaiian Nationalism in Hawai'i', pp. 15–34 in Ulla Hasager and Jonathan Friedman (eds) *Hawai'i: Return to Nationhood*. Copenhagen: IWGIA Document no. 75.

Trask, Mililani B. 1994. 'The Politics of Oppression', pp. 71–91 in Ulla Hasager and Jonathan Friedman (eds) *Hawai'i: Return to Nationhood*. Copenhagen: IWGIA Document no. 75.

Wilmsen, Edwin (ed.). 1989. *We Are Here: Politics of Aboriginal Land Tenure*. Berkeley: University of California Press.

3 MULTICULTURALISM, INDIVIDUALISM AND HUMAN RIGHTS: ROMANTICISM, THE ENLIGHTENMENT AND LESSONS FROM MAURITIUS

Thomas Hylland Eriksen

The term 'multiculturalism' covers a number of current political trends in North America and elsewhere which, although they are quite different in their aims and ideological content (see Goldberg 1994 for an overview), share a positive evaluation of cultural traditions and, particularly, the cultural or ethnic identities of minorities. Multiculturalism is evident in literature and the arts as well as in politics, and it seeks to revalorise the artistic and intellectual contributions of hitherto silent minorities as well as supporting their quest for equity in greater society. Related to the critical Hegelianism of the early Frankfurt School, to feminist critiques of epistemology and to postmodernist trends inspired directly or indirectly by Derrida, multiculturalist thought is often accused of inspiring nihilism (see for example Bloom 1987) since it seems to relativise absolute value judgements.

This chapter is restricted to a discussion of one particular political aspect of multiculturalism, and investigates under which circumstances multiculturalist ideas may be at odds with individual human rights (as depicted in the original UN charter). As a consequence, it is necessary to review the concept of 'culture' invoked in multiculturalist thought. This conceptual discussion (which has practical ramifications) forms the head and tail of the article, the main body of which is devoted to a critical presentation of multiculturalist practices and debates in Mauritius, which is used here as an exemplar of multiculturalist dilemmas and opportunities.[1]

49

Cultural Variation as a Political Challenge

For many years, it was commonplace within post-evolutionist comparative cultural research – cultural and social anthropology – to assume that cultures were generally sharply delineated and distinct, relatively homogeneous and stable. The world was thus depicted as a vast archipelago of cultures, each possessing its own internal logic and its own values, and which could exclusively be understood in its own unique terms. Variations in morality, custom and tradition were thus regarded as evidence of people's ability to adapt to the most variable environments and to shape their existence in a multitude of ways, and it was emphasised that there was no 'objective' standard available for the evolutionary ranking of cultures or the moral evaluation of actions. Value was defined from within. This line of thought, which is historically associated with the great German-American anthropologist Franz Boas (1858–1942), is usually spoken of as cultural relativism or historical particularism.

Recently the classic perspectives from cultural relativism have become increasingly problematic (cf. also Wilson's Introduction to this volume), and cultural theory from the 1980s and 1990s tends to emphasise (now approaching the point of irritating reiteration) that 'cultures' are neither clearly bounded, tightly integrated nor unchanging. An important contributing cause, or at least a major catalyst, in bringing this change about, is the intensification of the globalisation of culture since the Second World War. The globalisation of capitalism and the modern state, along with innovations in communication technology (jet planes, TV satellites and various wireless telecommunications are key innovations), have been crucial for these changes to come about. When former 'tribals' now apply for mortgages, follow North American TV series, take their Higher School Certificates, elect local governments and are imprisoned for criticising the government, it becomes intellectually and morally indefensible to seek refuge in the fiction of assuming that cultures are isolated and committed to their 'proper logic': political discourse has, to a great extent, become globalised.

The situation may be even more problematic to handle intellectually for persons steeped in Boasian relativism when very tangible expressions of global cultural variation suddenly appear at our doorstep, which indeed is happening in most industrialised societies due to labour migration and to the ongoing influx of political refugees. This new polyethnic situation has, especially in European countries, provoked discrimination as well as a revitalised cultural nationalism

and chauvinism in segments of the majority, but many – 'indigenes' as well as new arrivals – have also responded by developing ideological and practical models for polyethnic coexistence. Original alloys mixing anthropological cultural relativism, nationalism, modern individualism and human rights thought have thus, in the course of the past 20 years, created ideologies and theories dealing with 'multicultural society'. In this milieu of social and political thought, *difference* is seen not only as politically legitimate, but is also frequently invoked as justification for specific political rights. In this regard, multi-culturalist thought could be seen as post-nationalist, since it acknowledges the existence of several 'cultures' within one and the same political system. At the same time, multiculturalism may easily conflict with values seen as universal in modern liberal states, especially those to do with human rights and the rights and duties associated with equal participation in the institutions of society.

The basic dilemma of polyethnic societies can be phrased like this: on the one hand all members of a liberal democracy are (in principle if not in practice) entitled to the same rights and opportunities. On the other hand, they also have the right to be different – and in the 1990s, the rights of minorities to maintain and promote their cultural specificity, and to be visible in the public sphere, including the media, school curricula and so on, are increasingly insisted on. A crucial challenge for multi-ethnic societies therefore consists in allowing cultural differences without violating common, societally defined rights; in other words, the challenge consists in finding a viable compromise, for the state as well as for the citizens (representing power and agency, respectively, in the framework proposed in Wilson's Introduction), between equal rights and the right to be different.

This contradiction is as old as nationalism itself. Nationalism, the ideology holding that states ought to be culturally homogeneous (Anderson 1983; Gellner 1983), has a double origin in German Romanticism and French Enlightenment thought, which emphasise, respectively, cultural (in many cases ethnic as well) uniformity, and shared territory and citizenship, as the basis for national integration and as the source of political legitimation. According to classic Enlightenment thought, there existed a universal human civilisation, which was in principle accessible to all humans. According to German Romanticism, represented in the works of Herder above all, every people (*Volk*) had its proper linguistic and cultural character and the right to defend it. This view of culture, incidentally, was developed largely as a defensive response to French universalism, which was locally perceived as a form of cultural imperialism (probably not without a certain justification). This perspective and its derivatives

(including cultural relativism in its 'strong' variants) are currently expressed through ideologies arguing the importance of cultural homogeneity for political identity. This applies whether they are nationalist and champion the idea of homogeneous states, or ethnopolitical and insist on ethnically based rights for minorities within existing states. ·

However, the difference between 'German' and 'French' nationalism, so often stressed in the literature (see Kohn 1945 for a classic statement), is not absolute: in actually existing nations, the two principles are generally mixed, and even in principle, French territorialism is far from being culturally innocent. Insofar as the French universalist civilisation insists on speaking French, it has certainly not been perceived as culturally neutral among non-French speakers in Brittany, in Côte d'Ivoire and elsewhere. Modern human rights thinking is no more neutral either, incidentally, as it assumes global sharing of a specified set of societal values.

The contradiction between the demands for equal rights and for the right to be different is accentuated at present by two main tendencies. First, it has finally become clear in public discourse – nearly 80 years after Woodrow Wilson famously announced the right to self-determination of peoples – that hardly any ethnic group has its territory by itself. States are polyethnic, and any ideology stating that only people 'of the same kind' should live in a country is potentially dangerous. This problem was recognised already by Renan (1992 [1882]), but it has acquired unprecedented importance since the 1960s. Second, the current processes of cultural globalisation break down cultural boundaries and make it difficult to defend the idea that a 'people' is culturally homogeneous and unique. Cultural creolisation (or 'hybridisation', or again 'bastardisation' if one prefers), migration and increased transnational communication are important keywords here.

A widespread counter-reaction against the perceived threat of boundary dissolution through globalisation consists in ideological emphases on 'cultural uniqueness'. In this sense, cultural homogenisation and ethnic fragmentation take place simultaneously; they are consequences of each other and feed on each other in dynamic interplay (cf. Friedman 1990).

In other words, modern societies are by default 'multicultural' – or so it may seem. I shall nevertheless argue that 'multiculturalist politics' have to be universalistic in their very nature. The position to be defended below argues that culture is not a legitimating basis for political claims, and that cultural singularities among minorities and majorities in modern societies can only be defended to the extent

that they do not interfere with individual human rights. All societies are indeed 'multicultural', whether they contain diverse ethnic groups or not, since different citizens hold different values and different world views. Multiculturalism, a term describing doctrines which argue the importance and equivalence of cultural heritages *and* the decentralisation of defining power as to what is to count as one, may in practice be a strong form of individualistic thinking about personhood – the world seen as a smorgasbord of identity options. This line of thinking, described as 'critical multiculturalism' by Turner (1994), may enable diverse groups to participate in public life, with their 'cultural heritage' or 'cultural identity' as their legitimated symbolic capital, and it can thereby be liberating for formerly silenced or unarticulate groups, including non-ethnic groups such as women and homosexuals. If, on the other hand, institutionalised differences form the core of multiculturalist practices, it is liable to regress into nihilism, apartheid and/or the enforced ascription of cultural identities. As the empirical discussion below will argue, the former alternative has many virtues in relation to human rights, which the latter does not.

The Politicised Concept of Culture

Culture, Raymond Williams has written (1976: 87) in a much quoted passage, is one of the two or three most complex words of the English language. The meaning of the word, Williams shows, has gone through many changes since the original Latin *colere*, which referred to the cultivation of the soil. Today, the word has several, if related, meanings.

One of the most common meanings of culture posits it as synonymous with the way of life and world view the members of a particular group or community have in common, and which distinguishes them from other groups. This definition may at first seem plausible, but it does not survive closer scrutiny. Within nearly every 'group' or 'people' there are varying ways of life and world views; the rich differ from the poor, the men from the women, the highly educated from the illiterate, the urban from the rural and so on. Additionally, it is often extremely difficult to draw boundaries between 'cultures'. If one argues that a Norwegian culture exists and is by default different from Danish culture, one will need to show what it is that all Norwegians share with each other but not with a single Dane. That is not an easy thing to do. Finally, culture is naturally not a solid object, even if the word unhappily is a noun. Culture is

something which happens, not something that merely exists; it unfolds through social process and therefore also inherently changes.

Problems of this kind have made such a conceptualisation of culture difficult to manage, and many scholars have ceased to use it, while others insist on using culture in the singular sense, seen as that which all humans have in common, defining them as a species as opposed to nature in general and other species in particular.[2]

However, ideologists and political entrepreneurs of many shades have embraced this Romantic concept of culture. In recent years, 'culture' and 'cultural identity' have become important tools for the achievement of political legitimacy and influence in many otherwise very different societies – from Bolivia to Siberia. It is used by political leaders of hegemonic majorities as well as by the spokesmen of weak minorities.

Indigenous peoples all over the world demand territorial rights from the states in which they live, emphasising their unique cultural heritage and way of life as a crucial element in their plea. Immigrant leaders in Europe occasionally present themselves as the representatives of cultural minorities, demanding, *inter alia*, special linguistic and religious rights. The hegemonic elites of many countries also refer to their 'national culture' in justification of warfare or oppression of ethnic minorities. 'Cultural pleas' are, in other words, put to very different political uses.

A frequently mentioned 'paradox' concerning the break-up of Yugoslavia and subsequent war is the fact that the fighting parties, Serbs, Croats and Bosnian Muslims, are culturally very similar, yet justify their mutual hatred by claiming that they are actually profoundly different. This kind of situation, where ethnic relations between groups which are culturally close take on a bitter and antagonistic character, is more common than is widely assumed. In Trinidad, in the southern Caribbean, the following development has taken place in recent years (Eriksen 1992a). The two largest ethnic groups, Africans and Indians (originally from India; they are not American Indians), have gradually acquired more and more in common, culturally speaking; in terms of language, way of life, ambitions and general outlook.

At the same time, they have become ever more concerned to express how utterly different they are; culture and cultural differences are spoken about more often, and cultural differences are brought to bear on daily life, public rituals and political organisation to a greater extent than was earlier the case. Partly, this is because the groups are in closer contact than earlier and compete for the same scarce resources; but it is also partly because members of the two groups feel that their

cultural boundaries are threatened by tendencies towards creolisation and therefore feel an acute need to advertise their cultural differences. The groups have *simultaneously* become more similar and more different. This paradox is characteristic of globalisation processes, whereby differences between peoples are made comparable and therefore come to resemble each other, and where 'small' differences are 'enlarged'. It could, in line with this, be said that the entire discourse over 'multiculturalism' is embedded in a shared cultural framework encompassing, and bringing out the contradictions between, the Romantic notion of culture and the Enlightenment notion of individual rights. To put it somewhat more crudely: to make demands on behalf of a self-professed 'culture' indicates that one subscribes to a shared global political culture. The logic of multiculturalism and ethnopolitics shares its dual origins with the logic of nationalism in the Enlightenment and Romantic thought of early modern Europe.

In order to illustrate and further develop the preceding points, I shall now turn to an extended empirical example, which brings out many of the tensions and contradictions inherent in ideas of multiculturalism.

Ethnicity in Mauritius

Since Mauritius was permanently settled by French planters and their African and Malagasy slaves in 1715, this island in the south-western Indian Ocean has been a polyethnic society, and still is very much so, as witnessed in official symbolism as well as many aspects of everyday life (Eriksen 1988; Bowman 1990). The currency is the rupee, and the text on the bank notes is in English, Hindi and Tamil. However, Mauritian newspapers tend to be in French, but the video shops offer mostly Indian and East Asian films. A leisurely walk through the capital, Port-Louis, may bring one past, within half an hour or so, a Buddhist pagoda, a Sunni mosque, an Anglican church and a Catholic one, and two Hindu temples – one North Indian, one Tamil. And it is by no means uncommon that Mauritians have names like Françoise Yaw Tang Mootoosamy.

Contemporary Mauritius, with a surface of some 2,000 square kilometres, has about a million inhabitants. Their ancestors came from four continents, and they belong to four different 'world religions'. According to official categories, the largest ethnic groups are Hindus from North India ('Hindi-speaking', 42%), 'Creoles' of largely African descent (27%), Muslims of Indian origin (16%), Tamils and Telugus of South Indian descent (9%), Chinese (3%), *gens de couleur* (2%) and

Mauritians of French descent (2%). Mauritius, independent since 1968 and a republic since 1992, is a liberal multi-party democracy and a capitalist society (meaning, in this context, that both labour and consumption are mediated by money) which was impoverished, relatively overpopulated and dilapidated, with a vulnerable single export economy (sugar cane) and a high level of unemployment during the first decades after the Second World War. Mauritius has undergone an astonishing economic transformation since the early 1980s, and is now a relatively prosperous society with a dynamic economy based on sugar, textiles and tourism.

Mauritius is one among many peaceful polyethnic societies in the world. Although many of the country's inhabitants are concerned with their cultural identity, their 'roots' and the maintenance of local ethnic boundaries, compromise and tolerance are important ingredients in the shared Mauritian political culture. Notions which form part of a shared cultural repertoire include the admission that it would have been impossible to win a civil war, that secessionism would have been absurd, and that the country's political stability rests on a precarious balance between ethnic group interests. Therefore Mauritians have developed many more or less formalised methods for the maintenance of this balance (see Eriksen 1992b for details).

Ever since France lost Mauritius (then Ile-de-France) to Great Britain during the Napoleonic wars, the recognition of difference has been an explicit tendency in its politics; first *vis-a-vis* the French settlers, since the 'niggers and coolies' were not initially endowed with rights. When the French capitulated in 1814, the Britons guaranteed the settlers that they would be allowed to retain their religion, their language, their customs and their civil rights. That the British kept their promise is evident today, as Mauritius is still much more French-influenced than Anglicised. Even the legislative system appears as a unique blend of British law and the *Code Napoléon*.

During the twentieth century, and particularly since the extension of the franchise after the Second World War and the accession to full independence in 1968, policies relating to inter-ethnic tolerance have been extended so as to include the entire population. There is a continuous search for *common denominators* (Eriksen 1988) in legislation and in everyday social life, which are necessary for societal and national integration to be at all possible ('multicultural' or not, people need to have something in common if they are to have a society), and those universalist principles are balanced against the alleged conventions and culturally specific rights claimed by certain members of each constituent group.

Modes of Inter-ethnic Compromise

The electoral system in Mauritius is more or less a carbon copy of the British Westminster system, with simple majorities rather than proportional representation. The parties are largely organised along ethnic lines, and very many Mauritians vote for politicians who they feel represent their ethnic (sectional) interests. Attempts at creating inter-ethnic alliances or supra-ethnic alternatives (based on, for example, class) have generally been short-lived.

Although ethnic competition is in this way thematised in politics, there is nevertheless wide agreement over the political rules, and electoral results are respected. The Creoles, who are Christians, and the Muslims accept being governed by Hindus, who are politically dominant by virtue of numbers. At this level, there is no 'multiculturalism'. There is a shared discourse through which cultural variation and political disagreements may be articulated.

An important element in the Mauritian political system is the so-called *Best Loser* arrangement, which guarantees the representation of all ethnic groups through allotting a limited number of parliamentary seats to runners-up at General Elections. The 'best losers' are selected so as to ensure the representation of all ethnic groups in the Legislative Assembly. In this way, the importance of ethnic differences is made an integral part of the electoral system.

As in many other multi-ethnic societies, questions concerning schooling, religion and language are among the most complicated and controversial ones in Mauritius. It is perhaps here that the dilemma of equal rights and cultural differences is most evident. In all three fields, compromises of various kinds have been developed.

Regarding religion, the popular idiom *Sakenn pé prié dan so fason* ('Everyone prays in his/her own way') has nearly achieved legal status. As mentioned, four 'world religions' are represented in the island, and three of them (Christianity, Islam and Hinduism) are divided into a large number of sects and congregations. Religious groups receive state funding according to the size of their membership. In this field, a consistent compromise has been established, where no religion is given priority by the state.

The Mauritian schooling system represents a different kind of compromise. Here, equality is emphasised rather than differences. Thus core curricula are uniform island-wide, as are exams. However, classes in 'ancestral languages' are offered as optional subjects. As a matter of fact, a growing majority of Mauritians speak *Kreol*, a French-lexicon Creole, as their first language, and scarcely know the language

of their ancestors, but Kreol is rarely written. It could be said, therefore, that Mauritian schooling stresses equal opportunities yet allows for the expression of symbolic differences. It represents a compromise not only between ethnic groups, but also between a Romantic and an Enlightenment view of society.

A third kind of compromise is expressed in language policies. Officially, as many as fifteen languages are spoken in Mauritius; in practice, at least four or five are the mother-tongues of various groups. When Mauritius was to become independent from Britain in the late 1960s, in practice the new government faced four possibilities. First, it could have opted for Hindi, which is the ancestral language of the largest ethnic group (although many Mauritian Hindus do not understand it). Second, it could have chosen Kreol, which, in spite of its being held in low esteem, is by far the most widely spoken language. Third, French could have been an alternative, having been the dominant written language throughout the history of Mauritius.

In the end it was the fourth alternative, English, which was to win. English is an international language, and is learnt by Mauritians in the same way as non-native speakers elsewhere in the world learn English as a foreign language. This means that most Mauritians master it only partially. More importantly, perhaps, English was nobody's ethnic language, the few Anglo-Mauritians (most of them colonial civil servants) having either returned or become assimilated into the Franco-Mauritian group. By choosing English, an ethnically neutral language, as the language of the state, Mauritians avoided turning nation-building into a particularistic ethnic project at the beginning.

The other languages are nevertheless also supported through the state and its agencies. Public radio and TV broadcasting alternates between the major languages of Mauritius, and French still dominates in the written mass media. North American films are dubbed in French. There is in other words a clear, but negotiable division of labour between the non-ethnic language English, the supra-ethnic languages Kreol and, to some extent, French, and the ethnic languages, chiefly Bhojpuri/Hindi, Urdu, Tamil, Mandarin and Telegu.

Contradictions and Paradoxes

This will have to do as a general introduction to public policies relating to ethnic differences and national cohesion in Mauritius. I now turn to some of the problems, controversies, paradoxes and contradictions which inevitably arise during this kind of ongoing balancing act between demands for similarity and claims of difference.

The Catholic priest and ecumenic Henri Souchon became famous domestically when, at the height of the legendary 'race riots' of 1968, he admonished his congregation to visit the nearby mosque in order to familiarise themselves with a Muslim way of thought and thereby mitigate the mutual suspicion between Christians and Muslims. He called for contact and a possible 'merging of horizons', to use Gadamer's term, between the antagonists.

More than two decades after the riots, Souchon sees two possible scenarios for Mauritius regarding the relationship between ethnic boundaries and the formation of identity categories oblivious to ethnicity.[3] He calls them the fruit salad and the fruit compote, respectively. In the fruit salad, the components are clearly distinct; ethnic boundaries are intact, and reflexively 'rooted' identities are secure and stable. In the fruit compote, on the other hand, the different fruits are squashed and mixed together with substantial use of force. (This metaphor, it may be noted, is a variant of the American melting pot metaphor.) The result of the *compote de fruit*, in *père* Souchon's view, would be uprootedness, nihilism and confusion. He himself therefore supports the fruit salad variety, although he goes further than most in expanding the compass of the common denominators or, to stretch the fruit salad metaphor a bit, thickening the syrup. In order to have a dialogue, Souchon argues, one needs a firm position to conduct it from.

Some kind of fruit salad metaphor, or a rainbow metaphor which politicians are fond of invoking, is hegemonic in Mauritius. Yet conflicts between equality and difference are inevitable since the tension between sharing and difference is endemic to the island. Allow me to outline a few examples.

Most Mauritian schools are public, but private schools also exist, many of them run by religious organisations. There are anti-discrimination laws. It is nevertheless well known that Catholic schools have tended to prefer Catholic applicants for teaching positions, although they have also occasionally hired Muslims and Hindus. This policy was tried in court when an unsuccessful applicant filed a suit against a Catholic school in 1989 because she suspected having been by-passed on religious grounds.

In court the following year, the defence argued that it was necessary to have faithful Catholics in certain teaching jobs because a part of their job consisted in turning the pupils into good Catholics. The prosecutor asked whether this was also relevant with respect to subjects such as French, English and mathematics, which the school's lawyer admitted was not the case. In his testimony, the Archbishop, Mgr Jean Margéot, argued that the colours of the Mauritian rainbow

had to be kept separate 'for the *arc-en-ciel* to remain beautiful'. The Catholic school won the case, and succeeded in this way in creating a precedent for differential treatment on religious grounds in a limited part of the labour market. The principle of difference here won over the principle of equality.

Another nationally famous case from the same period concerned the controversial Muslim Personal Law (MPL), introduced during British rule, which allowed Muslims to follow customary Muslim law in family matters. A characteristic consequence of this law was that it became nearly impossible for women, but relatively easy for men, to obtain a divorce. In the course of the investigations of a Commission of Inquiry set up in the mid-1980s, it became clear that the opposition to the MPL was significant even among Mauritius's Muslims. Not unexpectedly, many women and young Muslims were against it, arguing that they were entitled to the same rights as other Mauritian citizens. In the end, the law was abolished, and universalist (Enlightenment) principles won over multiculturalist (Romantic) ones.

This second example is the most interesting one in this context. Here, the fundamental paradox of multiculturalist ideology becomes highly visible: it presupposes that the 'cultures' are homogeneous and 'have values and interests'. The mere fact that the formal leaders of an ethnic group invoke particular values and traditions does not imply that all members of the group support them. This is why it can be dangerous to accord special rights to *groups*, for groups inevitably consist of persons with often highly discrepant values and interests.

A third example highlights the relationship between particularist identities and universalist principles in a somewhat different way. Some intellectual Mauritians, tending towards the 'fruit compote' as an ideal, have experimented with mixing religions and cultural conventions in novel way, such as the radical music group Grup Latanier, which performs an essentially Creole *séga* music with strong Indian elements.

One leading Mauritian intellectual decided, some time during the 1980s, to challenge the rigid boundaries between different religions, reasoning that the island needed a 'shared culture' for a proper national identity to come about. On Christmas Day, therefore, he went solemnly to church, bringing bananas and incense as a sacrifice to the Hindu gods. This act was, naturally, frowned upon by Hindus as well as Christians, who both felt insulted by the blasphemous syncretism implied. If anything, they felt further apart after the experiment than before it. The ideal of the 'fruit compote' thus cannot be enforced against people's wishes. It should nevertheless be noted that universalist principles have been adopted by the Mauritian population

with respect to political culture. In so far as discrepant religious or otherwise cultural practices do not interfere with the universalism guaranteeing individuals equal rights, there is no good reason to chastise them.

Dilemmas of Similarity and Difference

The Mauritian attempt at creating a synthesis between liberal principles of individual equality and a cultural relativist principle is remarkable and unusual, and it certainly deserves international attention.[4]

The examples sketched in the previous section suggest that *both* equal rights and the right to be different may in particular situations lead to discrimination and the violation of commonly agreed upon individual human rights. If one insists on shared civil rights as the basis of citizenship and nationality, as the French revolutionaries did, one will tend to oppress minorities by forcing them to assimilate to a public culture (language, rules, hierarchies and conventions) which they perceive as alien and intrusive. If, on the other hand, one opts for differential treatment on the basis of religion or ethnicity, the risk is the opposite: those affected may lose their equal rights. South African apartheid policies are a good example of this; South Africans were encouraged to use their vernacular languages at all levels, and the majority of blacks were thereby in practice excluded from national and international political discourse. The hidden variable in this puzzle is, naturally, power discrepancies.

Additionally, it should be pointed out that political leaders and others are frequently prone to exploiting notions about cultural uniqueness strategically to strengthen their positions. In a critical study of ethnopolitics in the US, Steinberg (1981) concludes that persons and organisations generally invoke principles of cultural relativism when they themselves have something to gain from differential treatment, and that they will otherwise support equality principles. 'Tradition', 'rooted culture' and similar catchwords are positively evaluated in the political discourse of our time, and are often used rhetorically to justify privileges and political positions. On the other hand, this warning should not be taken to mean that there are never legitimate reasons for wishing to protect oneself against cultural domination. We just need to distinguish carefully between the right to a cultural heritage and particularistic politics.

Another, related point, which is also relevant for all polyethnic societies, concerns identification with collectivities in general. As a matter of fact, many Mauritians generally feel quite at ease as members of what they see as an emerging 'fruit compote', and do not long for

roots and purity. They would prefer to be cultural hybrids to the extent they wish, to be recognised as individuals and not as the representatives of a particular group. The legitimacy of this kind of strategy was tried out by members of the small radical socialist party *Lalit* ('The Struggle') before the General Elections of 1991. The militants on the list first refused to register their ethnic identity (which is compulsory, partly because of the Best Loser system), arguing it was irrelevant, and then proceeded to draw lots deciding their ethnic identity. The result was not devoid of Theatre of the Absurd qualities. For example, one of their leaders, to all appearances a white Mauritian of foreign birth, turned out to be a Hindu on the election rolls.

The neo-Romantic ideological climate influencing many parts of the world today – either viciously nationalist or equally viciously multiculturalist – is such that persons may virtually be forced to take on an ethnic identity whether they want to or not. Indeed, authoritarian culturalism may be just as oppressive in an ostensibly multi-ethnic and tolerant 'rainbow society' as in an ethnically hegemonic nation. The right to have an ethnic identity must also include the right not to have one. Here, perhaps, lies the greatest paradox of multiculturalism: in its apparently benevolent focus on 'the wealth of cultures and traditions' present in society, it neglects the Salman Rushdies of the world, so to speak; those persons who spend their entire lives midway between Bombay and London without wishing to, or indeed being able to, land.[5] It excludes the 'mongrels', anomalies and idiosyncratic individuals who are numerous and necessary as inter-ethnic brokers and in the forging of cross-cutting or non-ethnic alignments, and who represent the possible future of many societies.

Finally, cultural relativism gives no moral advice. To make it the source of public morality would imply that any practice would be acceptable as long as it can be justified by reference to 'a culture'. This kind of position is tantamount to no position at all, and is an inherent danger of falling into communitarianism.

Individualism as a Key Factor

It has often been asked why Mauritius is such a stable democracy, incorporating, as it does, a vast number of religious groupings and people originating from different continents. The question is wrongly asked, and it reveals an inadequate understanding of culture. At the level of everyday representations and practices, Mauritian culture can actually be described as quite uniform in the sense that there is a wide field of shared premises for communication encompassing most of the population: there is a shared political culture and a standardised

and standardising educational system, there is considerable linguistic uniformity, and recruitment to the labour market is increasingly based on individual skills. It is generally not difficult to argue the virtues of individual human rights among Mauritians; they tend to share similar, Western-derived notions of justice. It is, in other words, only superficially (if noisily) multicultural even if it may be profoundly multi-ethnic.[6]

It should be noted that the 'multiculturalist' model of coexistence, as practised in Mauritius and elsewhere, collapses unless the constituent groups share basic values of individualism and, in all likelihood, a shared *lingua franca*. For instance, it is widely believed, not least in that country itself, that the US has been capable of absorbing a great number of different nationalities without homogenising them culturally. This is wrong, and generally, migrants to the US have changed their language within two generations. One could perhaps say that the descendants of late nineteenth/early twentieth-century immigrants to the US have been assimilated to a degree of 99%, and have been allowed to use the remaining 1% to advertise their cultural uniqueness, which exists largely as a set of symbolic identity markers. As a Norwegian from Norway, I have often met Americans who identify themselves as 'Norwegians' but who unfailingly seem to betray, in their verbal and non-verbal language, lifestyle and values, a strong attachment to the moral discourses of US society.

If political multiculturalists favour equal individual rights, the 'culture' in their rhetoric is but a thin cosmetic film. If, on the other hand, they seriously defend the right of ethnic minorities to run their own political affairs according to a cultural logic of their own, they run the risk of defending practices which conflict with the human rights of individual group members.

The solution, or rather, the 'good multiculturalism', must arrive at a blend of sharing and difference. It requires common denominators in key sectors, including politics, education and the labour market, and it must institutionalise a dialogic principle (see Giddens 1994 on 'dialogic democracy') enabling a variety of voices to be heard on an equal footing. This is not relativism, but rather the recognition and democratisation of different value orientations in society, in the manner acknowledged as necessary and non-relativistic by Bauman (1993) when he notes the ill effects of the attempts at extending the Western 'ethical code over populations which abide by different codes ... in the name of one all-human ethics bound to evict and supplant all local *distortions*' (Bauman 1993: 12, italics in the original). It is a question of striking a proper balance between the demands for

formal equality and the demands for justice in a more general sense, including the equivalence of cultural heritages *as well as* the right not to acknowledge a heritage. The keyword is dialogue, which, it should again be noted, presupposes the existence of common denominators or shared meaning at the outset.

On Similarities and Differences

In the foregoing discussion, I have argued the importance of universalist human rights in modern state settings, and have alleged that political multiculturalism is a very fuzzy concept as it presupposes, yet explicitly and self-contradictorily resists, the presence of powerful processes of cultural integration. The very statement 'I have a culture worthy of protection' betrays a considerable degree of integration into a modern, reflexive way of thinking about the individual, human rights and politics. At the end, I would like to reflect on the question, tangential to the foregoing discussion, of whether the promotion and spreading of individual rights is morally objectionable in the case of societies which are multicultural in the sense that they contain people who are not integrated into a capitalist mode of production, have not been exposed to individualism and modern education and so on.

Debates about indigenous notions of personhood in anthropology have frequently oscillated between positions stating, on the one hand, that remote peoples are 'just like ourselves'; and, on the other hand, that they are qualitatively and fundamentally different. Of course, both positions can be defended convincingly, given the appropriate selection and interpretation of empirical material. Regarding human rights issues, it is an often debated question whether or not they are or ought to be universal, and if so, whether they should be 'adapted' to local circumstances because of socioculturally conditioned differences in the constitution of the person. Be this as it may, the situation in societies where there are still groups which have been spared the mixed blessings of individualism, is not similar or directly comparable to the situation in Mauritius, the US or other thoroughly modern 'multicultural' societies where personal autonomy is considered an absolute value.

As many anthropologists have shown (see for example Dumont 1980; Strathern 1992; Morris 1994), concepts of personhood vary dramatically cross-culturally. In India and Melanesia, for example, a dominant view on the individual emphasises that he or she is a product of social relations and far from that self-sustaining, independent and inviolable 'monad' the Western individual is seen as. In such societies, the community rather than the individual is

accorded rights, and the individual has duties rather than rights. In such societies, individual human rights can be seen as truly alien, even if they are often promoted and adopted by some segments of society, usually educated middle-class elites.

In his very beautiful and melancholy book *Danubio* (Magris 1986, Eng. trans. 1989), Claudio Magris writes that a fascist is a person who has best friends but cannot understand that others may be just as good friends; who feels love for his homestead but cannot understand that others may feel the same kind of love for theirs; and so on. It may therefore be proposed, as a general principle, that 'human rights missionaries' have an obligation to gain some understanding of the world views and value systems current among their target groups. They would then discover that virtually all peoples are, like Mauritian Muslims, divided on important issues. Some of their members would have gone to school and acquired individualist categories; some would have learnt about women's rights in remote countries; some might see a solution in a Marxist revolution or a liberal multi-party system, and yet others might refuse to question tradition.

As Samir Amin has written (Amin 1989), individualist thinking and social criticism is just as 'rooted' in Islamic history as fundamentalism. And as Salman Rushdie (1991) and others have reminded us, one scarcely does southern or eastern peoples a favour by continuously telling them that individual human rights are really a 'Western' invention and far from an aspect of their culture. This kind of attitude essentialises 'other cultures' and alienates the growing numbers in those societies which hold positive views of individual human rights at the same time as they resist cultural neo-colonialism.

Integration in a modern state with a liberal constitution may create a dialogical situation where human rights principles become a common denominator for the many groups and individuals which make up the state. If this sounds like blunt cultural imperialism, it should be noted that the most likely alternative, in my view, consists in a form of segregation whereby the exertion of power is left to persons such as the old men who are the formal leaders of Mauritian Muslims, and where there is a mounting risk of ethnic conflict because of the inter-group competition implied by segregation.

In most contemporary societies, processes of cultural homogenisation are taking place in some social fields (such as consumption, education and the media), while the demarcation of boundaries and the symbolic strengthening of 'identity', 'roots' and 'tradition' takes place in other fields. It is this process I described at the beginning of this article as the dual movement of cultural homogenisation and ethnic fragmentation. In this context, the

Mauritius I have described may perhaps serve as a microcosm or an ideal type of a modern society: Mauritian society is simultaneously characterised by conflicts and contradictions, pluralism and value conflicts along several axes, and one cannot offhand say what kind of values or morality 'society as such' represents. For this kind of society to be cohesive at all, common denominators are necessary, and a recognition of cultural diversity which does not interfere with the principle of universal, individual human rights may actually be the best alloy available. It is the blatant non-recognition of cultural heritages which leads to ethnic revitalisation and fundamentalism, not their institutionalisation through the state.

India was mentioned above as an example of a society where Western human rights thinking seems outlandish and alien. It might therefore be appropriate to end by stating that Marxist, feminist, liberal and other kinds of individualist human rights related movements enjoy great support in Indian society. Such groups are no less 'authentic Indian' than those of traditionalists who dream of a reawakened Hindu millenarian kingdom where ancient hierarchies are respected in minute detail.

Perhaps it would be useful to speak of a 'weak' and a 'strong' variant of political multiculturalism. The former is the one practised in some liberal modern states, including Mauritius, where a high degree of cultural homogeneity is taken for granted. The latter, which I have argued against, would be a kind of political rhetoric rejecting liberal individualism and human rights ideology on the basis of alleged tradition.[7] (Recall Tiananmen Square if in doubt.) The former, 'weak' variety is, however, also hard to defend as a political project seen within a human rights perspective. It may, as I have argued with reference chiefly to Mauritius, (1) contribute to freezing ethnic distinctions and thereby heighten the risks of ethnic conflict, (2) remove the protection and entitlement of shared societal institutions from the members of minorities, (3) strengthen internal power discrepancies within the minorities, (4) direct public attention away from basic contradictions in society, notably economic ones, and (5) contribute to a general moral and political disqualification of minorities in society: since they are not accorded the same rights and duties as everybody else, there is no apparent reason why they should be treated as equals in other respects either. The conclusion is, thus, not that cultural variation in itself should be combated, but that politicised culture is incompatible with the individual rights which modern states are, or ought to be, based on. The slogan could be 'cultural nationalism, political cosmopolitanism', to borrow a turn of phrase from Gellner (1994).

This final statement, I now realise, provides a starting-point for further discussion pivoting on the meaning of 'politicised culture'. Is marriage politics? If so, should, for example, arranged marriages in liberal individualist societies be seen as incompatible with human rights? Trusting that the reader will be able to draw on the preceding discussion in exploring further issues, I leave the problem here, partly unresolved.

Notes

1. Fieldwork in Mauritius was carried out in 1986 and 1991–92. I acknowledge funding from the Norwegian Research Council on both occasions. Thanks are also due to Richard Wilson for his perceptive and useful comments on an early version of the chapter.
2. Science encountered similar problems with regards to the concept of race about a century ago, and modern anthropologists from Boas and Malinowski onwards have not used it as an analytical concept, but it was finally abandoned by geneticists more recently.
3. I have his views from conversations which took place in 1991–92.
4. For example, a consideration of Mauritian politics and ideology might have made a wonderful section in Charles Taylor's now famous essay on multiculturalism (Taylor 1992).
5. Someone asked Salman Rushdie about his roots during a TV interview. He pointed downwards and said something like this: 'What do I have at the end of my legs? Roots? What I see are feet.'
6. This recalls a memorable passage by V.S. Naipaul, where he writes, bitterly: 'Superficially, because of the multitude of races, Trinidad may seem complex, but to anyone who knows it, it is a simple colonial philistine society' (Naipaul 1979 [1958]).
7. This distinction is similar to Turner's (1994) distinction between what he calls 'difference multiculturalism' and 'critical multiculturalism'. He sees the latter as a perfectly reasonable progressive movement for social and intellectual justice, and the former as a dangerous 'licence for political and intellectual separatism' (Turner 1994). Cf. also Parens's distinction between 'egalitarian antiessentialists', their 'fellow travellers' and 'separatist essentialists' (Parens 1994), the latter corresponding roughly to Turner's concept of 'difference multiculturalism'.

References

Amin, Samir. 1989. *L'Eurocentrisme: Critique d'un idéologie*. Paris: Anthropos.

Anderson, Benedict. 1983. *Imagined Communities*. London: Verso.

Bauman, Zygmunt. 1993. *Postmodern Ethics*. Oxford: Blackwell.

Bloom, Allan. 1987. *The Closing of the American Mind: How Higher Education has Failed Democracy and Impoverished the Souls of Today's Students*. Harmondsworth: Penguin.

Bowman, Larry. 1990. *Mauritius: Democracy and Development in the Indian Ocean*. Boulder, CO. Westview Press.

Dumont, Louis. 1980. *Homo Hierarchicus*, TEL edition. Chicago: University of Chicago Press.

Eriksen, Thomas Hylland. 1988. *Communicating Cultural Difference and Identity. Ethnicity and Nationalism in Mauritius*. Oslo: Department of Social Anthropology, Occasional Papers in Social Anthropology, 16.

—— 1992a. *Us and Them in Modern Societies. Ethnicity and Nationalism in Trinidad, Mauritius and Beyond*. Oslo: Scandinavian University Press.

—— 1992b. 'Containing Conflict and Transcending Ethnicity in Mauritius', in Kumar Rupesinghe (ed.) *Internal Conflicts and Governance*. London: Macmillan.

Friedman, Jonathan. 1990. 'Being in the World: Globalization and Localization', in Mike Featherstone (ed.) *Global Culture. Nationalism, Globalization and Modernity*. London: Sage.

Gellner, Ernest. 1983. *Nations and Nationalism*. Oxford: Blackwell.

—— 1994. Personal communication.

Giddens, Anthony. 1994. *Beyond Left and Right*. Cambridge: Polity.

Goldberg, Theo (ed.). 1994. *Multiculturalism: A Critical Reader*. Oxford: Blackwell.

Kohn, Hans. 1945. *The Idea of Nationalism*. New York: Macmillan.

Magris, Claudio. 1986. *Danubio*. Milano: Garzanti. (English edition: *Danube*, London: Collins Harvill, 1989).

McLuhan, Marshall (1994 [1964]) *Understanding Media: The Extensions of Man*. London: Routledge.

Morris, Brian. 1994. *Anthropology of the Self*. London: Pluto.

Naipaul, V.S. 1979 [1958]. 'London', in Robert D. Hamner (ed.) *Critical Perspectives on V.S. Naipaul*. London: Heinemann.

Parens, Joshua. 1994. 'Multiculturalism and the Problem of Particularism', *American Political Science Review* 88(1): 169–81.

Renan, Ernest. 1992 [1882] *Qu'est-ce qu'une nation?* Paris: Presses Pocket.

Rushdie, Salman. 1991. *Imaginary Homelands*. London: Granta.

Steinberg, Stephen. 1991. *The Ethnic Myth: Race, Ethnicity and Class in America*. New York: Atheneum.

Strathern, Marilyn. 1992. *After Nature: English Kinship in the Late Twentieth Century*. Cambridge: Cambridge University Press.
Taylor, Charles. 1992. *Multiculturalism and the 'Politics of Recognition'*. Princeton, NJ: Princeton University Press.
Turner, Terence. 1994. 'Anthropology and Multiculturalism: What is Anthropology that Multiculturalists Should be Mindful of It?' in Theo Goldberg (ed.) *Multiculturalism: A Critical Reader*. Oxford: Blackwell.
Williams, Raymond. 1976. *Keywords*. London: Fontana.

4 LIBERALISM, SOCIO-ECONOMIC RIGHTS AND THE POLITICS OF IDENTITY: FROM MORAL ECONOMY TO INDIGENOUS RIGHTS

John Gledhill

The 1948 UN *Universal Declaration* contained a number of articles relating to 'socio-economic' and 'cultural' rights. In 1948, however, the definition of cultural rights focused on education and the right to participate in 'cultural life' in the sense of the arts and sciences, rather than on respecting cultural difference and making redress to colonised peoples. The modernist ethnocentrism of the *Universal Declaration* rested, as so many commentators have noted, on foundations in Western conceptions of society and 'natural law'. Its authors unreflectively assumed that rights should be vested in individuals rather than collectivities (Messer 1993), and some of the articles, such as Sixteen, which deals with marriage and the family, showed scant concern for non-Western sensibilities. The articles on socio-economic rights were an expression of liberal as well as socialist voices within the Western tradition which argued that 'market society' could not be left to secure human welfare unassisted. Although they were essentially a charter for welfare state and labour policies which became a matter of broad consensus within the post-war metropolitan capitalist world, they seemed radical enough at the time for the United States to refuse to ratify the legal instruments for their implementation.

Today this consensus seems increasingly formal rather than real in the wake of the neo-liberal offensive which accompanied the abandonment of the Fordist–Keynesian mode of economic regulation in the old core industrial economies. In the aftermath of the collapse of communism and widespread disenchantment of metropolitan 'progressives' with Marxist grand narratives of historical progress and

emancipation, many on the left have come to see 'welfarism' in a more positive light, seeing struggles to defend welfare rights not simply as a means of pursuing 'class struggle' within a capitalist order which has been immeasurably strengthened by the collapse or market transformation of the 'actually existing' socialisms, but as positively empowering bases for building new multi-class mass movements and advancing the interests of women (Block et al 1987). The view of the capitalist state implicit in this position is more positive (and instrumentalist) than that enshrined in the writings of Marx. It is also broadly consistent with a trend towards replacing the old politics of class with a new politics of 'rights' based on a politics of identity. As Richard Wilson points out in his introduction to this volume, some examples of rights-based movements, such as the indigenous movement in Guatemala, do not focus their campaigns on national state institutions but on transnational institutions and agencies, since they represent groups which have been historically excluded from participation in national politics. Yet the global role of the United Nations agencies and non-governmental organisations poses the same questions of how 'power inhabits meaning' as the role of the national state. The Northern progressives who see struggles to defend welfare rights as intrinsically emancipating have, as Wendy Brown puts it:

largely foresaken analyses of the liberal state and capitalism as sites of *domination* and have focused instead on their implication in social and economic inequalities. At the same time, progressives have implicitly assumed the relatively unproblematic instrumental value of the state and capitalism in addressing inequalities. (Brown 1995: 10, emphasis in original)

The problem Brown poses here extends to the whole field of rights and identity politics:

While rights may operate as an indisputable force of emancipation at one moment of history – the American Civil Rights movement, or the struggle for rights by subjects of colonial domination such as Black South Africans or Palestinians – they may become at another time a regulatory discourse, a means of obstructing or coopting more radical political demands, or simply the most hollow of empty promises. ... The point is that rights converge with powers of social stratification and lines of social demarcation in ways that extend as often as attenuate these powers and lines. (Brown 1995: 98)

My purpose here is not to argue against the pursuit of any kind of politics of rights but to argue against settling for the politics of rights alone under liberal political institutions which embody various kinds of regulatory power and which are also tied in a fundamental way to capitalist social property relations. Individualism and individuation

are inscribed in existing structures of domination and those structures shape the kinds of rights movements which appear to be most challenging of their individualistic premises, notably struggles for recognition of the collective legal personalities of indigenous peoples. I will also argue against the exclusion of critical discussion of capitalist social property relations from any discourse on human rights, not on the grounds that the class form of social power determines all other modes of domination, but because it remains a constitutive part of the positioning of social subjects in the arena of struggles over rights.

The Politics of Poverty

The renewed emphasis on struggles for 'welfare rights' within the left in the United States reflects the way in which developments over the past two decades have increased the gap between reality and the standards embodied in the 1948 UN *Declaration*.[1] In 1990, the US Gross National Product reached an historic high, following a decade of growth which brought more than a 25% increase to the nation's wealth. In the same decade, child poverty increased by 21%, so that by 1991 one in five American children, a total of 14.3 million individuals, lived in poverty.

Although there is a clear pattern of ethnic disadvantage in the United States, a majority of poor children remains white, most of them have a parent that works, and most live outside large cities, in rural and suburban America, even though the inner cities have become sites of concentrated deprivation (US Bureau of the Census 1992). Of all Americans 14.2% (35.7 million people) lived below the official poverty line in 1991, half of them under 18 years of age; the country ranked fourteenth in the world in terms of life expectancy and twentieth in terms of infant mortality (UNICEF 1992). Despite the existence of Medicaid, 28.6 per cent of the poor in 1991 reported that they had no medical insurance of any kind (US Bureau of the Census 1992). Although the number of agencies providing emergency food supplies in cities like New York increased more than fifteen-fold during the 1980s, half of the cities surveyed in a 1992 study reported that they were unable to supply sufficient food to meet a demand for emergency assistance from families with children which was rising at an annual rate of 19% in 1988 and 1989; 75% of the cities turned people away from their facilities (United States Conference of Mayors 1992). In 93% of the cities, emergency facilities were providing long-term support to families and individuals (United States Conference of Mayors 1992). The total number of Americans suffering from hunger increased by 10 million, to 30 million, between 1985 and 1992. Those in deepest

poverty frequently failed to obtain the recommended dietary allowances of the National Academy of Sciences Food and Nutrition Board, for mean intakes of food energy, calcium, iron and zinc (US Department of Agriculture, Human Nutrition Information Service 1985); biometric studies indicate significant differences in child growth between poor and non-poor households (Jones et al 1985).

Point-in-time estimates of the numbers of people in the US making use of shelters and soup kitchens or congregating on the streets ranged from 400,000 to 600,000 in the late 1980s; measures based on counting the number of people who have experienced homelessness over a given period of time suggest that between 4.95 million and 9.32 million Americans experienced homelessness in the latter half of the 1980s (US Department of Housing and Urban Development 1994). Nearly two-thirds of poor families with children spend more than half their income on securing shelter, reducing their capacity to feed and clothe themselves adequately (Johnson et al 1991). As for the UN Declaration's plea for special consideration for motherhood, irrespective of marital status, 54% of all the poor families in the United States in 1991 were maintained by women with no husband present, the proportion rising to 78.3% in the case of Black families (US Bureau of the Census 1992).[2]

The United States is a country where a universal welfare 'safety-net' supposedly exists, at least for citizens.[3] Yet the background of the progressive increase in poverty, hunger and homelessness during the 1980s was not simply changing labour market structures and increasing polarisation of income distribution, but deep cuts in the core federal 'safety-net' programme budgets, including Aid to Families with Dependent Children (AFDC), Medicaid and Unemployment Compensation. At the same time as the federal welfare contribution fell, middle-class flight to the suburbs reduced the local fiscal resources available to alleviate poverty in the inner cities, reinforcing the ethnic concentration of poverty (Davis 1993). What these tendencies reflect is the lack of electoral political value of the poor in contemporary American democracy and the unwillingness of better-off Americans to pay the taxes required to ensure the less fortunate minimum standards of welfare.

The United States compares unfavourably in terms of poverty indicators with less wealthy countries such as Britain, but there is a general downward trend in the extent to which all metropolitan countries are delivering basic socio-economic rights. Globally, the figures are staggeringly bleak: a quarter of a million deaths from malnutrition every week and 1.2 billion people living below the threshold of absolute poverty as defined by the United Nations

(UNICEF 1992). In 1995, six months after it announced that it would be extending its programmes for the first time to the United Kingdom, Oxfam launched a new campaign to secure ten 'basic rights' for the people of the world: 'enough to eat'; 'clean water'; 'a livelihood'; 'a home'; 'an education'; 'health care'; 'a safe environment'; 'protection from violence'; 'equality of opportunity'; and 'a say in their future'. Some shifts of focus are manifest in Oxfam's stress on the environment and the specific rights of 'indigenous peoples', whilst its mission is now presented as one of 'supporting poor people in their efforts to work themselves out of poverty', but most of these ten fundamental rights were enshrined in the 1948 UN *Declaration*.

A recent position statement of the American Anthropological Association (AAA 1992) closely mirrors Oxfam's language, asserting the basic right of all people to adequate nutrition and food security as a pre-condition for a 'dignified and meaningful' social existence. Thus, 48 years after the UN *Declaration*, the campaign to deliver a set of socio-economic rights deemed 'basic' and 'fundamental' to enjoyment of a fully human life remains broadly the same, and perhaps further than ever from success.

Basic Rights: A Problem for Capitalist Societies?

The burden of anthropological comparative argument (and of the work of writers like Polanyi who drew on anthropological and comparative historical research) has been that access to adequate nutrition and shelter were generally less problematic in pre-capitalist societies. Deficits were seen as normally resulting from 'natural' catastrophes rather than social arrangements, although Polanyi noted that the growth of market-based grain trading could produce famines because of distributional failings rather than absolute shortfalls of production even in the ancient world (Polanyi 1977: 250). The 'moral economy' thesis advanced in the early work of James Scott (1976) seems to reinforce this conclusion.

Scott argued that exploitation in pre-capitalist agrarian class-based societies did not cross the bounds set by the principle that 'everyone has the right to basic subsistence' and sought to demonstrate that the principle was undermined by colonial capitalist relations. From this perspective, 'the right to basic subsistence' emerges as a candidate for universal status as a 'human right' enshrined in all pre-capitalist cultures but denied, at least in frequent practice and not merely in its formative period, by the cultural order of capitalism. Things are, however, somewhat more complicated. The usage of 'moral economy' in modern academic debate takes its cue from E.P. Thompson's classic

paper 'The Moral Economy of the English Crowd in the Eighteenth Century', originally published in 1971.[4] As Thompson points out, in response to two decades of critical commentary on this work:

My object of analysis was the *mentalité*, or as I would prefer, the political culture, the expectations, traditions, and, indeed, superstitions, of the working population most frequently involved in actions in the market; and the relations – sometimes negotiations – between crowd and rulers which go under the unsatisfactory term of 'riot'. My method was to reconstruct a paternalist model of food-marketing, with protective institutional expression and with emergency routines in times of dearth, which derived in part from Edwardian and Tudor policies of provision and market-regulation; to contrast this with the new political economy of the free market in grain, associated, above all, with the *Wealth of Nations*; and to show how, in times of high prices and hardship, the crowd might enforce, with a robust direct action, protective market-control and the regulation of prices, sometimes claiming a legitimacy derived from the paternalist model. (Thompson 1993: 261)

Thompson's original analysis was thus of what particular historical actors did in a particular time and in a particular place, on the basis of particular inherited historical conditions and within a particular balance of class forces, not a general theory of 'pre-capitalist moral economy'. Scott's early work was not really focused in the same way on confrontations and negotiations and it is really *Weapons of the Weak* (1985) which marks his own engagement with a more general debate on how (changing) class relations are negotiated (Thompson 1993: 344).

For many critics of the 'moral economy' approach, the 'error' supposedly committed by Thompson and Scott alike is romanticisation of the (popular) past and an inability to see at least some of the lower-class actors as individuals capable of playing the emergent market economy to their own advantage. Whether we are talking about the eighteenth century or more recent developments, it seems quite clear that such individuals exist, and that their strategies may shatter communities, although usually with a little help from outside forces. These are not, however, appropriate grounds for rejecting analyses which have no intrinsic commitment either to the idea that subalterns act in terms of a uniform and unchanging set of historically rooted 'norms' or that pre-capitalist communities are devoid of social conflict.

Thompson's version of the 'moral economy' approach seems perfectly consistent, for example, with the thinking underlying Florencia Mallon's recent study of why indigenous communities in the Sierra Norte de Puebla region of Mexico took the apparently paradoxical step of allying themselves with the liberal elites which sought to abolish village communal land tenure (Mallon 1995). Mallon

starts from the premise that such peasant 'communities' were divided along lines of age, gender, ethnicity and wealth. As a political construct, the 'community' is the provisional and contingent outcome of a hegemonic process, itself the outcome of contested definitions of power relations and cultural meanings, even as it plays a counter-hegemonic role (in whole or in part) in broader coalitions contesting power at the regional and national level. In the Puebla case, peasant communities could ally themselves with liberals because they constructed their own 'discourse of entitlement': they produced an alternative interpretation of liberal land law which was the antithesis of 'possessive individualism'; they articulated their rights to resources and political participation as their recompense for sacrifice and defence of the nation. In both Thompson's and Mallon's work, we, as analysts, discover popular 'discourses of entitlement' which contest the (equally morally grounded) discourses offered by elite actors pushing for change, such as the followers of Adam Smith's arguments for laissez-faire in the grain market in the English case. We discover, in other words, a series of propositions within popular discourses which seem to be about 'rights', 'duties', 'reciprocities' and 'mutual obligations'. However, as Thompson points out, this language is 'mostly our own' (1993: 350). To the extent that these populations had yet to interiorise the premises of individualism but maintained an holistic, hierarchic model of 'society' in Louis Dumont's sense (Dumont 1986), we may not be using an appropriate language from the standpoint of grasping the cognitive structures and motivations of the actors concerned. Indeed, we cannot even be sure that the different actors involved in shifting alliances between social strata at the time were talking the same language even where they used the same words.

Thompson himself raises the issue of what happens to the 'moral' part of the moral economy approach when it is transposed from a Judaeo-Christian environment to a hierarchic one in his discussion of the implications of Greenhough's studies of Bengal famines in the 1940s (for example, Greenhough 1982). Greenhough used the hierarchic model to explain why Bengalis reacted to famine by abandoning less-valued family members and clients, and ultimately resigning themselves to death, rather than by rioting. He criticises Scott's early work for translating indigenous Asian ideas into a Western juridical language of rights and duties. Thompson, for his part, argues that Greenhough's position is based on a 'reconstruction of the value-system of Bengali peasants [which] bears the mark of a certain school of holistic anthropology and allows no space for variety and contradiction', and suggests that he is as guilty as Scott of confusing the language of the historical subjects and academic interpreter (Thompson 1993: 347, 349). Whilst he concedes that Greenhough's

work provides a salutary warning against separating out an economic category 'subsistence' from 'the social, sacral and even cosmic links' that food preparation and commensality may represent, Thompson is not willing to countenance the argument that the Asian rice economy is 'more truly moral' in this respect than its European analogues (1993: 349–50).

It is, nevertheless, difficult to deny that there *is* a fundamental difference between an holistic and an individualistic model of society, and that Western ruling classes have been fundamentally concerned with making the latter hegemonic in the sense of getting people to interiorise it fully in the practices of social life. As Marx argued, the transition from feudal to bourgeois society depoliticised civil society in the sense that the political revolutions removed elements such as lordship, castes and guilds from political life in the name of a formal equality which created the sovereign individual (Brown 1995: 112). Civil society and the unequal social powers which exist within it become naturalised through their depoliticisation (Brown 1995: 145); it is this naturalisation which is at the centre of a bourgeois moral order in which the positively defended property rights of individuals who are capitalists and landlords circumscribe those of individuals who are workers and tenants. Pre-capitalist societies effect different kinds of naturalisation of social relations and, as Corrigan and Sayer (1985) demonstrate for the English case, the construction of bourgeois society requires a 'cultural revolution' in which people are re-formed as subjects of bourgeois power. If this process is not carried through fully, then it seems problematic to talk about human social problems in terms of a universal language of 'justice' and 'entitlements' founded on Western liberal premises, even if many contemporary forms of 'resistance' to 'Western values' may, on closer examination, be seen as effects of a Western hegemony which structures them in profoundly important ways.

Romanticisation of the pre-capitalist world is certainly best avoided. During the great famine suffered in the Valley of Mexico under Aztec rule in the years 1450–54, the rulers released the peasants from their tribute obligations, but thousands still died from starvation and thousands of others sold themselves or their children into slavery (Katz 1972: 151). Sahagún records that even some nobles sold their children, directing their wrath against the merchants who: 'purchased men for themselves. The merchants were those who had plenty, who prospered; the greedy, the well-fed man, the covetous ... the mean, the stingy, the selfish' (cited in Clendinnen 1991: 135).

Hierarchically organised societies are clearly not lacking in socio-political conflicts, and pre-Hispanic Mesoamerican empires generally

ended in peasant demonisation of ruling classes which had manifested their loss of the mandate of heaven, with the ritualised dismembering of elite symbols and sometimes elite persons. Yet there are fundamental differences between the agrarian social crisis of the 1450s in the Valley of Mexico (which did not provoke a rebellion) and that which occurred at the end of the eighteenth century in the Bajío region, which became the epicentre of the popular insurgency that began the movement for Mexican independence in 1810.

The most diversified and economically dynamic region in the colony (Wolf 1955), the Bajío had offered estate workers, tenant farmers, artisans and miners comparatively enviable conditions until increasing demographic density and Bourbon mercantilism created the social conditions which underlay the death of 15% of the rural population when the rains failed for a second year in succession in 1786 (Tutino 1986). This catastrophe was a product of a development of 'market relations' quite unlike anything known in the Aztec world. Unable to compete with peasant family farms in the maize market, estate owners had switched to growing wheat and vegetables for the urban upper income market, taking advantage of their monopoly control of irrigation water. This meant that the landlords' storehouses no longer contained maize stocks to distribute as food aid, but even had they possessed the means to help, they lacked the will. Much of the growing rural population was now expendable from the landlords' point of view, eking out an existence on the margin of subsistence survival as insecure tenants and squatters on estate land. Totally dependent on landlord power, unlike the communal peasants of Central Mexico, this rural underclass may not have received much sympathy from established tenants and resident estate workers initially, but the ruthless exercise of the rights of property was soon to increase the insecurity of all.

Having already taken advantage of growing demographic pressure to raise rents and lower wages, at the end of the eighteenth century the landlords began to evict even more prosperous tenants whose families had lived for generations on the estates, leasing their land to people with capital: merchants, owners of textile workshops, officials and tax collectors. We are back on the terrain of 'moral economy': the peasants believed that tenancy arrangements had a morally binding force of custom and even of 'contract'; the evictions fuelled feelings of moral outrage against landlords who were condemning people to starve so that already wealthy 'speculators' could farm the land that had given them a livelihood in selfish pursuit of surplus wealth. The Bajío did not rise in 1786, or even in 1800, and to analyse the case more fully it would be necessary to consider a

counter-factual: what would have happened had the colonial political system not entered what appeared to the peasants to be a crisis of intra-elite conflict, which turned a *criollo*-led political rebellion into a popular social revolution in which the target of the slogan 'Kill the Spaniards!' was the entire agrarian ruling class without distinction between *criollos* and *peninsulares*? Yet the case does point somewhere historically: it fits into a global pattern of transformation we recognise as symptomatic of the birth of an order of 'possessive individualism'. As it happens, both peasants and elites made serious misjudgements about the fields of social force implicated in 'modernising' Mexico in the long term, but it is no accident that at a time when dispossession is again on the agenda in the Mexican countryside, liberalism is again being invoked to provide it with an ethical basis.

Liberalism, Individualism and Social Justice

Liberalism is a far from uniform doctrine as far as conceptions of social justice are concerned. Some 'libertarian' neo-liberal theorists whose names are frequently invoked by the New Right, notably Friedrich Hayek, have regarded *any* redistributive principle of justice as incompatible with liberty and deny meaning to the very term *social* justice itself in 'a society of free men whose members are allowed to use their own knowledge for their own purposes' (cited in Lukes 1991: 53). Hayek's definition of 'freedom' as 'the state in which a man is not subject to coercion by the arbitrary will of another or others' (in Lukes 1991: 53), can lead to conclusions of the following kind on the issue of 'basic socio-economic rights':

[a] person who cannot afford to buy food may well have a justifiable grievance which ought to be rectified politically, but it would be misleading [*sic*] to describe his grievance as lack of freedom. (Joseph and Sumption, cited in Lukes 1991: 68)

The point, as far as libertarians are concerned, is that freedom means personal autonomy or full 'self-ownership', a concept which was integral to the Enlightenment view of 'freedom' which I will discuss in more detail below; the hungry man is not deprived of his own freedom where his poverty is the unintended consequence of others acting within their rights. Hayek, indeed, would be likely to reject even the idea that the hungry man's situation should be rectified politically, since the implementation of any scheme of distribution based on a concept of 'social justice' is, in his view, dependent on a central authority's coercive imposition of its own assessment of the needs of different individuals or group, and thereby leads down the path to

totalitarianism (Lukes 1991: 57–8). The libertarian takes inequality of resource endowments between individuals as a normal (natural) condition. The hungry man could only claim that his 'rights' had been violated and that his hunger was a consequence of lack of freedom if someone had coercively and arbitrarily imposed his condition – by stealing his wallet, for example. In this rigorously methodological individualist conception, involuntary, structurally imposed situations are convenient fictions dreamed up by totalitarian wolves masquerading as liberal humanist sheep.

These extraordinarily narrow conceptual restrictions seem designed to close off all possibilities of debating the kinds of questions raised by egalitarians:

Are lives not also rendered less autonomous by unintended actions, by social relationships and by impersonal and anonymous processes that may radically restrict people's alternatives of thought and action, and may even shape people's beliefs and preferences: and also by the lack of resources, including skills and motivations? Why ... should we conceive of their 'essential interests' as what narrowly conceived rights protect and narrowly conceived opportunities promote? Why should they not include basic needs, or the conditions of normal 'functioning', and their access to wider opportunities and a fuller life, and why should these not have a more urgent claim on society's resources to the extent to which they remain unmet? And why, finally, should the domain of disadvantage that is beyond their control – comprising luck, on the one hand, and exploitation on the other – be thought of as the 'natural' background to the practice of non-discrimination, or equal consideration, rather than as the field in which it should be practised? (Lukes 1991: 69)

Yet the libertarians' conceptualisations bear a recognisable relationship to the seven assumptions of 'possessive individualism' defined by C.B. Macpherson in his classic study of seventeenth-century thought, the central premise of which is that 'society consists of a series of market relations' (Macpherson 1962: 263–4). Their extremity results from insisting that only facts about individuals are acceptable as foundations for explanations of social processes (since 'society does not exist') and the axiomatic nature of their specific view of property rights: that individuals have an unrestricted right to an unlimited quantity of any goods they may accumulate by exercising their personal capacities. In many ways, this is a return to the ideas of the dawn of the capitalist era.

In the seventeenth century, freedom was defined in terms of proprietorship of the person and non-subjugation to the will of others. Although the Levellers, representing a class of small independent producers, challenged the bourgeois elite's definition of the property qualifications required for voting rights, they conceded that the

alienation of one's labour power constituted a partial alienation of property in the person, though not a complete one. Those who entered a wage-contract (or became dependent on poor relief) were 'included in their masters' as far as having a voice in government was concerned, since, in the Leveller view, the primary function of government was to enforce rules which enabled men to make the most of their autonomous capacities. They should thus be excluded from the franchise but not denied the civil and religious liberties to which all men had a 'natural' right (Macpherson 1962: 142–8). The Levellers were, however, unable to accept the 'image of the good' which might logically have stemmed from their possessive individualist assumptions, great inequality in the distribution of wealth: they clung to a Christian social ethic premised on relative equality and 'communitive Happinesse' (Macpherson 1962: 266). They did not see that:

a possessive market society necessarily puts in a dependent position not only wage-earners but also all those without a substantial (and by the natural operation of the market, an increasing) amount of capital. (Macpherson 1962: 267)

As Roger Rouse notes, Macpherson highlights the way in which 'the fundamentally relational view of personhood dominant in medieval society' was progressively supplanted under the cultural revolution involved in the creation of bourgeois society by a 'conception of the individual as essentially the proprietor of his own person and capacities' (Rouse 1995: 360). The long-term effects of this transformation were to turn the emancipatory and counter-hegemonic discourse of bourgeois rights versus the absolutism of the old regimes into a new model for naturalising and depoliticising social power based on private property which 'organized mass populations for exploitation and regulation' (Brown 1985: 99).

It was Locke who contributed the defence of the moral rationality of unlimited accumulation to an emergent liberal doctrine. Locke's position is all the more remarkable because his argument begins by appearing to set limits on individual appropriation on the grounds that: 'Men, being once born, have a right to their Preservation, and consequently to Meat and Drink, and such other things, as Nature affords for their Subsistence' (*Second Treatise of Government*, cited in Macpherson 1962: 200). If everyone has the right to preservation in this sense, then it appears that no one should appropriate more than he or she needs, since this prejudices the preservation of others. This was indeed Locke's position as far as the appropriation of produce and land was concerned in 'the First Ages of the World'. Locke

proceeds to argue, however, that these rules of 'natural law' ceased
to apply, when, still in the state of nature, human beings voluntarily
introduced money. Money, unlike perishable natural products, is an
asset which never spoils. It is therefore rational to accumulate it
(along with land) as capital, overcoming one of the grounds for
denying individuals surpluses above their immediate needs
(Macpherson 1962: 207–8). But the other apparent natural law barrier
to unlimited individual accumulation, the argument that accumulating
land may deprive others of the right to perservation, appears more
intractable. Locke overcame this difficulty by arguing that larger and
'improved' extensions of land increased the 'common stock' of
mankind through their superior productivity. He then assumes that
the enlarged (individually appropriated) product will be distributed
in such a way as to ensure that people left without sufficient land to
maintain themselves will be guaranteed at least a basic livelihood as
labourers and suggests that they will in fact enjoy a higher standard
of living as a result of increased (social) productivity (Macpherson
1962: 212).

Since the rights of all to enough land for subsistence were derived
from a more fundamental right to self-preservation and subsistence,
Locke can argue that class-divided societies are perfectly consistent
with natural law. By introducing the institutional infrastructure of both
merchant and agrarian capitalism into his 'state of nature' (Macpherson
1962: 209), Locke not only provides an apparent moral basis for
capitalism, but projects back into a state of nature a difference of
rationality between classes which he used to justify the political
exclusion of the labouring class and its subjection to both legal
sanctions and a tutelary Church. This is the consummate naturalisation
of differences in social power within civil society. The difference in
the moral and reasoning capacities of the propertied and labouring
classes derives from their distinct conditions of life: wage-workers
cannot develop their capacities for reason and moral life because
they are preoccupied by the exigencies of a hand-to-mouth existence.
If, however, 'by nature', all men are equally capable of shifting for
themselves, those who fall behind only have themselves to blame. Thus
it became 'possible to reconcile the justice of the market with the
traditional notions of commutative and distributive justice'
(Macpherson 1962: 245).

A number of the sleights of hand in Locke's argument continue to
underpin contemporary argument in bourgeois societies. An obvious
one is the assumption that gains in social productivity achieved
through private accumulation will be distributed throughout society
in such a way as to benefit all those who are disadvantaged.

Admittedly, Locke's judgements on these matters oscillated between the realistic and the patently ideological: English labourers are living like the Kings of primitive lands on one page and too close to the subsistence to entertain a rational thought or resist depravity on another. Yet he did at least recognise that distribution was an issue which needed addressing, and continued to maintain a theory of natural rights to basic subsistence, in contrast to libertarians who try to put the issue beyond debate.

The 'Copernican revolution' which gave birth to the doctrine of the liberal state as a 'rights-based' state is premised in a fundamental way on individualism. Not only do individuals possess rights which do not depend on the institutions of sovereignty, but the rights they hold in the 'state of nature' precede the establishment of society itself, which is the creation of individuals to promote the satisfaction of their interests and needs and to permit them the full exercise of their 'natural rights' (Bobbio 1990: 8–9). As a political doctrine, liberalism is concerned with the limits of the state's interventions in 'civil society' (either in the sense of the limits of state power – the 'rights-based state' – or the limits of state functions – the 'minimalist state'). But it is a political doctrine which depends fundamentally on a social doctrine, a rejection of organicist and holistic conceptions which see society as taking ontological (and political) precedence over the individual (Bobbio 1990: 7–8).

The fantasies of 'natural rights' theorists did not, however, prove acceptable to a later generation of liberal theorists taking their lead from Bentham, whose 'principle of utility' was developed in direct opposition to the Declaration of Rights produced by the French Revolution. In the hands of John Stuart Mill, utilitarianism focused on 'social utility' (Bobbio 1990: 59), and his late writings sought to reconcile liberalism and socialism. Mill was, however, wedded, like all liberals, to the idea that state intervention represents a potential menace to the self-realising and self-creating capacities of individuals. His version of utilitarian doctrine asserts that the state may only legitimately interfere with the pursuit of an individual's interests and projects if they are harmful to others, and it is anti-paternalist in the sense that actions which cause harm solely to the individual concerned should not be sanctioned. The boundary between public and private drawn by Mill therefore tends, in principle, towards a relatively libertarian position, yet there is a twist, since, like Locke (and indeed, Aristotle), Mill did not regard 'barbarous' segments of humanity as worthy subjects for such freedoms, because their faculties and capacities were insufficiently developed (Bobbio 1990: 61). Within societies which had achieved a degree of 'progress', universal education

could, Mill thought, eventually justify the inclusion of the labouring classes in the franchise, but illiteracy and dependence on parish relief remained valid reasons for excluding persons from participation in government; Mill's notion of liberal democracy even countenanced the idea that the better-educated should be entitled to more than one vote. Furthermore, the 'social' version of utilitarianism could itself be paternalist: Mill argued that women should have the vote because, as the weaker sex, they were more in need of society's protection if they were not to suffer harm at the hands of men (Bobbio 1990: 65). Nineteenth-century political liberalism therefore by no means equates with democracy, and Mill's emphasis on maximising the happiness of all citizens preserves the fundamentals of earlier individualistic formulations whilst leaving the question of who is to make the decisions about the 'social good' uncomfortably ill-defined.

What does, however, emerge from Mill's model of 'historical progress' and 'improvement' is an argument for the (eventual) inclusion of the lower (working and tax-paying) classes in the political community, along with the idea that the political representation of a plurality of conflicting interests is a pre-condition not merely for avoiding 'despotism' but for securing *continuing* progress. Macpherson argued that the political exclusion of the working classes – in effect, the denial of their individualism – was what spurred attempts to reformulate the liberal problematic in the centuries after Locke, and made the tensions between liberalism, democracy and social equality increasingly central to the debate. Yet the problems confronting the modern capitalist metropolis again seem to be ones of the relationship between social exclusion and political representation and participation, as growing proportions of the populations resident within national territories occupy social positions which less and less resemble the 'improving' working classes which Mill felt were proper subjects for enfranchisement.

At the forefront of modern attempts to reconcile liberal concerns with 'liberty' and social equality is the work of John Rawls, which represents the antithesis of the Hayekian neo-liberal position. Rawls's theory begins from the premise that the citizens of modern societies are generally divided by differing 'comprehensive doctrines' of the good, that is, that they support deeply conflicting religious, philosophical and moral conceptions. Given these profound differences, Rawls asks how a just and stable society of free and equal citizens can endure. He argues that 'political liberalism' in his terms provides the only viable solution to this dilemma because it provides a basis for social cooperation based around an 'overlapping

consensus' which does not entail society uniting around any one comprehensive doctrine (Rawls 1993: 201).

The 'overlapping consensus' of constitutional liberal democratic regimes is a consensus on 'political virtues', such as toleration and freedom of speech, which the state may take measures to protect (by acting against racial discrimination, for example). Rawls concedes, however, that the liberal state cannot avoid taking actions which may have the practical effect of diminishing support for particular comprehensive doctrines and certain forms of life as it strives to sustain social cooperation. He also recognises that there may be practical difficulty in preventing state actions designed to ensure that all citizens understand the substance of their constitutional and civic rights from simultaneously inculcating substantive values of 'autonomy' and self-realising individualism, values which belong to a comprehensive liberal doctrine of the kind advocated by Kant or Mill rather than to the more limited set of virtues and values necessary for an overlapping consensus (Rawls 1993: 193–5, 199–200). An example of the latter type of problem would be the compulsory public education of children born to parents who were members of religious sects which were radically opposed to the kinds of 'modern' values embodied in the curriculum. Nevertheless, Rawls argues, the *aim* of political liberalism (as distinct from a comprehensive liberal doctrine) is not to favour one comprehensive doctrine over another, but to secure the conditions for authentic pluralism. This will, however, inevitably lead to the extinction of any conceptions of the good which actually conflict with the principles of justice embodied in political liberalism (such as slavery); furthermore, some forms of life will disappear simply because they will progressively lose adherents because of their incompatibility with the public culture of constitutional democratic regimes. In accepting that 'social influences favoring some doctrines over others cannot be avoided by any view of political justice', Rawls concedes that: 'We may indeed lament the limited space, as it were, of social worlds, and of ours in particular; and we may regret some of the inevitable effects of our culture and social structure' (Rawls 1993: 197). He thus at best treats what might, from a different theoretical perspective, be defined as the 'normalising' tendencies of modern disciplinary societies (Brown 1995: 66) as a matter of unavoidable sociological fact, whilst conceding that the liberal state cannot be 'neutral' in significant respects.

Rawls is, however, a strong advocate of redistributive policies, seeking to reconcile liberty and equality with a theory of 'justice as fairness' which rests on methodological individualist premises. Rawls supposes that all members of a democratic society have a rational plan

of life which enables them to allocate their personal resources so as to pursue their conceptions of the good over a complete life, taking into account 'reasonable expectations' of their future circumstances (Rawls 1993: 177). Society itself is seen as a 'fair system of cooperation over time, from one generation to the next'; the conception of political justice defines what terms of cooperation are fair; all persons are 'free' in the sense that they possess powers of moral judgement and reason; and they are 'equal' in the sense that they possess them to the minimum degree necessary to be fully cooperating members of society (Rawls 1993: 16–19). In order to free the discussion from 'distracting details', Rawls also treats societies as closed, self-sufficient and temporally self-reproducing systems, which people enter on birth and leave on death, their ability to plan rationally over a complete life being dependent on both this closure and self-sufficiency. He envisages any extension of his theory of justice beyond these constraining assumptions as a matter of addressing 'just relations between peoples'. Rawls thus frames the problem of justice in terms of the national state and the rights of its citizens, excluding consideration of the rights of non-citizens and the problems posed by agencies and populations which move across national boundaries. Given that framework, however, he argues that only an egalitarian form of liberalism can serve as the basis for a stable system of social cooperation based on overlapping consensus. This entails not merely equal basic rights and liberties and fair rather than formal equality of opportunity, but also the 'difference principle': 'that the social and economic inequalities attached to offices and positions are to be adjusted so that, whatever the level of those inequalities, they are to the greatest benefit of the least advantaged members of society' (1993: 6–7). Justice as fairness thus requires an equalisation of life chances and the maximisation of benefits to the least advantaged. Unless the 'basic needs' of citizens are met, they will be unable to understand and 'fruitfully exercise' their rights and the liberties. Some interpret this as an argument for socialism, although Rawls himself rejects this inference (1993: 7–8 ff.).

Working out of what citizens 'need' to fulfil their roles as moral and rational cooperating members of society cannot, however, rest on any comprehensive doctrine of the good (the domain of value conflict within the 'reasonable pluralism' which Rawls regards as integral to democratic society). He therefore draws up a list of 'primary goods' which represent a 'partial similarity in the structure of citizens' permissible conceptions of the good' (1993: 180). These include freedom of movement and choice of occupation, income and wealth and 'the social bases of self-respect'; they offer a 'practicable public basis of interpersonal comparisons based on *objective features of citizens'*

social circumstances' (1993: 181, emphasis added). The purpose of the list is to construct an index against which we can measure the extent to which societies' 'basic structures' – their main political, social and economic institutions – deliver to all citizens the means for 'the adequate development and exercise of their moral powers and a fair share of the all-purpose means essential for advancing their determinate (permissible) conceptions of the good' (1993: 187). Primary goods thus provide a baseline for implementing the Difference Principle.

Rawls's account of primary goods as a condition for the 'normal functioning' of a citizen in a system of social cooperation takes up many of the issues raised earlier in Lukes's list of questions egalitarians would ask of the libertarians. It remains questionable, however, whether it is possible to construct indices of this kind which are flexible enough. As Lukes observes, variations in the conditions of individuals which limit their real opportunities in life, and are therefore candidates for compensation in the interests of fairness in Rawls's sense, are diverse in their causes and in the forms of compensation which would seem appropriate or reasonable (Lukes 1991: 62). Is incapacitation by illness or accident, for example, always a matter of individual bad luck rather than socially determined disadvantage, and what form and level of compensation is required? Furthermore, in actually existing constitutional democracies, it seems clear that the level of practical consensus on what claims it is appropriate for citizens to make on 'society' and what 'society' is obliged to deliver is formal rather than real in areas that are central to the notion of 'primary goods'.

First, reductions in welfare compensation to the elderly and unemployed are justified by principles of 'fairness' to taxpayers to which many taxpayers can readily be induced to subscribe, and programmes of 'positive discrimination' tend to provoke backlashes. To some extent these represent a spontaneous clash of values (premised on differentiation of social positions) but they can also be politically orchestrated by a variety of actors ranging from the 'respectable politicians' of the right to racist and fascist organisations beyond the frontiers of institutional party politics. As I argued earlier, even if we restrict ourselves to the political field defined by 'respectable' party politics, we need to recognise that an electorally significant 'consensus' has now been produced in favour of policies which diminish enjoyment of 'basic rights' in countries such as the United States. Whether or not most electors fully subscribe to what this appears to entail – acceptance of the substantive values embedded in neo-liberal comprehensive doctrines – is less important in practice than how they respond to the kinds of 'choices' offered to them by those who are effective players

in politics. In both the United States and Britain, the range of what is on offer from the major political parties has now narrowed to the point where the dominant discourses of mainstream political life share an emphasis on limiting welfare provision to the 'truly needy' and encouraging 'responsibility'. In this kind of framework, redistributive policies go off the agenda, the persistence of poverty and low wages is accepted, and the debate on 'basic rights' becomes a question of entitlement and the division of public and private responsibilities. The state, speaking in the name of 'society', now argues that (normalised) families have private responsibilities towards individuals which should not be transferred to society at large, and that local 'communities' must shoulder more of the burden of care of the poor and incapacitated within their midst. At the same time, a remorseless insistence on individual responsibility not merely constructs certain categories of welfare subjects (such as unmarried mothers) as morally undeserving, but enjoins us to be good Rawlsians by making long-term private financial provision for our care in age and infirmity. There are some evident ironies here. The poor have been stereotypically accused of living 'without thought for the future' (and castigated in the past for practices which suggested they did otherwise, such as having large families). Yet they are clearly not capable of 'planning for the future' by buying that security which the market can offer, and the fact that others are able to protect themselves in this way not merely ameliorates the fiscal problems of the late capitalist state but reinforces the moral stigmatisation of poverty – through discourses of personal responsibility which at the same time ethically validate voting on lines of immediate self-interest.

Second, conflicts over rights which involve appeals to 'fairness' do not necessarily simply involve individuals (singly or as members of a socio-economic category), but may involve more intractable claims based on collective rights and fundamental arguments about the virtues of different forms of life. Rawls assumes that the overlapping consensus common to exponents of different comprehensive conceptions of the good creates a framework in which these differences can be tolerated and rationally discussed. Yet this assumption seems more plausible in his abstract philosopher's world of rational individuals in closed citizen-societies than in the fractured social worlds which frame postcolonial rights politics, where sustained refusal of real equality and fundamental capitalist interests intervene, an issue to which I will return in the next section.

Third, experience of persistent discrimination can erode the foundations for overlapping consensus even between citizens. This is particular clear in the case of the Black population of the United

States, much of which is manifesting an increasingly separatist consciousness and rejecting the core symbols of 'national unity'. Poverty alone clearly does not explain this situation: Latinos fare worse than Blacks on aggregate in terms of the kind of poverty indicators which I discussed earlier. It is difficult to know what would have happened in the United States had the policies which created large urban concentrations of poor Blacks not been implemented, but the limited fruits of the politics of Black civil rights and social advancement have now created a climate in which a dialogue in terms of shared commitments to Rawlsian 'political virtues' may no longer be possible. Today, even delivery of more jobs, let alone more welfare, might not be sufficient to assuage accumulated feelings of oppression and exclusion.

Finally, even some of the actions which Rawls proposes to combat disadvantage and apply the Difference Principle require closer scrutiny: the radical forms of social engineering which some deem necessary to eliminate structural causes of the 'lack of capability' to function 'normally' in society attributed to the so-called 'urban underclass' seem problematic because they imply the 'normalcy' of forms of life and behaviour which are part of a hegemonic (and class-based) 'comprehensive conception of the good' (Gledhill 1995: 177–8). To what extent are 'features of citizens' social circumstances' truly 'objective', rather than effects of the taxonomic practices of bureaucratic power? If constitutional democracies are not characterised simply by a 'reasonable pluralism' of conceptions of the good but by structures of power which do seek to impose 'comprehensive doctrines' on members of society, then it makes little sense to start with individuals or even groups pursuing conceptions of the good which are seen as their property, competing for support on a level playing field.

Richard Rorty has argued that the merit of Rawls's philosophy is that it is thoroughly historicist and anti-universalist, beginning with liberal democratic society as it exists historically and looking for the ideas and principles actually implicit in its known convictions, such as religious toleration and rejection of slavery (Rorty 1991: 180). Rawls does not attempt to ground his conception of justice in metaphysics or a view of man's essential nature. Thus 'no such discipline as "philosophical anthropology" is required as a preface to politics, but only history and sociology' (Rorty 1991: 181). Yet it is a particular kind of history and sociology. Even if one believes that the framework of liberal democracy offers the best prospects history has produced for addressing questions of justice and fairness in social affairs, it remains an open question whether real history is really going the way of Rawls and Rorty on the basis of the evidence I have

presented thus far on the realities and politics of poverty, even in the countries which come closest to realising liberal ideals.

A major problem raised by Rawls's argument is that of defining 'reasonable pluralism'. Many other liberals who follow Mill in asserting the need for civilised societies to address problems of socio-economic inequality also follow him in emphasising the dangers posed for 'the development of man [*sic*] as creative and self-directing beings' by any kind of state-directed social project. Isaiah Berlin, for example, writes:

Today the very virtues of even the best-intentioned paternalistic state, its genuine anxiety to reduce destitution and disease and inequality, to penetrate all the neglected nooks and crannies of life which may stand in need of its justice and bounty ... have narrowed the area within which the individual may commit blunders and curtailed his liberties in the interest (the very real interest) of his welfare or his sanity, his health, his security, his freedom from want and fear. His area of choice has grown smaller ... in order to create a situation in which the very possibility of opposed principles, with all their unlimited capacity to cause mental stress and danger and destructive collisions, is eliminated in favour of a simpler and better regulated life, a robust faith in an efficiently working order, untroubled by agonizing moral conflict. (Berlin 1969: 38)

But Berlin's response to modernity's 'iron cage' is to suggest that:

What the age calls for is not (as we are so often told) more faith, or stronger leadership, or more scientific organization. Rather it is the opposite – less Messianic ardour, more enlightened scepticism, more toleration of idiosyncrasies, more frequent *ad hoc* measures to achieve aims in a foreseeable future, more room for the attainment of their personal ends by individuals and by minorities whose tastes and beliefs find (whether rightly or wrongly must not matter) little response among the majority. (Berlin 1969: 39–40)

Berlin thus insists that minorities (rather than simply individuals) should be allowed more space than that allowed by Rawls: freedom means expanding the space of our social worlds.

The movement for indigenous rights represents a stern test of what liberal societies can offer 'minorities'. In at least some cases, indigenous movements challenge a central liberal principle: that rights are ultimately enjoyed by individuals who remain equal under the law but may be assigned special rights *as individuals* in a certain category. In the current negotiations between the Zapatista Army of National Liberation (EZLN) and the Mexican government in Chiapas, a central demand is to give communities rather than the individuals which constitute them a legal personality. Abolishing the legal personality of indigenous communities was one of the chief objectives of nineteenth-century liberalism in Mexico and other parts of Latin

America. Although agrarian reform partially undid the privatisation of communal land effected under liberal reforms, the official *indigenista* ideology of the post-revolutionary Mexican state was assimilationist. 'Material progress' – delivery of basic socio-economic rights – was offered as a compensation for extinction of indigenous identities in favour of a single 'national' identity. I now wish to focus on the possible limits of the emancipation promised by an indigenous rights politics which has developed as a reaction to the continuing non-delivery of socio-economic fairness.

The Post-Colonial State and the Politics of Rights and Identity

The government side in the dialogue established with the EZLN in San Andrés Larráinzar had, by October 1995, conceded that the existing political party system did not provide adequate representation for indigenous communities and that the key to ending indigenous marginalisation within Mexican society was to create 'equitable conditions in property in land and territory' (*La Jornada* 21 October 1995). Consensus was, however, more apparent than real, leaving aside any doubts about the sincerity of the government's commitment to negotiation.[5] The previous administration had modified Constitutional Article Four to declare Mexico a 'multicultural' society, but the progress of legislation to date falls far short of the provisions of UN Agreement 169 and the hemispheric indigenous movement's demand for 'autonomy' and recognition of collective rights. The government continued to insist that no national government could tolerate 'a nation within the nation' which might give rise to separatist tendencies; the example of Quebec was invoked by both government spokespersons and the right-wing National Action Party as an example of where concessions in Chiapas might lead. It also continued to treat 'indigenous rights' as rights which would be granted to individual citizens belonging to the category 'indigenous people', a position which immediately raises the issue of how claims to indigenous status are to be adjudicated and by whom.

The criteria proposed have included biological descent, language use, dress and other 'cultural traits'. The search for taxonomic criteria makes sense in terms of the bureaucratic structures of the modern state, but little ethnohistorical sense in a country like Mexico: people who see themselves as 'indigenous' may not speak an indigenous language or look particularly folkloric, and the relatively 'open' nature of many historical indigenous communities makes biological criteria peculiarly inappropriate. 'Race' is, however, significant in other senses. 'National identity' is built around the notion of 'race mixing' (*mestizaje*):

historically, the presumption of the ideology of *mestizaje* was that national 'progress' equated with 'whitening' (Lomnitz-Adler 1992), but the official ideology of *indigenismo* also placed symbolic value on the 'indigenous past' and the notion of a creative 'cultural fusion'. It is therefore possible to rework parts of this established discourse of identity and argue that the real, 'deep' Mexico remains indigenous, as more romantically inclined anthropologists, such as Guillermo Bonfil (1990), have done. Yet the role of racist ideologies in social practice makes it unlikely that most lower-class Mexicans will spontaneously rediscover themselves as '*indígenas*'. Nor is the problem trivial from the viewpoint of the state and the elites which lie behind it. If special rights, including rights to economic resources, are to be granted to persons in the 'indigenous' category, then the bureaucratic definition of who is included becomes crucial: too inclusive a definition could open the floodgates to the manipulation of legislation to serve popular agendas inimical to dominant economic interests.

The state therefore cannot accept self-ascription as a basis for claiming rights as an 'Indian'. Furthermore, the forms of identity self-ascription are themselves conjunctural and situational. The category '*indio*' was a label originally imposed by colonisers, with negative connotations which the term '*indígena*' (original inhabitants of a territory) sought to transcend. Indigenous peoples continued to divide themselves into distinct ethnic groups (*etnias*) and in many contexts, more local, community identities took precedence over feelings of inclusion in broader ethnic categories (Wilson 1993). Movements articulating higher levels of ethnic inclusion, such as the pan-Mixtec and pan-Maya movements (Kearney 1986; Watanabe 1995), the growth of a transnational, continental movement and the positive revalorisation of the '*indio*' label, are products of socio-economic change, state-building and globalisation. Even so, politicised identities are contested. Some leaders of organisations representing Michoacán's Purhépecha Indians, for example, emphasise their culture's opposition to the Nahua identity which, they claim, has been privileged by the association of the Aztecs with the official *indigenismo* of the national state in Mexico City (Zárate Hernández, 1991).

The EZLN negotiators, backed by academic advisers, including anthropologists, deny the charge that their position is 'anti-national'. The issue of indigenous autonomy was only part of the programme advanced by the EZLN-convened National Democratic Confederation (CND), which met for the first time, in Chiapas, in August 1994. The CND brought together the same kind of broad coalition of social movements and opposition political activists as the National Democratic Front which supported the presidential campaign of

opposition leader Cuauhtémoc Cárdenas in 1988, but it was a novel development in the sense that it was a movement associated with indigenous people which now drew Mexico's fragmented and conflictive left together (Stephen 1995: 88, 96). The CND programme embraced workers' and women's rights as well as those of indigenous peoples; it also called for a radical programme of democratisation beyond the limits of electoral politics alone and for reform of the police and judiciary (Stephen 1995: 92–3, 95). The coalition subsequently fragmented, with the EZLN distancing itself from the CND organisation in general and in particular from the elements within it allied to the centre-left Party of the Democratic Revolution (PRD). The Zapatistas have, however, continued to argue that the demand for indigenous 'autonomy' in the political sphere – that the state 'respect the uses and customs of communities in electing their own authorities' – is part of a larger project to establish a new federalism based on popular sovereignty: the goal of the dialogue is a new constitution, but the dialogue itself is an example of popular sovereignty in practice, since the state is being forced to talk to 'Indians' and to respond to their demands rather than engage in the empty practice of 'consulting' their opinion of official proposals (*La Jornada* 21 October 1995)

This claim is, however, problematic. The EZLN's leadership of the non-official peasant movement in Chiapas is contested (Tello Díaz 1995), and its relations with the PRD, which also enjoys substantial grassroots support, deteriorated drastically after the 1995 state elections. Although the EZLN has made great play of 'taking issues back to the communities' for final decision by communal assemblies, its right to speak for those communities is dependent on 'communal hegemony' in Mallon's sense. Here it is important to note that the origins of the repressive 'bossism' (*caciquismo*) found in many indigenous communities in the Central Highlands of Chiapas lies in interventions by the national state in the 1930s under the radical president Lázaro Cárdenas. The state's objective was to reduce the power of the regional elite. Young bilingual Indians promoted to leadership positions as a result of this intervention were later able to defend their monopoly of local power by rejecting 'outside interference' in the 'internal affairs' of communities which possessed their own 'traditional institutions' for settling disputes (Rus 1994). A similar link between a *caciquismo* aligned with the ruling Institutional Revolutionary Party (PRI) and 'indigenous autonomy' developed in Oaxaca state, where mayors in indigenous communities have long been elected according to the 'uses and customs' of consensus in communal assemblies.

The violence associated with this process of maintaining 'communal hegemony' through a 'defence of tradition' which both national and regional elites may find it convenient to support is strikingly exemplified by the case of San Juan Chamula, where a new outbreak of violence between Catholic 'traditionalists' and Protestant dissidents took place during the November round of San Andrés negotiations (Rus 1994: 299–300; *La Jornada* 21 November 1995).[6] As Rus points out, the association of 'the traditional community' with *caciquismo* in the Central Highlands means that those who are seeking a new way of doing things are seeking to define 'post-traditional' forms of community (*La Jornada* 21 November 1995). Yet all contending parties may appeal to 'community autonomy' and 'tradition' (Collier 1994), and opposition groups as well as entrenched leaderships may seek leverage for their position from outside parties, including the state and the radical wing of the Catholic Church. If it is undeniable that new forms of community organisation have been built and rebuilt over the generations in Chiapas, it also seems important, at least from an analytical point of view, not to ignore the fact that all forms of 'communal consensus' rest on conflict. It appears that the achievement of 'communal consensus' in those communities which agreed to commit themselves to the EZLN insurrection of January 1994 entailed the expulsion of those who refused to participate (Tello Díaz 1995: 186). This does not mean that the resulting new expressions of communal will are 'inauthentic' products of manipulation of passive and credulous 'Indians': this, the stereotypic view of the non-Indian ranchers of states like Chiapas and Guerrero, is belied by long-standing histories of conflict and resistance and by the presence of people born in indigenous communities in leadership roles (Harvey 1994; Stephen 1995). The EZLN's own switch from a focus on national and class perspectives towards a more exclusive focus on indigenous rights reflects the way it has been increasingly captured by its base, as hopes for a wider response to the rebellion have receded. It does, however, mean that what are popular, emancipatory demands at one historical moment can turn into new forms of oppression. The Mexican regime has always displayed the utmost ruthlessness and cynicism in exploiting this fact.

The EZLN demands that communities be granted legal personality not simply in the agrarian field, but in the management of all the resources in their territories. This challenges the past role of the state as well as private interests, and fits into a broader global pattern. Such demands may be met by offering indigenous groups a share of the income generated by exploiting minerals or forest resources rather than by offering any real participation in management. The radical

alternative, to allow indigenous communities the choice of leaving their resources unexploited, has not generally been on the agenda.[7] How satisfying such arrangements prove is dependent on context. In the the Northern Territory of Australia, for example, title to the land comprising the Uluru National Park, which contains Ayers Rock, was transferred to the Mutitjulu Community in 1983, on an arrangement under which the Aborigines agreed to lease the Park back to the government for an annual fee plus a percentage of the entrance fee charged to tourists: since, however, the Aborigines also objected to the way tourists vandalised the site and treated their persons with patronising contempt, the creation of an Aboriginal Board of Management to co-administer the Park with the National Parks and Wildlife Service did not prove a mere formality but led to the imposition of new controls (Whittaker 1994: 316). Yet even this case, which involves a relatively small number of beneficiaries, and little challenge to major economic interests or private property relations, proved controversial. White Australians can also appropriate Ayers Rock as a national symbol, and argue against the rights of Aboriginals in terms of discourses of equality and fairness, reinforced by critiques of the interventionist state. If liberals who sympathise with the Aborigines produce a discourse of compensation and moral restitution, interest groups opposed to land claims (including transnational corporations) find much of the Australian public receptive to the argument that extension of land rights to people who might prevent the exploitation of the mineral resources threatens national prosperity (Whittaker 1994: 320–4).

All these arguments draw on moral precepts. Some of them, such as the sanctity of Ayers Rock for 'all Australians', are reactions to the discourse on sacredness embedded in Aboriginal rights discourse; others reflect divergent 'comprehensive conceptions of the good' and a clash between individualistic and non-individualistic accounts of the foundations of society (Whittaker 1994: 328). One of the most significant underpinnings of controversy relates to the socio-economic dimensions of the rights assigned to indigenous people. Poor whites may see themselves as equally deserving of additional sources of income, whilst the power of money may play a significant role in the future management of resources where indigenous rights to participate are recognised: as Mexican experience demonstrates only too clearly, those who achieve dominance in the construction of communal hegemony may well be coopted. Furthermore, claiming special rights for 'indigenous people' may seem less problematic because indigenous people are particularly poor and marginalised: other 'ethnic minorities' may have claims to compensatory treatment, and it is often difficult

to separate arguments about indigenous rights from arguments about the need for income redistribution and poverty alleviation on grounds of social equity alone.

Indigenous rights arguments rest on special case reasoning about the rights of indigenous peoples as colonised peoples. These are not simply arguments about the need for material compensation but about the need to respect indigenous 'tradition' and to conserve differences in cultural practice. In the case of Australian land claims, the arguments have gravitated around the question of how 'traditional' Aboriginal relations to land differed from private property relations. The extent to which, in practice, Aborigines are being offered the chance to live in a 'traditional' way under the kinds of arrangements described above are clearly debatable – even assuming that 'we', as anthropological 'experts', or 'they', as living exponents of a (presumably living and developing) culture, can define what traditional relations with land were, either in general or for a given region. Yet the obvious problem with an argument that cultural difference should be respected in the case of colonised peoples is that concessions are to be encapsulated within an unchanged dominant socio-economic system: indigenous rights discourse does not offer other members of society the choice of recreating some kind of pre-capitalist agrarian lifestyle (unless, perhaps, they do it through market mechanisms by purchasing land for a commune).

Another obvious danger in indigenous rights discourse is that of essentialising 'indigenousness'. This is clearly the case with the overtly separatist wing of the continental indigenous movement, whose demands for autonomy replicate the language of state and nation-building of superordinate *criollo* and *mestizo* political culture (Hale 1994). The emancipatory and democratic projects of the EZLN appear to be broader, but if the alliances they have sought with other sectors of Mexican society continue to fail to prosper, they may find themselves trapped by the logic of maintaining their place in the politics of Chiapas and by an indigenous rights platform which can be contained politically and stripped of its broader potential to challenge the structures of social power.

The negotiation of further special political and legal arrangements for indigenous communities would run counter to the neo-liberal project of creating a fully 'modern' civil society, and any further modifications to Constitutional Article 27, which was revised to create the legal framework for a privatisation of the land reform communities in 1991, might also be seized upon by non-indigenous communities. But the costs for the state should be measured against the fact that Mexico is now a largely urbanised society and has a long

historical record of successful circumvention and perversion of the law by those who possess wealth and power. Nevertheless, the EZLN's claim that recognition of 'indigenous autonomy' could be made part of a wider democratising project in which a 'new federalism' offers grassroots empowerment to all citizens in Mexican society does deserve to be taken seriously. It would be far easier to frustrate a ruling-class strategy of containing the radical content of indigenous demands by building an 'overlapping consensus' within the popular movement itself which did not relegate the demands of indigenous people (or women, for that matter) to secondary importance. The model of the 'autonomous indigenous community' might seem to fit the Lacandón jungle rather better than great cities like Mexico City and Guadalajara, but the peasant communities of Chiapas have, for some time, been participating in larger regional organisations which have combined class-based and indigenous demands. Large urban spaces do not necessarily make it impossible to establish face-to-face representative assemblies as part of a hierarchy of representative institutions, although contemporary urban social organisation makes such a project more difficult because of high rates of residential mobility: the latest evidence from Mexico City suggests that only 30% of the total population are long-established neighbours. There are, however, other problems. The tensions which so rapidly emerged within the CND in part reflected the fact that a national political party like the PRD was only willing to commit itself to a model of popular power built from the base up in a rhetorical way. Establishing concrete arrangements to underpin the 'new federalism' would also raise long-established questions about the limits of direct democracy in a large-scale society, the distinction between representatives and delegates and all the other age-old questions posed by liberal theories of political representation. On these grounds, the kinds of liberal political institutions defended by Rorty and Rawls may seem more realistic targets for reformers.

Yet there is little in liberal versions of history and sociology which really explains why indigenous peoples are demanding their own spaces in our modern social worlds. The political theory of indigenous autonomy in Chiapas appears to rest on the simple fact that indigenous communities do have their own ways of doing things, which are recognisably different from the way things are done, for example, in land reform community assemblies which conform to the 'legal-rational' norms of procedure laid down by the post-revolutionary state. We have seen that this situation is, in fact, related to the interventions of external powers historically, but that this is not the whole of the story, since 'community' is continually being reinvented at the

grassroots. Actual indigenous practices are never unaffected by the practices of the larger society (particularly, the communities of the Selva Lacandona, which have little historical depth, mix together people who bear distinct 'ethnic identities', and have experienced extensive influences from outside organisations). Nor, as Richard Wilson stressed in his introduction, are contemporary local developments unaffected by the global diffusion of rights discourse and transnational legal practices, although the interesting questions relate to the ways in which these national or transnational flows are appropriated, manipulated and reinterpreted situationally. As I noted earlier, some indigenous communities were making their own readings of liberal discourses in Mexico in the nineteenth century. This enabled them to turn liberalism to their advantage in some respects, but it also brought down repression when they tried to implement their model 'on the ground' in a way which resisted the long-term social project of the liberal elite in Mexico City. Their conception of the good was ultimately utterly inconsistent with the 'modern (substantive) values' enshrined in this, hardly atypical, liberal regime.

This returns us to the question of the kind of resolution of underlying problems which might result from the 'dialogue' in Chiapas. Twentieth-century regimes can probably afford to be more flexible about making special arrangements for indigenous communities in terms of property law and systems of political representation than their nineteenth-century predecessors, since capitalism and the national state are now firmly consolidated. It is, however, not yet clear whether the EZLN will negotiate enough concessions from the national state to be able to convince its base that a settlement should be reached, enabling it to establish itself as an institutional political interlocutor within the bounds of the 'reasonable pluralism' envisaged by Mexico's current rulers. This is not simply a question of whether the radical demands for socio-economic justice embedded in the original Zapatista declarations will eventually be toned down and subject to compromise. What at least part of the EZLN's base wants is a kind of 'social dignity' which it may prove difficult to deliver in full simply by political and juridical reform, poverty alleviation programmes, or even more jobs and land reform. Within the social logic of *mestizaje*, the social dignity of other poor people has been tied to their distancing themselves from the Indian identity which is the inferior part of themselves, the 'darkness' which distinguishes them from the elites. To break down the barriers this poses to the achievement of indigenous social dignity requires not simply a new and more genuine *popular* pluralism, but a counter-hegemonic shift in non-indigenous identities, so that both specific indigenous and other

kinds of social identities can provide a basis for mutual respect between individuals. This is not a completely impossible dream. My own experience of studying rural social movements which mobilise land claimants suggests that *mestizos* and *indígenas* can display very concrete solidarity, seeing each other as people who share common (class) problems of poverty without losing their senses of 'difference'. Yet even in the countryside, other patterns of social differentiation are still associated with everyday, racially coded, practices of discrimination and negative stereotyping; North–South and rural–urban divides magnify these problems, despite the fact that there is a two-way movement of the poor between rural and urban places which has had a significant historical impact on the development of the indigenous movement itself (Gledhill 1995: 217). Given that context, an insistence on the value of Indian alterity which did not contribute to a reframing of 'popular' identities in general, could have very negative consequences, even if it brought some immediate material benefits to the EZLN's base and was seen by that base as the best way to respond to persistent oppression and denigration.

To pursue this argument further it is necessary to renew the critique of liberal accounts of sociology and history in a more depth. At first sight, history does indeed seem to favour the creation of forms of life which correspond to liberal assumptions. As I stressed earlier, through the bureaucratic and taxonomic practices embodied in the state apparatuses, modern ruling classes strive to shape the subjectivities of their citizens. As Foucault has shown us, individualisation is central to these processes. The burden of past state action on native communities has been to work for individuation against collectivism and holism, which anthropologists have generally seen as a process which undermines cultural coherence. 'Natives' become welfare-dependents, alcoholics, persons in need of treatment or food-stamps. They also become people whose identities are shaped by the state agencies on which they come to depend. The socio-economic marginalisation and political exclusion of indigenous people has, however, worked against such projects: the absence of a real will to assimilate (in consequence of both racism and exploitation and dispossession) has recreated boundaries which have sharpened collective identities and maintained a heterodox recreation of communitarian cultural practices. But the effects of domination continue to shape these contestations.

After six months of violence in which nine of their number have been assassinated and a 12-year-old boy had an ear slashed off by the wife of a leading *mestizo* politician, the Mixtec inhabitants of the municipality of Tlacoachistlahuaca, Guerrero, demanded a separate

municipio, although they constitute 60% of the population of the current, *mestizo*-dominated unit (*La Jornada* 25 November 1995). This separatist demand was accompanied by protestations of continuing loyalty to the national and state governments, but it is, in a clear sense, a product of the existing system of domination (being seconded by the *mestizos* themselves following the Mixtecs' breaching of the established order by seizing the town hall, which they subsequently burned). Hector Díaz-Polanco (currently an EZLN adviser) has argued that, in general, the manipulation of ethnic identities is a strategy of power in Latin America:

Dominant elites have not ignored the sociocultural complexity of their national societies; on the contrary, they have based their domination on it in order to control the remaining sectors, including the so-called ethnic groups. Seen clearly in this light, ethnic groups are not – as traditional cultural anthropology has had it – mere complexes of cultural traits rooted in the past (customs, traditions, forms of social organization, world-views, etc.) but sociocultural realities constantly created and recreated by capitalism that cannot be understood without the critical factor of the control exercised over them by dominant groups. Without this factor, ethnic groups as now constituted would cease to exist. (Díaz-Polanco 1992: 18)

The imaginary of the indigenous community, with its distinctive forms of political organisation and claims to control territory and resources, does represent a powerful and attractive counter-hegemonic symbol in Mexico. This is not simply because of its apparent antithesis to the image of a corrupt political elite and rapacious capitalism, but because the 'progressive' imaginary of the 1910 Revolution (and the egalitarian liberal values it embodied) failed to materialise. Yet it is difficult to see where an indigenous rights politics can lead in Mexico, unless it is effectively articulated to a wider movement to achieve a major redistribution of income as a material basis for reshaping social attitudes. Under existing social conditions, 'privileges' for Indians are likely to be seen as divisive, since Indian collectivities will be seen by other disadvantaged groups simply as 'super-individuals' which have an advantage simply because they have a special identity which others cannot claim. As DaMatta (1991) has argued, the problem facing the Latin American poor is that they have been made into individuals not simply by changes in the law and adoption of liberal constitutions, but by processes of social change which have stripped them of reliable kin and patronage connections: it is not, in fact, simply people who identify themselves as *indígenas* who would like to maintain a more holistic model of society, but it is those who can still secure recognition (by the state and by anthropologists, among others) as *indígenas* who have the best chance of capitalising on such

a vision. Since their current position is one of heightened disadvantage, they deserve to succeed, even if they cannot take the rest of the disadvantaged with them or, unaided, force a collapse of the larger regime of possessive individualism. In a now heavily militarised Chiapas, the stakes are so high, and the antagonisms so great, that even minimal advances would be a great achievement.

Yet there are other issues to be considered. The collective rights enshrined in indigenous demands are in tension with the universal individual rights at the core of liberalism. Where the 'essentialist impulse' (Díaz-Polanco 1992: 19) of ethnic identity can lead is only too apparent in the other contexts, notably Bosnia and India. The violence which has been meted out to indigenous people in Latin America over the centuries is premised on dominant group assumptions about essential difference which lend the 'Indians' a dangerous quality. An essentialisation of difference which began as a reflex of colonial anxiety was reinforced by the adoption of liberal constitutions, since the notion that 'Indians are spiritually different' provided a means of framing their continuing exclusion from the rights enjoyed by free and equal citizens. Those indigenous movements which have responded to continuing exclusion by celebrating their own version of the principle of difference are clearly courting the risk of exacerbating latent tensions as well as restricting the scope of struggles based on common class oppression. There are therefore many pitfalls in the way a postcolonial sense of guilt supports the construction of 'indigenous peoples' as bearers of distinctive rights. Yet this is also one of the most practically effective positions from which it is possible to contest dispossession and exploitation under contemporary global conditions, precisely because it involves a kind of ('unnatural') injustice and discrimination which are incommensurable with the elements of overlapping consensus to which all who pretend to modern liberal (read civilised) values still feel obliged to subscribe.

The Politics of Social Justice in Late Capitalist Societies

As I have stressed, lamenting the decline of the welfare state at the expense of abandoning 'critical analyses of state paternalism and state management of capitalism's inequities' (Brown 1995: 15) is not a viable position because the forms of power embodied in the liberal state produce subjects in Foucault's sense, recodifying boundaries and extending protection to categories of persons defined by and in regulatory discourses (Brown 1995: 100). The neo-liberal discourse of the 'minimalist state' might be seen as a mask for expanded state domination, and its accompanying programmes of deregulation,

privatisation and 'outsourcing' as new and more effective techniques for managing a social body dismembered by capitalist restructuring (Brown 1995: 17–18). From this standpoint it could be argued that the current interest of the liberal state in giving space to 'indigenous rights' movements and other forms of 'identity politics' fits into a broader picture of the liberal state as a regulatory agency under late capitalist conditions, whose 'language of recognition of difference as no difference ... becomes a vehicle of subordination through individualization, normalization and regulation, even as it strives to produce visibility and acceptance' (Brown 1995: 66).

Let us briefly review the problem of 'basic needs'. One of the problems with any theory of 'basic needs' is that it tends to embody minimalist assumptions about what human beings deserve. Peasant beneficiaries of development projects, for example, have long learned that middle-class bureaucrats think that peasants deserve to subsist, but not to become middle-class themselves. It also seems odd to argue the need to promote 'self-help' among the poor, as if they possessed little intrinsic initiative, given the incredible amount of effort it has always taken to survive economically in the lower ranks of capitalist society. One of the things history and ethnography seem to teach us about the poor is that they also invest a considerable amount of energy in maintaining their social dignity, not merely in the eyes of their peers, but in their interactions with their superiors (whether the superiors recognise that the exchange has that significance or not). It is therefore not entirely true that one cannot lead a dignified life in conditions of poverty, though it will be certainly be a life which contains many moments of humiliation and physical and emotional suffering.

Nevertheless, many of the ways in which people 'contest' their humiliation and individuation, through violent and non-violent means, can be seen as effects of structures of domination and may be as destructive of the person as taking refuge in crack cocaine. Although modern states may be spending more on instruments of social containment in general, the chief targets of repressive legislation and state violence are organised groups, not least the organisations of supposedly moribund 'working classes'. The poor remain relatively powerless, and the politics of social welfare are a powerful legitimation of the state's protectionist role which, in draining poor people of autonomous identities and social diversity, deepens that powerlessness. The 'self-help' alternative to 'paternalism' is also generally individualising, as is the need of many to participate in the 'black' and 'grey' areas of the economy to survive. Both state tactics inhibit politicisation along fundamental lines of class cleavage. This

is why it is far from clear that a politics of rights focused on other kinds of identities – specific forms of injury, discrimination and social subordination on grounds of race, gender or sexual preference, for example – is any more emancipating: seeking redress through the law 'fixes the identities of the injured' as victims of injustice and 'casts the law in particular and the state more generally as neutral arbiters of injury rather than themselves invested with the power to injure' (Brown 1995: 27). To challenge domination, that is, to go beyond reactive 'resistance' within the framework of the existing order of domination, requires more than an appeal to the moral sensibilities and reason of the powerful. It requires a struggle not only for an alternative 'comprehensive conception of the good', but, as Brown puts it, 'an aspiration to power rather than a tendency to reproach it' (Brown 1995: 55).

Increasing sociocultural pluralism is not a conspicuous feature of the metropolitan countries of the North at the present time. It is true that some concessions have been made to internally colonised groups within national state borders, but there has been an equally obvious attempt to revalorise a notion of 'national' (majoritarian) culture, accompanied by increasingly strong measures against immigrants, asylum-seekers and refugees who might further 'dilute' national identity. As Michael Kearney (1991) has argued, the formation of transnational migrant populations problematises the regulation of their identities by the bureaucratic and disciplinary apparatuses of national states, but the unequal powers embedded in different national states still structure their lives in important ways (Basch et al 1994: 30).

It is difficult not to relate these developments to capitalist restructuring. Technological change and shifts in the centres of gravity of the world economy are leaving large segments of the potential 'native' metropolitan workforce unemployable in those sectors where higher earnings can still be secured; relocation of production and investment outside national frontiers is undermining the security of skilled working and middle classes accustomed to rising material standards of consumption. It is not, however, simply shifts within the capitalist world-system which make it increasingly hard to envisage a move back to redistributive policies in old or declining 'cores' at the present time. The political base for such policies has been eroded within democratic electoral regimes by the desire of professional politicians to appease 'the middle' as far as possible in the process of transition and to give such a strategy a moral basis. Since the liberal tradition embodies positions which are appropriate for such a purpose, we now find social democrats drawn into a consensus which has shifted towards the right of the possible spectrum of positions. To the

extent that socio-economic marginalisation has 'racial' dimensions (as it clearly does in Britain, Europe and the United States), the short-term advantages of attempts to 'reunite the nation' around a spurious majoritarian construction of 'national culture' is likely to exacerbate conflicts grounded in ethnic communities and the construction of antagonistic 'comprehensive conceptions of the good' of a 'foundationalist' kind. In the last analysis, however, what is happening in the old industrial core zones of the world economy is an intelligible consequence of the need to manage economic decline within the framework of preserving an existing class structure and maintaining the incomes of its upper strata.

The non-Western world is bound up with these processes of global economic restructuring in different ways, confronting them through distinct cultures of capitalism, sometimes under the aegis of elites which proclaim their rejection of liberal values. I will restrict my attention here to Latin America, a region in which these values have been formally embraced for at least a century. Given the legacies of history, one might argue that even the Latin American countries where the ethnic divide was deepest, such as Guatemala and Peru, are making strides towards achieving major gains in pluralism relative to the past, in the sense that indigenous peoples are achieving a political voice on the national stage. Mexico's human rights record has certainly not improved under the present administration (Amnesty International 1995), but one might nevertheless argue that it is a positive development that human rights issues are debated in public and that the dialogue on indigenous rights is taking place. I have argued, however, that a key issue is how demands for indigenous rights can be made part of a broader project of democratisation and the formulation of a popular alternative to neo-liberalism. By appropriating an identity which is a product of a colonial situation, Mexico's *etnias* can make their collective voice a more powerful one, nationally and internationally, but there is a price to be paid.

For the majority of Mexico's growing army of deracinated urban poor, the general class opposition between *'ricos'* and *'pobres'* has greatest salience to their conditions of life, and is reflected in at least some moments of their quotidian discourse. The problem is that it is subject to a high degree of interference by other mediations, amongst which may be counted the discourse of identity itself. As Rouse argues, state-sponsored 'ethnic pluralism' and the assumption that prejudice and disenfranchisement should be combated by the self-mobilising struggles of what are conceived as the homogeneous and horizontal collectivities which suffer from these problems, could be seen as aspects of a reworked hegemonic project of bourgeois-

dominated ruling blocs in the era of 'flexible accumulation' (Rouse 1995: 363, 374). It is, nevertheless, ironic, as Brown points out, that, in a postcolonial epoch in which 'modern liberal states fully realize their secularism' and 'the mantle of abstract personhood is formally tendered to a whole panoply of those historically excluded from it by humanism's privileging of a single race, gender and organization of sexuality':

the marginalized reject the rubric of humanist inclusion and turn, at least in part, against its very premises. Refusing to be marginalized, to render the differences inconsequential, to be depoliticized as 'lifestyles', 'diversity' or 'persons like any other', we have lately reformulated our historical exclusion as a matter of historically produced and politically rich *alterity*. (Brown 1995: 53)

Politicised identities are therefore both 'a production and contestation of the political terms of liberalism, disciplinary-bureaucratic regimes [and] certain forces of global capitalism'. But we still need to ask how basing claims to recognition on identity can avoid re-subjugating actors historically subjugated through identity; what kinds of politicisation, in what kinds of political context, could sustain subversion of the power structures producing such subjugation? (Brown 1995: 54–5).

Liberal political definitions of collective identity through categorical equivalence can be just as 'individualistic' in their foundations as the more obvious 'individualism' of the culture of consumerism promoted by the capitalist corporation. The possibilities of the dominant bloc in Mexico using the current struggle for 'indigenous autonomy' as a means of fragmenting a broader potential coalition of forces against the current model of capitalist development are apparent. This was not, however, the way that the EZLN began its insurgency against the government of Carlos Salinas de Gortari, on the day of the implementation of the North American Free Trade Agreement. The Mexican 'proletariat', and particularly a proletariat formed from the 'working poor' is not defunct, and the possibilities of forming broader cross-cutting popular coalitions were demonstrated by the large marches organised in Mexico City in the later months of 1995 by sacked bus-drivers and mechanics from the militant SUTAUR (Sindicato Único de Trabajadores de Auto-Transporte Urbano-Ruta 100) union, street-sellers displaced from the city centre by riot police, indigenous and *mestizo* peasants belonging to rural organisations linked to radical urban groups, a variety of public sector manual workers and school teachers. In a city in which 3% of the population forms an upper class which continues to enjoy its privileges in fortified suburbs patrolled

by private security guards, and the 20% who form the middle class have good reasons to believe that the neo-liberal model is not working for them, the formation of multi-class coalitions demanding redistributive policies, and perhaps even a transformation of social property relations, might not be an impossible dream.

In the polls, however, most of the middle classes are opting for the National Action Party, which embodies the strongest of commitments to possessive individualism. The centre-left Party of the Democratic Revolution is increasingly limited to the support of the poorest and most marginalised, including the indigenous rural communities of the states where the direct influence of the EZLN has been less significant than in Chiapas. And a large proportion of the lower classes are simply not voting at all. The struggle for electoral democracy and decency in public life does not, therefore, run parallel to the struggle for greater socio-economic justice. The electoral success of authoritarian (but not 'white') rule in the Peru of Alberto Fujimori suggests that much more complex relations exist between a desire for economic stability, civil liberties and an end to established social practices of social and political exclusion on lines of ethnicity than liberal models of a fair and pluralistic society allow. If the historical challenge in Latin America was to build a real and substantive connection between recognition of the universal rights enshrined in liberal discourse and the material progress and social dignity of all citizens, the challenge today may be that of convincing people that there is any point in seeking to participate in the larger political life of a society which offers them no place in its conception of the good.

Notes

1. Data for this discussion of poverty in the United States were acquired from the World Wide Web pages of the National Coalition for the Homeless, the Food Research and Action Center and the Hunger and Poverty Web pages compiled by Daniel Zalik of Brown University. The Oxfam Web pages were the source for the outline of that organisation's current campaign later in this section.
2. The lowest rate of female-headed households is found among Latinos, although their larger families, low pay and lack of access to health care reinforce relative disadvantage.
3. Current legislative proposals to deprive undocumented migrant families of access to most welfare facilities *inter alia* entail the abandonment of an earlier acceptance of 'the special rights of children'.
4. The text is reprinted without revision in Thompson (1993).

5. Leaving aside the role of the military in Chiapas itself, and the 'dirty war' being waged against the Peasant Organisation of the Southern Sierra (OCSS) and indigenous communities in general in the state of Guerrero under the auspices of governor Rubén Figueroa, compadre of President Zedillo, the government's approach to indigenous demands in other parts of the country did not mirror the spirit of 'dialogue' in San Andrés. A meeting of 200 indigenous delegates convened in November in Huautla, Hidalgo, by the Organización Independiente de Pueblos Unidos de la Huasteca (OIPUH) and the Frente Democrático Oriental Mexicano Emiliano Zapata (FDOMEZ), was impeded by road-blocks and constant overflights by helicopters. Its demands, seconded by national human rights organisations, were 'Justice and No More Murders' (*La Jornada* 23 November 1995).

6. Some of those expelled from Chamula and other highland communities for opposition activities had re-established themselves in the Selva Lacandona by the 1980s, along with colonists who had left areas of high demographic density to start a new life in this zone of colonisation in the previous decades. The basis for support for the EZLN in the Lacandón jungle was the growing land scarcity caused by the federal decision in the 1970s to create a huge reserve for the very small number of Lacandón Indians (in the cynical interest of opening up forest resources to state exploitation), followed by the designation of an ecological reserve (Tello Díaz 1995: 61). These decisions were, of course, justified in terms of the high principles of 'justice for marginalised minorities' and 'conservation'.

7. It should be conceded that, to the discomfort of some indigenous rights activists, support for leaving nature as it is is not generally forthcoming from indigenous movements, though their demands have been harnessed to ecological critiques of non-sustainable development. This raises the question of whether it is reasonable to expect poor people to subscribe to the kinds of value systems which make sense to middle-class intellectuals whose lifestyles are maintained at a great distance from the point of production of the resources that sustain the system of material civilisation in which they live.

References

American Anthropological Association. 1992. *Surviving Famine and Providing Food Security in Africa*. Position Statement. Washington, DC: American Anthropological Association.

Amnesty International. 1995. *Mexico. Human Rights Violations in Mexico: A Challenge for the Nineties.* AI Index: AMR 41/21/95. London: Amnesty International.

Basch, Linda, Nina Glick-Schiller and Cristina Szanton-Blanc. 1994. *Nations Unbound: Transnational Projects, Postcolonial Predicaments and Deterritorialised Nation States.* Langhorne: Gordon and Breach.

Berlin, Isaiah. 1969. *Three Essays on Liberty.* Oxford: Oxford University Press.

Block, Fred, Richard Cloward, Barbara Ehrenreich and Frances Fox Piven. 1987. *The Mean Season: The Attack on the Welfare State.* New York: Pantheon Books.

Bobbio, Norberto. 1990. *Liberalism and Democracy.* London: Verso.

Bonfil Batalla, Guillermo. 1990. *México Profundo: Una Civilización Negada.* México, D.F.: Editorial Grijalbo.

Brown, Wendy. 1995. *States of Injury: Power and Freedom in Late Modernity.* Princeton, NJ: Princeton University Press.

Clendinnen, Inga. 1991. *Aztecs: An Interpretation.* Cambridge: Cambridge University Press.

Collier, George A. 1994. 'The New Politics of Exclusion: Antecedents to the Rebellion in Mexico', *Dialectical Anthropology* 19(1): 1–43.

Corrigan, Philip and Derek Sayer. 1985. *The Great Arch: English State Formation as Cultural Revolution.* Oxford: Basil Blackwell.

DaMatta, Roberto. 1991. *Carnivals, Rogues and Heroes: An Interpretation of the Brazilian Dilemma.* Notre Dame and London: University of Notre Dame Press.

Davis, Mike. 1993. 'Who Killed LA? Part II: The Verdict is Given', *New Left Review* 199: 29–54.

Díaz-Polanco, Hector. 1992. 'Indian Communities and the Quincentenary', *Latin American Perspectives* 19(3): 6–24.

Dumont, Louis. 1986. *Essays on Individualism.* Chicago: University of Chicago Press.

Gledhill, John. 1995. *Neoliberalism, Transnationalization and Rural Poverty: A Case Study of Michoacán, Mexico.* Boulder, San Francisco and Oxford: Westview Press.

Greenhough, Paul R. 1982. *Prosperity and Misery in Modern Bengal.* Oxford: Oxford University Press.

Hale, Charles. 1994. 'Between Che Guevara and the Pachamama: Mestizos, Indians and Identity Politics in the Anti-Quincentenary Campaign', *Critique of Anthropology* 14(1): 9–39.

Harvey, Neil. 1994. 'Rebellion in Chiapas: Rural Reforms, Campesino Radicalism and the Limits to *Salinismo*', in Neil Harvey et al (eds) *Rebellion in Chiapas*, pp. 1–49. Transformation of Rural Mexico

Series, No. 5. La Jolla: University of California, San Diego, Center for US–Mexican Studies.

Johnson, C.M., L. Miranda, A. Sherman and J.D. Weill. 1991. *Child Poverty in America*. Washington, DC: Children's Defense Fund.

Jones, D.Y., M.C. Nesheim and J.P. Habicht. 1985. 'Influences in Child Growth Associated with Poverty in the 1970s: An Examination of NHANES I and NHANES II, Cross-sectional US National Surveys', *American Journal of Clinical Nutrition* 42(4): 714–24.

Katz, Friedrich. 1972. *The Ancient American Civilizations*. London: Weidenfeld and Nicolson.

Kearney, Michael. 1986. 'Integration of the Mixteca and the Western US–Mexico Region via Migratory Wage Labor', in Ina Resenthal-Urey (ed.) *Regional Impacts of US–Mexican Relations*, pp. 71–102. Monographs Series, No. 16. La Jolla: University of California, San Diego, Center for US–Mexican Studies.

Kearney, Michael. 1991. 'Borders and Boundaries of State and Self at the End of Empire', *Journal of Historical Sociology* 4(1): 52–74.

Lomnitz-Adler, Claudio. 1992. *Exits from the Labyrinth: Culture and Ideology in the Mexican National Space*. Berkeley: University of California Press.

Lukes, Steven. 1991. *Moral Conflict and Politics*. Oxford: Clarendon Press.

Macpherson, C.B. 1962. *The Political Theory of Possessive Individualism: Hobbes to Locke*. Oxford: Oxford University Press.

Mallon, Florencia E. 1995. *Peasant and Nation: The Making of Postcolonial Mexico and Peru*. Berkeley, Los Angeles and London: University of California Press.

Messer, Ellen. 1993. 'Anthropology and Human Rights', *Annual Review of Anthropology* 22: 221–49.

Polanyi, Karl. 1977. *The Livelihood of Man*. New York: Academic Press.

Rawls, John. 1993. *Political Liberalism*. New York: Columbia University Press.

Rorty, Richard. 1991. *Objectivity, Relativism and Truth*. Cambridge: Cambridge University Press.

Rouse, Roger. 1995. 'Questions of Identity: Personhood and Collectivity in Transnational Migration to the United States', *Critique of Anthropology* 15(4): 351–80.

Rus, Jan. 1994. 'The "Comunidad Revolucionaria Institucional": The Subversion of Native Government in Highland Chiapas, 1936–1968', in Gilbert M. Joseph and Daniel Nugent (eds) *Everyday Forms of State Formation: Revolution and the Negotiation of Rule in Modern Mexico*, pp. 265–300. Durham and London: Duke University Press.

Scott, James C. 1976. *The Moral Economy of the Peasant: Rebellion and Subsistence in Southeast Asia*. New Haven: Yale University Press.

110   Human Rights, Culture and Context

Scott, James C. 1985. *Weapons of the Weak: Everyday Forms of Peasant Resistance*. New Haven: Yale University Press.

Stephen, Lynn. 1995. 'The Zapatista Army of National Liberation and the National Democratic Convention', *Latin American Perspectives* 22(4): 88–99.

Tello Díaz, Carlos. 1995. *La Rebelión de las Cañadas*. Mexico, D.F.: Cal y Arena.

Thompson, E.P. 1993. *Customs in Common*. Harmondsworth: Penguin Books.

Tutino, John. 1986. *From Insurrection to Revolution in Mexico: Social Bases of Agrarian Violence*. Princeton, NJ: Princeton University Press.

United States Conference of Mayors. 1992 (December). *A Status Report on Hunger and Homelessness in America's Cities: 1992, a 29-City Survey*. Washington, DC: United States Conference of Mayors.

US Department of Agriculture, Human Nutrition Information Service. 1985. *Nationwide Food Consumption Survey: Continuing Survey of Food Intakes by Individuals: Women 19–50 Years and their Children 1–5 Years, 1 Day (Report 85-1)*. Washington, DC: US Department of Agriculture.

US Department of Commerce, Bureau of the Census. 1992 (August). *Poverty in the United States: 1991*. (Current Population Reports, Series P-60, No. 181). Washington, DC: Government Printing Office.

US Department of Housing and Urban Development, Office of Policy Development and Research. 1994. *Worst Case Needs for Housing Assistance in the United States in 1990 and 1991: A Report to Congress*. Washington, DC: Department of Housing and Urban Development.

UNICEF. 1992 (December). *State of the World's Children Report, 1993*. New York City: Oxford University Press.

Watanabe, John M. 1995. 'Unimagining the Maya: Anthropologists, Others, and the Inescapable Hubris of Authorship', *Bulletin of Latin American Research* 14(1): 25–46.

Whittaker, Elvi. 1994. 'Public Discourse on Sacredness: The Transfer of Ayers Rock to Aboriginal Ownership', *American Ethnologist* 21(2): 310–34.

Wilson, Richard. 1993. 'Anchored Communities: Identity and History of the Maya-Q'eqchi', *Man* 28(1): 121–38.

Wolf, Eric R. 1955. *The Mexican Bajío in the Eighteenth Century: An Analysis of Cultural Integration*. New Orleans: Tulane University.

Zárate Hernández, José Eduardo. 1991. 'Notas para la interpretación del movimiento étnico en Michoacán', in Victor Gabriel Muro and Manuel Canto Chac (eds) *El Estudio de los Movimientos Sociales: Teoría y Método*, pp. 111–29. Zamora and Coyoacán, D.F.: El Colegio de Michoacán and La Universidad Autónoma Metropolitana.

5 ON TORTURE, OR CRUEL, INHUMAN AND DEGRADING TREATMENT

Talal Asad

In this chapter[1] I discuss the modern conception of 'cruelty', in particular as represented in Article 5 of the *Universal Declaration of Human Rights*: 'No one shall be subjected to torture or to cruel, inhuman or degrading treatment or punishment.' In this statement the adjectives qualifying 'treatment or punishment' seem to indicate forms of behaviour that, if not quite equivalent to 'torture', at least have a close affinity with it.

Moral and legal judgements that derive from this rule have an interesting history in the West, to which I shall refer in what follows. I want to advance the thesis that the universal rules enshrined in the *Declaration* cover a wide range of qualitatively different kinds of behaviour. More precisely, I shall try to make four points: first, that the modern history of 'torture' is not only a record of the progressive prohibition of cruel, inhuman and degrading practices. It is also part of a more complex story of the modern secular concept of what it means to be truly human. The second point is this: the phrase 'torture or cruel, inhuman or degrading treatment' serves today as a cross-cultural criterion for making moral and legal judgements about pain and suffering. Yet it is given much of its operative sense historically and culturally. My third point is linked to the first two. It is that the new ways of conceptualising *suffering* (which include 'mental torture' and 'degrading treatment') and *sufferer* (a term that now refers also to non-humans, and even to the natural environment) are increasingly universal in scope but particular in prescriptive content. The final point is that the modern dedication to eliminating pain and suffering often conflicts with other commitments and values: the right of individuals to choose, and the duty of the state to maintain its interests.

Together, these four points aim at underscoring the unstable character of a central category deployed in modern, Western society.

The instability relates, in brief, to the fact that the ideas of torture, cruelty, inhumanity and degrading treatment are intended to measure what are often incommensurable standards of behaviour. In addition, they are applied in particular cases in a contradictory fashion.

I do not argue that there can be no such thing as cruelty. I am merely sceptical about the *universalist discourses* that have been generated around it. But my scepticism is intellectual, not moral. This chapter is not concerned with attacking the reforms that take their inspiration from the United Nations' condemnation of 'torture or cruel, inhuman and degrading treatment'. I am interested primarily in the way Western discourses about cruelty hang together, and the ways that the idea of torture can overlap with and substitute for ideas of cruel, inhuman and degrading treatment – as well as of the inflicting of pain and suffering on others. In my view such inquiries are necessary if we seek to clarify our transcultural judgements.

Two Histories of Torture

I begin with a discussion of two books which together show very different ways of writing histories of cruelty. The first, by G.R. Scott, represents physical cruelty as a feature of 'barbaric' societies – that is, societies that have not yet been humanised. The other book is by Darius Rejali. It makes a distinction between two kinds of physical cruelty, one appropriate to pre-modern and the other to modern societies, and describes that difference in the context of contemporary Iran.

Scott was a Fellow of several British learned societies, including among them the Royal Anthropological Institute. Scott's (1940) *History of Torture* is perhaps the first modern story of its kind. It deals at length with 'Savage and Primitive Races', ancient and early modern European peoples, and Asian 'civilisations' (China, Japan and India). On the one hand it tells a story of punishments now largely discontinued or suppressed; on the other it speaks of motives for inflicting suffering that are deep-rooted and pervasive. His indebtedness to Krafft-Ebing's ideas is evident not only in explicit form in his chapters on 'Sadism' and 'Masochism', but also in the general evolutionary scheme he employs according to which the primitive urge to inflict pain remains a latent possibility (sometimes realised) in civilised society.

Scott is somewhat unusual for his time in wanting to include the mistreatment of animals in his account of torture, and in describing their plight as a consequence of the non-recognition of rights, for like other moderns he sees the extension of rights to be crucial for the elimination of cruelty. But in the course of arguing this thesis he hits

on a profound and disturbing ambiguity. It is not entirely clear whether he thinks that human cruelty is merely an instance of bestial cruelty – that is a working out of the supposedly universal instinct of stronger animals to hunt or attack the weaker, or whether human cruelty is unique – not a characteristic of animal behaviour at all – and that everyday human ruthlessness towards animals is essential for justifying the persecution of vulnerable people (defeated enemies, uninitiated children, etc.) on the grounds that they are *not fully human*. In either case Scott disturbs liberal ideas of what it is to be truly human: humans are essentially no different from other animals, or they are different by virtue of their unique capacity for cruelty.

It is worth noting that the instances of physical pain Scott describes as 'torture' belong sometimes to the involuntary submission to punishment and sometimes to the practices of personal discipline (for example, rituals of endurance, asceticism). He makes no distinction between the two: pain is regarded as an isolable experience to be condemned for what it is.

In the encounter between 'Savage Races' and modern Euro-Americans, Scott has no doubt that 'torture' is something the former do to the latter – perhaps because it is synonymous with 'barbarity'. At any rate the suffering inflicted on Native Americans by white settlers and the expanding US state has no place in his history of torture.

This is not to say that Scott asserts torture to be entirely absent in the modern state. On the contrary, he is quite explicit about its use by the police to secure confession ('the third degree'). His position is that the story of modernity is in part a story of the progressive elimination of all morally shocking social behaviour – including what is now described in international law as 'cruel, inhuman and degrading treatment or punishment'. Scott does not claim that that intention has been fully realised, only that progress has been made. In this story of progress, he tells us, the state's definition and defence of rights is the most effective protection against cruelty.

In his important book, the Iranian political scientist Darius Rejali (1994) makes the interesting argument that, far from being a barbaric survival in the modern state as Scott's story suggests, torture is in fact integral to it. Although he classifies torture into two types, modern and pre-modern, he shares with Scott the view that the term 'torture' has a fixed referent. More precisely, both of them assume that to speak of torture is to refer to a practice in which the agent forcibly inflicts pain on another regardless of the place that the practice occupies within a larger moral economy.

Rejali offers a sophisticated account of the role of political punishments in Iran both before and after the inception of

modernisation in that country. Modern torture, he tells us, is a form of physical suffering that is an inseparable part of a disciplinary society. In Iran the practice of torture is as essential to the Islamic Republic today as it was to the Pahlavi regime it replaced. Both in their own way are modern disciplinary societies.

Rejali believes that his book refutes what Foucault (1979) had to say about torture in *Discipline and Punish*.[2] He maintains that torture does not replace discipline in modern society, as Foucault claimed, but persists in a major way. But this belief arises from a misreading of Foucault, whose central concern was not with 'torture' but with 'power': and consequently with a contrast between sovereign power (which needs to exhibit itself publicly) and disciplinary power (which works through the normalisation of everyday behaviour).

Public rituals of torture are no longer deemed to be necessary to the maintenance of sovereign power (whether they were in fact functionally necessary to the maintenance of 'social order' is, of course, another question). But Foucault's thesis about disciplinary power is not subverted by evidence of surreptitious torture in the modern state. On the contrary, precisely because torture carried out in secret is intimately connected with the extraction of information, it is an aspect of policing. Policing is a governmental activity directed at defending a fundamental 'interest of society': the ordinary and extraordinary security of the state and its citizens. It is also an institution in which knowledge and power depend upon each other, and where power – and this point is curiously neglected by Rejali – circulates in secret.

Modern torture as part of policing is typically secret partly because inflicting physical pain on a prisoner to extract information, or for any purpose whatever, is 'uncivilised' and therefore illegal. It is also secret because policing agents do not wish to advertise everything they learn from tortured prisoners. After all, the effectiveness of certain kinds of disciplinary knowledge depends upon its secrecy. The secret character of knowledge acquired in policing therefore relates at once to the uncertainty of outside critics as to whether, and if so how often, something illegal has been done by a bureaucratic power to obtain it ('torture is intolerable in a civilised society'), and also to how, when and where law-enforcing power chooses to act once it possesses that secret information ('every society must protect itself against criminal conspiracies').

Rejali's definition of torture as 'sanguinary violence condoned by public authorities' slips uneasily between the legitimate and public practice of classical torture on the one hand, and, on the other, the secret because 'uncivilised' character of policing torture in modernising

states like Iran. His fuller argument does not address this difference. Modern torture, he insists at length, is integral to what Foucault called disciplinary society. It is, if not itself quite identical with discipline, then very close to it.

There are valuable insights in Rejali's book relating to the brutalising aspect of the process of modernisation. Here I mention only two objections that might be made to his argument. The first is that his main example (twentieth-century Iran) relates to what many readers will identify as a 'modernising' rather than a 'fully modern' society. Whether all the transformations in Iran in the period covered by Rejali's book truly represent modernisation in the sense of moral improvement is – these readers will say – an open question, but shocking evidence of blatant torture in that country does not prove that torture is integral to modernity. Rejali's argument at this point would have been stronger if he had referred to a modern society, like Nazi Germany, rather than a society on the way to being modernised.[3] For although Nazi Germany was notoriously an illiberal state, it was certainly no less modern than any other.

The other objection is this: Rejali does not explain why, unlike discipline, modern state use of torture requires the rhetoric of denial. The brief answer to this question, surely, is that there is now a new sensibility regarding physical pain. Although it occurs frequently enough in our time, the modern conscience regards the inflicting of pain without 'good reason' (to perform a medical operation, say) as reprehensible, and therefore as an object of moral condemnation. It is this attitude to pain that helps define the modern notion of cruelty.

The modern conscience is also a secular conscience, a category that subsumes what we now know as modern religion. Christianity, which was traditionally rooted in the doctrine of Christ's passion, consequently finds it difficult to make good sense of suffering today. Modern theologians have begun to concede that pain is essentially and entirely negative. 'The secularist challenge', writes a modern Catholic theologian:

even though separating many aspects of life from the religious field, brings with it a more sound, interpretive equilibrium; the natural phenomena, even though sometimes difficult to understand, have their cause and roots in processes that can and must be recognised. It is man's job, therefore, to enter into this cognitive analysis of the meaning of suffering, in order to be able to affront and conquer it. ... Through his works, even before his words, Jesus of Nazareth proclaimed the goodness of life and of health, as the image of salvation. For Him pain is negativeness.[4]

The writer in this passage is clearly thinking of disease, but since pain can also be a consequence of human intention, it follows that such pain should be eliminated from the world of human interaction – even from religious disciplines, and from the enactment of martyrdom, where it once had an effective and honoured place. The secular Christian must now abjure passion and choose action. Pain is not merely negativeness. It is, literally, a scandal.

Abolishing Torture

Why has the infliction of physical pain now become scandalous? A well-known part of the answer is this progressivist story: two centuries ago critics of torture like Beccaria and Voltaire recognised how inhuman it was, and how unreliable as a way of ascertaining the truth in a trial. Thus they saw and articulated what others before them had (unaccountably) failed to see. Their powerful case against judicial torture shocked Enlightenment rulers into abolishing it. The theme of its intolerable cruelty emerged more clearly because the pain inflicted in judicial torture was declared to be gratuitous. Pain inflicted on prisoners to make them confess was immoral, it was argued, particularly because it was grossly inefficient in identifying their guilt or innocence.[5]

The Enlightenment reformers didn't necessarily condemn physical punishment as such, because it involved considerations other than simple instrumental ones, especially ideas of justice. Eventually, however, the evolution of modern ideas of justice were to contribute to growing hostility to painful punishment. But why was this gratuitous pain not condemned by critics earlier? What had prevented people from seeing the truth until the Enlightenment?

In his brilliant study *Torture and the Law of Proof*, John Langbein (1977) has provided a partial explanation. He demonstrates that torture was proscribed when the Roman canon law of proof – which required either confession or the testimony of two eyewitnesses to convict – declined in force in the seventeenth century. Increasing resort to circumstantial evidence secured convictions more easily and speedily. The abolition of judicial torture was thus in effect the moral condemnation and legal proscription of an extremely cumbersome and lengthy procedure that was now coming to be regarded as more or less redundant. Langbein implies that the moral truth about judicial torture was linked to the prior construction of a new concept of legal truth.

When torture was the object of vigorous polemic in the eighteenth century, Jeremy Bentham came to the conclusion that the pain of torture

is sometimes easier to justify than the suffering inflicted in the name of punishment. In the course of this justification he maintained, for example, that Courts of Law resorting to imprisonment in cases of contempt might find the application of physical pain, or even the threat of applying it, would secure obedience in a way 'less penal' than prison:

A man may have been lingering in prison for a month or two before he would make answer to a question which at the worst with one stroke of the rack, and therefore almost always with only knowing that he might be made to suffer the rack, he would have answered in a moment; just as a man will linger on a Month with the Toothach [sic] which he might have saved himself from at the expense of a momentary pang.[6]

It is not Bentham's apparent refusal to distinguish between voluntary and involuntary subjection to pain that should be noted here. It is the idea that subjective experiences of pain can be objectively compared. This idea is crucial for the modern understanding of 'cruel, inhuman and degrading treatment' in a cross-cultural context, although liberals today would strongly reject Bentham's view regarding the occasional preferability of torture to imprisonment. For it is precisely some notion of comparability in suffering that makes of long years in prison (including solitary confinement) a 'humane' punishment and of flogging an 'inhumane' one, even though the experience of imprisonment and of flogging are qualitatively quite different.

In an interesting passage in *Discipline and Punish*, Foucault (1979: 232) notes that in the nineteenth century imprisonment was compared favourably to other forms of legal punishment mainly because it was regarded as the most egalitarian. This was a consequence of the philosophical doctrine that freedom was the natural human condition. Penal reformers reasoned that since the desire for liberty was implanted equally in every individual, depriving individuals of their liberty must be a way of striking at them equally – that is, regardless of their social status or physical constitution. For just as fines were easier for the rich to pay, so physical pain could be borne better by the more sturdy. No form of punishment accorded so precisely with our essential humanity, therefore, as imprisonment did. That legal incarceration was considered to be equitable contributed to the sense that physical punishment was gratuitous. For this reason, although modern liberals must regard Bentham wrong in the conclusion he reached about torture, they must consider him right to have endorsed a quantitative comparison of very disparate kinds of suffering. It is not difficult to see how the utilitarian calculus of pleasure and pain has come to be central to cross-cultural judgement in modern thought and practice. For by a reductive operation the idea of a calculus has

facilitated the comparative judgement of what would otherwise remain incommensurable qualities.[7]

Humanising the World

The historical process of constructing a humane society, it is said, has aimed at eliminating cruelties. Thus it has often been observed that European rule in colonial countries, although not itself democratic, brought about moral improvements in behaviour – that is, the abandonment of practices that offend against the human.

Major instruments in this transformation were modern legal, administrative and educational practices. And a central category deployed in them was the modern category of customary law. 'Of all the restrictions upon the application of customary laws during the colonial period', writes James Read (1972: 175):

the test of repugnancy 'to justice or morality' was potentially the most sweeping: for customary laws could hardly be repugnant to the traditional sense of justice or morality of the community which still accepted them, and it is therefore clear that the justice or morality of the colonial power was to provide the standard to be applied.

Read points out that the phrase 'repugnant to justice and morality' does not have a precise legal meaning, and that early legislation in the colonies sometimes employed other expressions, such as 'not opposed to natural morality and humanity', to perform the same revolutionary work.

But moral and social progress in those countries has been uneven. Although Europeans tried to suppress cruel practices and forms of suffering that were previously taken for granted in the non-European world by making the practitioners legally culpable, the suppression was not always completely successful. Today the struggle to eliminate social suffering is taken up by the United Nations. So the story goes.

I want to propose, however, that in their attempt to outlaw customs the European rulers considered cruel, it was not the concern with indigenous suffering that dominated their thinking, but the desire to impose what they considered civilised standards of justice and humanity on a subject population – that is, the desire to create new human subjects.[8] The anguish of subjects compelled under threat of punishment to abandon traditional practices – now legally branded as 'repugnant to justice and morality' or as 'opposed to natural morality and humanity', or even sometimes as 'backward and childish' – could not therefore play a decisive part in the discourse of colonial reformers. On the contrary, as Lord Cromer (1913: 44) put it with

reference to the misery created among the Egyptian peasantry by legal reforms under British rule: 'Civilisation must, unfortunately, have its victims.' In the process of learning to be 'fully human' only some kinds of suffering were seen as an affront to humanity, and their elimination sought. This was distinguished from suffering that was necessary to the process of realising one's humanity – that is, pain that was adequate to its end, not wasteful pain.

Inhuman suffering, typically associated with barbaric behaviour, was a morally insufferable condition for which someone was therefore responsible; those requiring it (themselves inhuman enough to cause it to be inflicted) must be made to desist, and if necessary punished. That, at any rate, is the discourse of progressive reform. What individual colonial administrators actually felt, thought or did is another (though not entirely unrelated) matter. Most experienced administrators were prepared locally to tolerate various 'uncivilised' practices for reasons of expediency, but all were no doubt aware of the dominant progressivist discourse rooted in 'civilised' societies.[9]

In a recent unpublished paper by Nicholas Dirks there is a lucid illustration of just this discourse in late nineteenth-century British India. His account of the inquiry conducted by the colonial authorities into the ritual of hook swinging[10] contains this sober judgement by the presiding British official:

It is, in my opinion, unnecessary at the end of the nineteenth century and, having regard to the level to which civilisation in India has attained, to consider the motives by which the performers themselves are actuated when taking part in hook swinging, walking through fire, and other barbarities. From their own moral standpoint, their motives may be good or they may be bad; they may indulge in self-torture in satisfaction of pious vows fervently made in all sincerity and for the most disinterested reasons; or they may indulge in it from the lowest motives of personal aggrandisement, whether for the alms they might receive or for the personal distinction and local éclat that it may bring them; but the question is whether public opinion in this country is not opposed to the external acts of the performers, as being in fact repugnant to the dictates of humanity and demoralising to themselves and to all who may witness their performances. I am of the opinion that the voice of India most entitled to be listened to with respect, that is to say, not only the voice of the advanced school that has received some of the advantages of western education and has been permeated with non-Oriental ideas, but also the voice of those whose views of life and propriety of conduct have been mainly derived from Asiatic philosophy, would gladly proclaim that the time had arrived for the Government in the interests of its people to effectively put down all degrading exhibitions of self-torture.

The fact that the performers themselves declared that they felt no pain was irrelevant. So, too, was the plea that this was a religious rite.

Such claims to difference were not acceptable. It was the offence given by the performance to a particular concept of being human that reduced qualitatively different kinds of behaviour to a single standard.

Confirmation of its offensiveness was obtained by listening to some colonised voices only. The latter included Indians who were directly westernised. But, more significantly, confirmation was provided also by those who accepted a westernised exegesis of their 'Asiatic philosophy'.[11] From the point of view of moral progress, the voices of those who took up a reactionary position could not be attended to.

Clearly, in the cause of moral progress there was suffering and suffering. What is interesting, I think, is not merely that some forms of suffering were to be taken more seriously than others, but that 'inhuman' suffering as opposed to 'necessary' or 'inevitable' suffering was regarded as being essentially gratuitous, and therefore legally punishable. Pain endured in the movement towards becoming 'fully human', on the other hand, was necessary, in the sense that there were social or moral reasons why it had to be suffered. This view is of a piece with the post-Enlightenment concern to construct through judicial punishment the most efficient means of reforming offenders and of guarding society's interests.[12]

As the idea of progress became increasingly dominant in the affairs of Europe and the world, the need for measuring suffering was felt and responded to with greater sophistication.

Representing 'Torture', Acting with Deliberate Cruelty

Pain is not always regarded as insufferable in modern Euro-American societies. In warfare, sport and psychological experimentation – as well as in the domain of sexual pleasure – inflicting physical suffering is actively practised and also legally condoned. This makes for contradictions which are exploited in public debate. When transitive pain is described as 'cruel and inhuman' it is often referred to as *torture*. And torture itself is condemned by public opinion and prohibited by international law.

It is hardly surprising, therefore, that the many liberal-democratic governments[13] that have employed torture have attempted to do so in secret. And sometimes they have been concerned to redefine legally the category of pain-producing treatment in an attempt to avoid the label 'torture'. Thus:

Torture is forbidden by Israeli law. Israeli authorities say that torture is not authorised or condoned in the occupied territories but acknowledge that abuses occur and state that they are investigated. In 1987 the Landau Judicial

Commission specifically condemned 'torture' but allowed for 'moderate physical and psychological pressure' to be used to secure confessions and to obtain information; a classified annex to the report defining permissible pressure has never been made public.[14]

Needless to say, other governments in the region (for example, Egypt, Turkey and Iran) have also condoned torture and, unlike liberal-democratic governments, they have used it freely against their own citizens. But the remarkable feature of this case is the scrupulous concern of a liberal-democratic state with calibrating the amount of pain that is legally allowable. There is evidently a concern that *too much* pain should not be applied. It is assumed that 'moderate physical and psychological pressure' is at once necessary and sufficient to secure confession. Beyond that quantity, pressure is held to be excessive (gratuitous), and therefore presumably becomes 'torture'.[15] Other states in the Middle East are rarely so punctilious, or so modern in their reasoning.

The use of torture by liberal-democratic states relates to their attempt to control populations that are not citizens. In such cases torture cannot be attributed to 'primitive urges' – as Scott suggested. Nor to governmental techniques for disciplining citizens, as Rejali has argued. It is to be understood as a practical logic integral to the maintenance of the nation-state's sovereignty, like warfare.

The category of torture is no longer limited to applications of physical pain: it now includes psychological coercion in which disorientation, isolation and brainwashing are employed. Indeed 'torture' in our day functions not only to denote behaviour actually prohibited by law, but also desired to be so prohibited in accordance with changing concepts of 'inhumane' treatment (for example, the public execution or flogging of criminals, and child abuse, as well as animal experiments, factory farming and fox hunting).

This wider category of torture, or 'cruel, inhuman and degrading treatment', could in theory be applied to the anguish and mental suffering experienced by people in societies obliged to give up their beliefs and 'become fully human' (in the sense understood by Euro-Americans). But by a curious paradox it is a version of relativism that prevents such an application of the category. For the anguish is itself the consequence of a passionate investment in the Truth of beliefs that guide behaviour. The modern *sceptical* posture, in contrast, regards such passionate conviction to be 'uncivilised', as well as a perpetual source of danger to others and of pain to oneself. Beliefs should either have no direct connection to the way one lives, or be held so lightly that they can be easily changed.

One might be inclined to think that at least in humanising societies more sorts of inflicted pain come to be considered morally unacceptable with the passage of time. In some cases, however, pain-producing behaviour that was once shocking no longer shocks. Or if it does, then not in the way it did in the past. Putting large numbers of people in prison for more and more kinds of offence is one example. Inflicting new forms of suffering in battle is another.

Some writers on pain such as Elaine Scarry (1985: 61) have claimed that war is 'the most obvious analogue to torture'. However that may be, it is significant that the general concept of 'cruel, inhuman and degrading treatment or punishment' is not applied to the *normal* conduct of war – although modern, technological warfare involves forms of suffering, in numbers and in kind, that are without precedent. The Geneva Convention, it is true, seeks to regulate conduct in war.[16] But paradoxically, this has the effect of legalising most of the new kinds of suffering endured in modern war by combatants and non-combatants alike.

The military historian John Keegan (1978: 329–30) wrote of the new practices of 'deliberate cruelty' nearly two decades ago when he described some of the weaponry employed in twentieth-century warfare:

Weapons have never been kind to human flesh, but the directing principle behind their design has usually not been that of maximising the pain and damage they can cause. Before the invention of explosives, the limits of muscle power in itself constrained their hurtfulness; but even for some time thereafter moral inhibitions, fuelled by a sense of the unfairness of adding mechanical and chemical increments to man's power to hurt his brother, served to restrain deliberate barbarities of design. Some of these inhibitions – against the use of poison gas and explosive bullets – were codified and given international force by the Hague Convention of 1899;[17] but the rise of 'thing-killing' as opposed to man-killing weapons – heavy artillery is an example – which by their side-effects inflicted gross suffering and disfigurement, invalidated these restraints. As a result restraints were cast to the winds, and it is now a desired effect of many man-killing weapons that they inflict wounds as terrible and terrifying as possible. The claymore mine, for instance, is filled with metal cubes ... the cluster bomb with jagged metal fragments, in both cases because that shape of projectile tears and fractures more extensively than a smooth-bodied one. The HEAT and HESH rounds fired by anti-tank guns are designed to fill the interior of armoured vehicles with showers of metal splinters or streams of molten metal, so disabling the tank by disabling its crew. And napalm, disliked for ethical reasons even by many tough minded soldiers, contains an ingredient which increases the adhesion of the burning petrol to human skin surfaces. Military surgeons, so successful over the past century in resuscitating wounded soldiers and repairing wounds

of growing severity, have thus now to meet a challenge of wounding agents deliberately conceived to defeat their skills.

One might add to this that the manufacture, possession and deployment of weapons of mass destruction (chemical, nuclear and biological) must be counted as instances of declared governmental readiness to engage in 'cruel, inhuman, and degrading treatment' against civilian populations even when they are not actually used. In brief, cruel modern technologies of destruction are integral to modern warfare, and modern warfare is an activity essential to the security and power of the modern state, on which the welfare and identity of its citizens depends. In war, the modern state demands from its citizens not only that they kill and maim others but also that they themselves suffer cruel pain and death.[18]

So how can the *calculated* cruelties of modern battle be reconciled with the modern sensibility regarding pain? Precisely by treating pain as a quantifiable essence. As in state torture, an attempt can be made to measure the physical suffering inflicted in modern warfare in accordance with the proportionality of means to ends. The human destruction inflicted should not outweigh the strategic advantage gained. But given the aim of ultimate victory the notion of 'military necessity' can be extended indefinitely. Any measure that is intended as a contribution to that aim, no matter how much suffering it creates, may be justified in terms of 'military necessity'. The standard of acceptability in such cases is set by public opinion, and that standard varies as the latter moves in response to contingent circumstances (for example, who the enemy is, how the war is going).

I want to stress that I am making no moral judgement here. My concern is to identify the paradoxes of modern thought and practice that relate to the deliberate infliction of pain between states as well as within them. If I focus on state-condoned cruelty this is not because I assume that the state is its only source today, but because our moral discourse about cruel, inhuman and degrading treatment or punishment is closely linked to legal concepts and political interventions.

In the instances discussed so far, I have tried to suggest that the instability of the concept of physical suffering is at one and the same time the source of ideological contradictions and of strategies available for evading them. I now shift my attention to the domain of interpersonal relations that the modern state defines as 'private'. Here we meet with a contradiction that has deeper roots, and one which cannot be resolved simply by, say, redefining the concept of torture or by prohibiting calculated cruelty in military combat.

Subjecting Oneself to 'Cruel and Degrading Treatment'

While the category of 'torture' has in recent times been expanded to include cases of induced suffering that are primarily or entirely psychological, it has also been narrowed to exclude some cases of the calculated infliction of physical pain. This sometimes leads to contradictions. But there is another kind of contradiction which is characteristic of modern social life.

Moderns are aware of situations in which the sharp separation between the negative experience of pain and the positive experience of pleasure are inseparable. Sadomasochism is disturbing to many people precisely because here they are confronted with suffering that is no longer simply painful. It is at once pain and the opposite of pain. Two centuries of powerful criticism directed at the Utilitarians' calculus of pleasure versus pain has not destroyed the common-sense view that these two experiences should be mutually exclusive. Yet in the eroticisation of suffering the two are intimately linked, and it is actively sought by some.

Here is an extract from a sadomasochist text *The Leatherman's Handbook II* (Townsend 1989: 15):

Because I consider any attempt to define SM in a single concise phrase to be the ultimate exercise in futility – or masochism – I shall forego the temptation to add yet another version to the great discarded stack of unsuccessful, inadequate verbal garbage. Instead let me suggest a short list of characteristics I find to be present in most scenes which I would classify as SM:

1) A dominant-submissive relationship.
2) A giving and receiving of pain that is pleasurable to both parties.
3) Fantasy and/or role playing on the part of one or both partners.
4) A conscious humbling of one partner by the other (humiliation).
5) Some form of fetish involvement.
6) The acting out of one or more ritualised interactions (bondage, flagellation, etc.).

Notice that this text speaks not about *expressions* of pain, still less about conventional play-acting, but about pain experienced and inflicted, in which both partners, the active and the passive, are jointly agents. So why is sadomasochism not rejected by all moderns who condemn pain as a negative experience?

One answer, according to some interpreters, is that not everyone 'confuses the distinction between unbridled sadism and the social subculture of consensual fetishism. To argue that in consensual S/M

the 'dominant' has power, and the slave has not, is to read theater for reality' (McClintock 1993: 87).

However, the point of my question is not to dismiss the distinction between 'unbridled sadism' and the 'subculture of consensual fetishism'. It is to ask what happens when individual self-fashioning embraces every difference – including the difference between 'pain' and 'pleasure' – within an aesthetic whole. We are sometimes told that the hybridisation of categories, including those that organise our sensual experience, is a mode by which stable authority may be subverted in the name of liberty. But it is possible also that the eroticisation of pain is merely one of the ways in which the modern self attempts to secure its elusive foundation.

Recently, an article in a London newspaper gave the following account of a local performance by an American artist at the Institute of Contemporary Arts (ICA):

With his face set in a mask of concentration, Ron Athey allows his head to be pierced with a six-inch needle just above the eyebrow. You watch, transfixed, as the needle snakes along beneath the skin like water pulsing through an empty hosepipe. A droplet of blood wells up at the point where steel meets scalp. This is the first spike of Athey's crown of thorns – a body piercer's tribute to the power of Christian iconography, an ex-junkie's flirtation with the needle, and a gay man's defiance of infection with HIV.

By the time the macabre 'sketch' is finished, Athey is encrusted with needles, garlanded with wire and oozing blood, in what appears to be a parody of the crucifixion. Ah, but is it a parody, defined in the dictionary as 'an imitation so poor as to seem a deliberate mockery of the original'? Or is it – as Athey's supporters would claim – an exploration of the nature of martyrdom, as manifest to a worldwide gay community in the era of Aids? (Armistead 1994: 26)

What is remarkable about these opening paragraphs is that the writer of this account finds herself having to put the familiar theatrical word 'sketch' in quotation marks – but not so the equally familiar theological expression 'martyrdom'. The reader is given to understand that this is a *real* tribute to the power of Christian iconography, a *real* exploration of the nature of (Christian) martyrdom, but that it only 'appears' to be a form of theatre, an 'imitation'.[19]

I stress that I am not here challenging this claim but underlining the writer's recognition that in the discourse of modern self-fashioning, the tension holding 'real' and 'theatrical' apart can collapse. It is especially in a modern culture, where the split between the real and its mere representation has become institutionalised, that it becomes necessary to assert from time to time that a given performance is *merely* theatrical, or that another performance is *not really* theatre. My point

here, however, is that it is the difference between 'the real' and 'the mimetic' – like the difference between 'pain' and 'pleasure' – that is available to modern self-fashioning. And that consequently the tension between 'real' and 'pretend' bondage is itself aestheticised, and the clear distinction between consent and coercion problematised.

Of course S/M as defined in the text I quoted earlier is different from this performance at the ICA. For one thing, in the latter there is a separation between performers and observers. No experience of giving and receiving pain binds the two together in mutual pleasure. We find only a one-sided representation (presentation?) of an evocative image of suffering, which is preceded by a painful construction of that image on the stage. Furthermore, its intention is not the production of private pleasure. We can't know whether the various members of Athey's audience respond primarily to the icon of Christ's last passion, or to the painful construction of that icon on the stage – or to both. Nor can we tell what difference it would make to those who would like to ban this performance if they were to be told that Athey suffers from a malfunctioning of the nervous system so that he actually feels no pain. Or – more tellingly – that like a religious virtuoso he has learnt to experience it positively.

Think of the Shi'a Muslim flagellants mourning the martyrdom of the Prophet's grandson Hussain annually every Muharram. That instance of self-inflicted pain is at once real and dramatic (not 'theatrical'). It has even less to do with 'pleasure' than does Athey's performance. It differs from the latter in being a collective rite of religious suffering and redemption. It is not a secular act that borrows a religious metaphor to make a political statement about prejudice. Nor is it premised on the right to self-fashioning and the autonomy of individual choice. Yet both strike against the modern sensibility that recoils from a willing, positive engagement with suffering. Because for ascetics, as for sadomasochists, pain is not merely a means which can be measured and pronounced excessive or gratuitous in relation to an end. Pain is not action but passion.

These brief references to pain willingly endured in modern society help us to raise some questions at the transcultural level.

The interesting thing about the criteria enumerated in the S/M text I quoted above is that they come up against Article 5 of the *Universal Declaration of Human Rights*: 'No one shall be subjected to torture or to cruel, inhuman or degrading treatment or punishment.' This rule is not qualified by the phrase 'unless the parties concerned are consenting adults'. In the same way, and for the same reason, one may not consent to sell oneself into slavery, even for a limited period, and not even if the parties concerned find the relationship of bondage erotic.

So, too, the liberalised Church strongly disapproves of monks being whipped at the command of their abbot for penalisable faults – even when the penance has a ritual closure and a dramatic character. And even if the monks have taken monastic vows of obedience voluntarily. This follows from the modern rejection of physical pain in general, and of 'gratuitous' suffering in particular. But it is more precise to put it this way: the modern hostility is not simply to pain, it is to pain that does not accord with a particular conception of being human – and that is therefore in excess. 'Excess' is a concept of measure. An essential aspect of the modern attitude to pain rests on a calculus that defines appropriate actions.

Needless to say nothing I have said so far is an argument against S/M. I am not denouncing a 'dangerous' sexual practice.[20] Nor am I concerned to celebrate its 'emancipatory' social potential.[21] These antagonistic positions seem to me to assume that 'sadomasochism' has an essence. They are mirror images of each other. But the essence of what legal and moral discourse constructs, polices and contests as 'S/M' is not the object of my analysis. As in the field of 'abnormal and unnatural' sexual practices generally, state power is, of course, directly and vitally involved – helping to define and regulate normality. My concern here, however, is with the structure of public debate over the valorisation of painful experience in a culture that regards it negatively. In that debate argument is sharpened because, on the one hand, moderns disapprove of physical pain as 'degrading'. On the other hand they are committed to every individual's right to pursue unlimited physical pleasure 'in private' – so long as that conforms to the legal principle of consenting adults and does not lead to death or serious injury. Thus one way that moderns attempt to resolve this contradiction is by defining cruelty in relation to the principle of individual autonomy, which is the necessary basis of free choice. However, if the concept of 'cruel, inhuman and degrading treatment' cannot be consistently deployed without reference to the principle of individual freedom, it becomes relativised.

This becomes clearer in the transcultural domain. For here it is not simply a matter of eliminating particular cruelties, but of imposing an entire modern discourse of 'being human', central to which are its ideas about individualism and detachment from passionate belief. Thus while at home the principle of consenting adults within the bounds of the law works by invoking the idea of free choice based on individual autonomy, the presence of consenting adults abroad may often be taken to indicate mere 'false consciousness' – a fanatical commitment to outmoded beliefs – which invites forcible correction.

Yet only the suspicious individual – suspicious of others and of herself – can be truly autonomous, truly free of fanatical convictions. But continuous suspicion introduces instability at another level: that of the subject.

Concluding Comments

I have tried to problematise the basic idea underlying the United Nations declaration that 'No one shall be subjected to torture or to cruel, inhuman or degrading treatment or punishment.' I have suggested that the idea is unstable, mainly because the aspirations and practices to which it is attached are themselves contradictory, ambiguous or changing. Of course, the fact that an idea is unstable may not, in itself, be reason enough for abandoning it. But neither the attempt by Euro-Americans to impose their standards by force on others, nor the willing invocation of these standards by weaker peoples in the Third World, makes them stable or universal. It merely globalises them.

We need ethnographies of pain and cruelty which can provide us with a better understanding of how relevant practices are actually conducted in different traditions. Such ethnographies will certainly show us that cruelty can be experienced and addressed in ways other than as a violation of rights – for example, as a failure of specific virtues or as an expression of particular vices. They will also show us that if cruelty is increasingly represented in the language of rights (and especially of human rights), then this is because perpetual legal struggle has now become the dominant mode of moral engagement in an interconnected, uncertain and rapidly changing world.

Notes

1. An earlier version of this paper was read first in Bellagio at a conference on 'Social Suffering' in July 1994; I thank the organisers Arthur Kleinman, Veena Das and Margaret Lock for their helpful responses. Later versions were read at seminars in the New School for Social Research, the University of California at Santa Cruz, Johns Hopkins University, New York University and the University of Sussex at Brighton. I am grateful to each of these audiences for their criticisms and comments. In particular, I have benefited from critical suggestions made by the following: Jonathan Boyarin, Jeff Goldfarb, Vicki Hattam, Kira Kosnick, Jim Miller, Keith Nield, David Schneider, David Scott, Don Scott and Brian Street.

2. So too, Page DuBois (1991: 153–7).
3. In *Modernity and the Holocaust*, Bauman (1989) has explored the structures and processes of the modern state that made possible the distinctive modes of cruelty under Nazism.
4. A. Autiero (1987: 124). Incidentally, there is a curious paradox in invoking a metaphor of military violence ('to affront and conquer') to describe the compassionate work of healing. But such paradoxes abound in Christian history, of course.
5. Thus Beccaria (1986: 4) denounces 'the barbarous and useless tortures multiplied with prodigal and useless severity for crimes that are either unproven or chimerical'. And Voltaire (1818: 314), with characteristic sarcasm, remarks that 'On a dit souvent que la question [that is, torture] était un moyen de sauver un coupable robuste, et de perdre un innocent trop faible.'
6. See the two fragments first published as 'Bentham on Torture' in *Bentham and Legal Theory*, edited by M.H. James (1973: 45).
7. In her important work *Classical Probability in the Enlightenment* Lorraine Daston (1988) has described how, over two centuries, Enlightenment mathematicians struggled to produce a model that would provide a moral calculus for 'the reasonable man' in conditions of uncertainty. Although modern probability theory has become entirely divorced from this moral project since about 1840, the idea of a calculus continues to be powerful in liberal welfare discourse.
8. Lord Milner (1899: 23), Under-Secretary for Finance during the British Occupation of Egypt which began in 1882, described Britain's imperial task in that country as follows:

This then, and no less than this, was meant by 'restoring order.' It meant reforming the Egyptian administration root and branch. Nay, it meant more. For what was the good of recasting the system, if it were left to be worked by officials of the old type, animated by the old spirit? 'Men, not measures,' is a good watch-word anywhere, but to no country is it more profoundly applicable than to Egypt. Our task, therefore, included something more than new principles and new methods. *It ultimately involved new men.* It involved 'the education of the people to know, and therefore to expect, orderly and honest government – the education of a body of rulers capable of supplying it.'

Here Milner enunciates the government's need to create subjects (in both senses) as well as rulers informed by new standards of human behaviour and political justice. That this would involve the application of some force and suffering was a secondary consideration. I stress that my point is not that colonial

administrators like Milner lacked 'humanitarian' motives, but that they were guided by a particular concept of 'humanness'.

9. I am grateful to Jon Wilson for informing me that 'The word *expediency* is one that we find again and again in Imperial India's official documents, from the 1820s to the *Royal Commission on Agriculture of 1928.*' Resort to expediency, as to 'interest', indicated a distrust of passionate belief (see Hirschman 1977).

10. Hook swinging involves a ceremony in which the celebrant swings from a cross-beam built for the purpose on a cart, suspended by two steel hooks thrust into the small of his back (see Kosambe 1967).

11. In relation to the more celebrated British prohibition of *sati* (the self-immolation of Hindu widows on the funeral pyre of their husband) in 1829, Lata Mani (1985: 107) notes that

    Rather than arguing for the outlawing of *sati* as a cruel and barbarous act, as one might expect of a true 'moderniser', officials in favour of abolition were at pains to illustrate that such a move was entirely consonant with the principle of upgrading indigenous tradition. Their strategy was to point to the questionable scriptural sanction for *sati* and to the fact that, for one reason or another, they believed its contemporary practice transgressed its original and therefore 'true scriptural meaning'.

    Thus it was a modernised 'Hinduism' that was made to yield the judgement that *sati* was a cruel and barbarous act.

12. 'Reformative theory presented punishment to offenders as being 'in their best interests' while utilitarian theory cast it as an impartial act of social necessity. In rejecting retributive theory, the reformers sought, in effect, to take the anger out of punishment. As it was legitimized to the prisoner, punishment was no longer to be, in Bentham's words, '"an act of wrath or vengeance", but an act of calculation, disciplined by considerations of the social good and the offenders' needs'. (Ignatieff 1989: 75).

13. For example France in Algeria, the US in Vietnam, Israel in Gaza and the West Bank, Britain in Aden, Cyprus and Northern Ireland.

14. US Department of State, *Country Reports on Human Rights Practices for 1993*, p. 1204.

15. This is precisely Bentham's (1973: 45) argument about the rationality of torture in comparison with punishment:

    The purpose to which Torture is applied is such that whenever that purpose is actually attained it may plainly be seen to be attained; and as soon as ever it is seen to be attained it may immediately be made to cease. With punishment it is necessarily otherwise. Of punishment, in

order to make sure of applying as much as is necessary you must commonly run a risque of applying considerably more: of Torture there need never be a grain more applied than what is necessary.

16. It should not be forgotten that medieval warfare also had its rules (for example, see Contamine 1984). In one sense the moral regulation of conduct in warfare was even stricter in the early Middle Ages: killing and maiming, even in battle, was regarded as a sin for which the Church demanded penance (see Russell 1975).

17. Of the mushrooming or 'dum-dum' bullet, invented in British India in 1897, Dàniel Headrick (1979: 256) observes: 'This particular invention was so vicious, for it tore great holes in the flesh, that Europeans thought it too cruel to inflict upon one another, and used it only against Asians and Africans.'

18. The paradox here is that the modern citizen is a free individual and yet he is obliged to forgo the most important choice a free human being can make – that affecting his life or death. The modern state can send its citizens to their unwilling deaths in war, and forbid them from willing to end their own lives in peace.

19. Cf. McClintock (1993: 106) 'S/M is the most liturgical of forms, sharing with Christianity a theatrical iconography of punishment and expiation: washing rituals, bondage, flagellation, body-piercing, and symbolic torture.' But why only *symbolic*?

20. See for example Linden et al (1982). See also the legal judgements in the Spanner case in England, now being appealed against in the European Court.

21. The radical social criticism allegedly expressed by S/M is eloquently argued for in McClintock's article, but the liberatory implications of S/M are explicitly retracted at the end. (See also the clever book by Angela Carter, 1979, entitled *The Sadeian Woman*.) While such writings typically provide radical political decodings of S/M narratives, they also seem to be saying that, as a mode of obtaining orgasm, S/M is the product of socially distorted and sexually repressive relations.

References

Armistead, Claire. 1994. 'Piercing Thoughts', *Guardian Weekly*, 17 July: 26.

Autiero, A. 1987. 'The Interpretation of Pain: The Point of View of Catholic Theology', in J. Brihaye, F. Loew, H.W. Pia (eds) *Pain*. Vienna/New York: Springer-Verlag.

Bauman, Z. 1989. *Modernity and the Holocaust*. Ithaca: Cornell University Press.

Beccaria, Cesare Marquis of. 1986. *On Crimes and Punishments*, ed. and trans. by D. Young. Indianapolis: Hackett.

Bentham, Jeremy. 1973. 'Bentham on Torture', in *Bentham and Legal Theory*, edited by M.H. James. Belfast: *Northern Ireland Legal Quarterly*.

Carter, Angela. 1979. *The Sadeian Woman*. London: Virago.

Contamine, P. 1984. *War in the Middle Ages*. Oxford: Blackwell.

Cromer, Lord. 1913. 'The Government of Subject Races', in *Political and Literary Essays, 1908–1913*. London: Macmillan.

Daston, Lorraine. 1988. *Classical Probability in the Enlightenment*. Princeton, NJ: University of Princeton Press.

Dirks, N. n.d. 'The Policing of Tradition: Colonialism and Anthropology in Southern India', unpublished ms., pp. 9–10.

DuBois, Page. 1991. *Torture and Truth*. New York: Routledge.

Foucault, Michel. 1979. *Discipline and Punish*. New York: Vintage Books.

Headrick, Daniel. 1979. 'The Tools of Imperialism: Technology and the Expansion of European Colonial Empires in the Nineteenth Century', *Journal of Modern History* 51.

Hirschman, A.O. 1977. *The Passions and the Interests*. Princeton, NJ: Princeton University Press.

Ignatieff, Michael. 1989. *A Just Measure of Pain*. Harmondsworth: Penguin Books.

Keegan, J. 1978. *The Face of Battle*. Harmondsworth: Penguin Books.

Kosambe, D.D. 1967. 'Living prehistory in India', *Scientific American* 216 (2).

Langbein, J.H. 1977. *Torture and the Law of Proof; Europe and England in the Ancien Regime*. Chicago: University of Chicago Press.

Linden, R.R. et al (eds). 1982. *Against Sadomasochism: A Radical Feminist Analysis*. San Francisco: Frog in the Well.

Mani, L. 1985. 'The Production of an Official Discourse on *Sati* in Early Nineteenth-century Bengal', in F. Barker et al (eds) *Europe and Its Others. Vol. 1*. Colchester: University of Essex Press.

McClintock, A. 1993. 'Maid to Order: Commercial Fetishism and Gender Power', *Social Text* 37 (Winter).

Milner, Lord. 1899. *England in Egypt*. London: Edward Arnold.

Read, J. 1972. 'Customary Law under Colonial Rule', in H.F. Morris and J.S. Read (eds) *Indirect Rule and the Search for Justice*: Oxford: Clarendon Press.

Rejali, D.M. 1994. *Torture and Modernity; Self, Society, and State in Modern Iran*. Boulder, CO: Westview Press.

Russell, F.H. 1975. *The Just War in the Middle Ages.* Cambridge: Cambridge University Press.

Scarry, Elaine. 1985. *The Body in Pain.* Oxford: Oxford University Press.

Scott, G.R. 1940. *The History of Torture Throughout the Ages.* London: T. Werner Laurie.

Townsend, L. 1989. *The Leatherman's Handbook II.* New York: Carlyle Communications Ltd.

US Department of State, *Country Reports on Human Rights Practices for 1993.* Washington, DC.

Voltaire, François-Marie Arouet de. 1818. *Oeuvres complètes de Voltaire,* Vol. 26. Paris: New Edition.

6 REPRESENTING HUMAN RIGHTS VIOLATIONS: SOCIAL CONTEXTS AND SUBJECTIVITIES

Richard A. Wilson

Legalism in Human Rights Reporting

… whatever it is that the law is after it is not the whole story. (Geertz 1983: 173)

This chapter examines the genre of human rights reporting with reference to two cases of murder in Guatemala. It is argued that category of 'human rights violation' does not exist independently of its representation in human rights reports. The process by which an event becomes textualised is highly selective, organising signs in such a way as to codify an event according to an universal template. The language in which most cases are represented is generally realist and legalistic, and it engages in a decontextualisation of events. Accounts of human rights violations are characterised by a literalism and minimalism which strip events of their subjective meanings in a pursuit of objective legal facts. Such observations have been made of law, though not yet to my knowledge of human rights law, by anthropologists such as Clifford Geertz (1983: 170–4) who has referred to the 'skeletonization' and 'sterilization' of fact in legal processes.

Although human rights organisations constantly review their policy on the language used in their publications, there seems to be nothing like the debate about representation that exists for depictions of the Nazi Holocaust.[1] Those such as LaCapra (1992: 111) have argued that conventional techniques of historiography are not sufficient to capture the 'reality' of the Holocaust: 'Nowhere more than with reference to the Holocaust do positivism and standard techniques of narrowly empirical-analytic inquiry seem wanting.' Many literary works on the Holocaust eschew documentary realism in preference

for an 'allusive' or 'distanced' realism, where reality is presented through the filter of memory.

These issues are not only of relevance for academic commentary on human rights texts, since they parallel debates that human rights organisations have had internally for years. Discussions about the content and style of reports have become more acute recently – for instance Amnesty International's present General Secretary has advocated a shift in Amnesty's policy towards a greater degree of contextualisation in AI reports. In the last few years, Amnesty International Council Meetings have passed resolutions calling for more context in reports. I would like to see this chapter as a contribution to the debate between the 'legalists', who advocate the narrow circumscribing of information to that which is relevant for the prosecution of violations and the 'contextualists', who argue for the inherent value of including a wider scope of social and contextual material. This chapter suggests that part of the brief of anthropology is to restore to accounts of political violence both the surrounding social relations and an associated range of subjective meanings.

An objection might be raised on the grounds that legal rhetoric prevails in human rights reporting precisely because its intended audience is governments and international bodies such as the UN, and law is the dominant language of national and international governance. At least formally, states and transnational institutions are only willing to take seriously knowledge produced according to a 'culture of scientism' and represented in a universally classified and usually quantified manner. I seek to challenge this 'pragmatist' adherence to legalism and positivism on two grounds; that it inherently displaces questions of ethics and values from what is claimed to be an ethical endeavour (human rights reporting); and that since governments are not the sole recipients of human rights reports, a wider range of reporting styles is both defensible and necessary.

Chronicle of a Death Retold

I originally had no intention of studying human rights in Guatemala, but instead focused on religious conversions and ethnic identities in the department of Alta Verapaz (See Wilson 1995). Yet I was repeatedly placed in the position of bystander – witnessing or hearing personal testimonies of violent expressions of state power within my immediate social network. One such case occurred late on a Sunday afternoon on 20 March 1988, while I was watching a local football game with a friend in the highland town of Cobán (see map on p. 216).

March is a comfortable month in the Guatemalan highlands, when the rains are far away and the summer heat is not yet intense, and the football pitches are full of local teams competing for prestige. A few minutes before the final whistle, I heard several loud bangs, but disregarded them as the common sounds of a misfiring truck. After the game, the crowd began to aimlessly drift off home, but then it rapidly gathered around a street corner only 50 yards from the football ground. My companion went to find out what had happened, and he returned shocked and agitated. He told me that a local member of the elite, a certain Waldemar Caal Rossi, had just been murdered. Rossi had also been watching the game and while on his way home, had been shot repeatedly at point-blank range in the head. My friend urged us to leave quickly before the army arrived to disperse the crowd by force.

In the days after the murder I sought out local people's views on Waldemar Rossi's death in private discussions, and encountered a bewildering plethora of responses. Instead of a common consensus, there were five main theories about who had carried out the murder:

1. *Military repression thesis*: the extreme right and/or the army had killed him for being a prominent civilian politician in order to destabilise the electoral process which had replaced over 20 years of army rule. Rossi was on the executive board of the centre-right UCN party and had stood for mayor in the local elections two years previously. The evidence put forward for this view was that a 9 mm revolver was used, which was the conventional instrument of extra-judicial murder. I was told that this handgun was standard army issue. Also, in the local lexicon of violence, shots to the head suggested a political assassination rather than a common crime.

2. *Party political explanation*: the ruling Christian Democrat government had killed Rossi for being a leader of the UCN, the party due to win the upcoming local elections in the department of Alta Verapaz. The government had been accused of procedural irregularities and harassment of opposition parties during the run-up to the local elections in March. For instance, the legal papers and other municipal election materials sent by the Supreme Electoral Tribunal to another centre-right party, the PR, were robbed from the bus station in Cobán. Shrill complaints had appeared in the national paper *El Grafico*, which was owned at the time by the leader of Rossi's UCN party, Jorge Carpio Nicolle, who was himself assassinated in 1993. Proponents of this theory also pointed out that Rossi's assailant drove off speedily to the capital in a car. It was said that this proved that the government was involved

instead of just the army, which would have used a local agent and not worried unduly about hiding him.

3. *Intra-state rivalry theory:* Rossi was killed by the ruling civilian government for being an agent of the army. Little evidence was offered for this view except to point out that the civilian and military authorities had clashed on repeated occasions. However, such pronouncements proved to be somewhat prophetic, as a few months later, in May 1988, hardline army factions rolled towards the capital in tanks and armoured personnel carriers in an attempt to oust the civilian president.

4. *Inter-elite rivalry hypothesis:* Rossi had been killed in a family feud, for simply being a Rossi, by one of the other prominent elite families of the area. Rossi was a key member of one of the few families which historically dominated the local economy, political party system and government bureaucracy. Rossi himself held a high position in the national electricity company, INDE. With names like Rossi, Leal, Hempstead and Deisseldorff, most of the local elite had originally descended from German, Italian and British entrepreneurs who built a coffee agro-export economy at the end of the nineteenth century. Yet like the Rossi family, most of them had intermarried with the local Maya-Q'eqchi' population and also had indigenous surnames. Thus Rossi was an Italian 'Rossi', but also a Q'eqchi' 'Caal'. The stability of traditional elite power had started to waver in the 1970s when the cardamom export industry generated a new class of entrepreneurs. In the late 1980s, this fragmentation was accelerated as Cobán became a centre for drug smuggling and the financial laundering of illicit profits.[2]

5. *Moral economy explanation:* the members of the house I was staying in at the time disagreed with all of the above views and stated simply that he was killed for being rich, by someone who was poor, perhaps a disgruntled employee, a thief who wanted to rob him, or simply someone who was jealous of his wealth. The Q'eqchi' matriarch who sold tortillas to supplement her household budget said, 'See! It's better to be poor and not have all that envy around you.' The father, a retired craftsman, replied quickly, 'Ah ... but it is the poor who get killed most!' And so the family commentary on the local moral economy went on, with the implicit view that there are webs of social reciprocity at work in the community which only the rich can hope to escape from, but sometimes at the cost of their lives.

Some responses are not included in this orderly catalogue of accounts since they were highly idiosyncratic to the point of being

bizarre. A few were completely incomprehensible and I felt that some people, when faced with stressful questions, spoke without any intention of making sense.

My own view at the time was that the 'military repression' or 'party-political' explanations were the most probable accounts of the murder. In contrast, local views tended overwhelmingly towards the last two theories of inter-elite rivalry and the moral economy, that is, which reproduced the traditional language of local politics with its emphasis on patron–client relations and reciprocity. It could be of course, that most people did not trust me enough to make an explicit denunciation of the army or government. Yet my feeling is that in Cobán, local discourses on Rossi's death prevailed over the national ones. The people I knew best, who had in the privacy of their home often derided the army, perceived the event through the prism of local class politics.

As I discovered in the days after the death of Waldemar Rossi, each murder draws on a heterogeneous field of interpretations and memories, in a social space where meaning is contested, assertions are vague and polysemous, and where anyone and everyone could have had a motive. Narratives on murder then serve to crystallise social relations and feed off perceived tensions and discordance. As in the television murder mystery genre, the message is usually that, despite apparently calm external appearances, something is rotten in Denmark.

In such situations, a social researcher is much more likely to doubt the search for definitive lines of determinacy than a human rights researcher, and instead seek to contextualise an event rather than codify it. In the local reporting of a death, reliability becomes problematic, since individuals' statements are often more indexical than true or false. In the context of murder of a prominent local politician in Cobán, this means that some people are trying to express their position in relation to an overall situation of elite rule, death squad murders, militarisation and guerrilla war. Others, however, lose themselves behind a smoke screen of incomprehensible utterances in order to avoid taking a position at all.

Several weeks later, while on a short break in Mexico, I communicated my tentative understanding of the Rossi murder to a small international human rights agency. Without even apportioning blame to one of the parties, the mere appearance of the murder on a human rights report would have indicated that it was not a 'common crime' but that it was somehow related to the political process. In the Guatemalan context, the finger of suspicion would point towards governmental institutions – especially the security apparatus. Yet I have not come across any report on this case by a major human rights organisation;

Amnesty International for instance has no record of the killing. Somehow, the fate of Waldemar Caal Rossi did not become an item of information flowing through the networks of human rights agencies.

This exclusion led me to contemplate in more depth how an event becomes a publicised human rights violation. The most obvious reason for Rossi's exclusion was that social life in Alta Verapaz is thoroughly militarised, and at the time of the event there were no human rights offices or agency workers. National and international agencies receive reports through established networks of local people who are considered reliable sources; including their own staff, journalists and occasionally church workers and local development organisations. Perhaps the place-bound explanations of Rossi's murder won out, their centripetal force confining the information to a small area.

In remote areas of rural Latin America, the absence of individual contacts means that much information derives from secondary sources. Often human rights agencies can only respond quickly to events they learn about through press reports, and therefore are bound to reproduce their language. It is possible to see this replication in a quick assessment of the content of the first line of denunciation; Amnesty International's 'Urgent Action' – a 1–2-page document which is released within hours or days of a murder or kidnapping. In Latin America this usually means that the offending agents are referred to as *'desconocidos'*, or 'unknown persons'. The reports mention briefly what the assailants were wearing, but there is little space for contextual information on each case.

These deliberations led me to consider in more detail how human rights violations are constructed – not in the sense that the Rossi murder did not actually happen, nor that we can never know that it happened, nor that political assassinations are not a regular occurrence in Guatemala. Instead, my meaning is that human rights agencies have to piece together contradictory fragments of information and act on the basis of already formulated criteria about what kind of murder victim, and manner of murder, is likely to constitute a human rights violation. The indeterminacy of the event and the heterogeneous nature of bystanders' narratives hamper the coherence of a single integrated plot, which is highly disconcerting for those seeking actionable certainties.[3] Human rights reports must therefore impose meaning on the chaos and incoherence of events. Further, occurrences are universalised, that is, they are re-presented in human rights reports in such a way that the event can be comprehended by readers on the other side of the globe.

The complexities of the Rossi case have not been presented in order to contend that human rights claims for epistemological concreteness are false and unwarranted. Nor do I want to echo the claims of governments that the language of human rights is being used by other nations to slander them, or more usually in Latin America, as part of a phantom international communist conspiracy. Instead, I have explored the contingency around one act of violence in order to examine the limitations generally on representations of 'human rights violations'. In my view, there is a need to examine the powerful representational claims articulated within human rights discourses, so as to drag them down from the rarefied epistemological and moral high ground, and include them in more sociological debates about the interpretation, understanding and explanation of empirical evidence and the limits of its representation.

The Category of 'Human Rights Violation'

The whole concept of human rights violation is constructed around state involvement, in opposition to the category of 'common crime'. Human rights organisations recognise both the difficulty of establishing culpability, and the blurred nature of the boundary between state and criminal acts. Amnesty International (1989: 8) often writes in its reports: 'In many cases, for example, it is not possible to establish precisely who carried out a particular killing, although circumstantial evidence and a pattern of similar killings by government forces often appears clearly to indicate official responsibility.'[4]

Despite the recognition of the difficulties of establishing official responsibility,[5] accusations of state involvement rest upon a clear distinction between the 'state' and 'civil society' which is not the way that either society or violence are organised. In some instances, there is direct evidence of state involvement in a violation, such as that of the murder of seven members of a Jesuit household in El Salvador in November 1989. As in the Jesuit case, most death squads in Latin America are made up of regular police and military officials operating in plain clothes under orders from their superiors. Yet not all groups involved in extra-judicial acts of violence are under such direct orders from the security apparatus. They can also be para-statal, *ad hoc* groupings of ultra-right political parties and members (or ex-members) of the security forces. In Guatemala, human rights organisations tend to attribute responsibility to the state for acts of violence or intimidation carried out by para-statal civil defence patrols. Civil patrols were set up by the army in highland villages in the early 1980s and are made up of local men, many of whom perform

their role due to coercion or neutral acquiescence. Others, however, are utterly convinced that they are protecting their village from the guerrillas and communism.[6]

Some writers have argued that regimes are repressive precisely because they are 'weak' and lack the more sophisticated surveillance and control techniques of industrialised states (see Giddens 1985; Asad 1992). In such 'weak states', acts of violence may be carried out independently by landowners or private security forces, often against employees involved in trade union activities. In countries where the administrative apparatus does not permeate the whole territory (for example, Brazil, Nicaragua, Guatemala), non-state adjudication is meted out at the 'frontier' by the patrimonial authorities of economic enclaves. In these contexts, violence emerges from both inside and outside state institutions, and these forms can be organised relatively independent from each other.

In all of these cases, the category of human rights violation is constructed in opposition to the category of 'common crime'. This is not an unproblematic distinction either, since these binary categories are not hermetically sealed, static or universal, but are overlapping and are mutually constitutive. As Jennifer Schirmer shows in this volume, the Guatemalan military has historically both conflated and maintained the boundaries between 'criminals' and 'subversives', and intertwined emergency counter-insurgency legal measures with the conventional criminal justice system.

The categories of ordinary crime and state crime share a common semiotics of violence, and draw upon the same lexicon of conventional signs. Human rights organisations have come to recognise that political killings are often made to look like common homicides. Amnesty International (1989: 8) has written that in Guatemala: 'perpetrators of political killings were now apparently resorting to stabbing, machetes, or even poison to conceal their political motives and make it appear that those killed were the victims of common crime'. Conversely, it has been noted that 'criminals' in Guatemala have plagiarised from the stock symbolism of politically motivated murders, and one report refers to how 'many common homicides may be committed with shots to the back of the head'.[7]

At the risk of echoing standard government evasions of responsibility, it must be recognised that for a variety of reasons, it is problematic to discern a 'criminal' from a 'political' murder in many cases. In a similar vein, Judith Zur (1994: 12) argues that in a context of legal impunity, juridical 'concepts of innocence and guilt lose their meaning'. Generalised fear and violence dissolve narratives around justice. Normative juridical distinctions are the distinctions

of established liberal democracies which do not have recent traditions of habitual political murder or mass criminal violence. As such, liberal categories, however desirable, may have little bearing on the experiences of punishment and surveillance during decades of militarised state rule. Where terror rules, normative categories of justice are abolished, undermining frameworks designed to conceptualise them, much less act upon them.

Since state-directed murders often operate in a context of extreme epistemological doubt, human rights organisations operate more or less reflexively with a set of criteria of what profile of person and what kind of murder is likely to be 'indicative of security force involvement'. In so doing, the discourse of human rights constructs its subjects as much as it reacts to events, since these criteria promote a selective process which screens out certain cases and homes in on others. In particular human rights texts construct the category of 'victim', and many Amnesty International country reports list violations against trade unionists, students, refugees or political activists under the umbrella heading of 'The Victims'.

Like the discourse of development, the human rights literature draws upon Manichean dualisms (violated/violator; powerless/powerful) to construct its subjects as innocent victims. Both share similar images of their subjects as in 'need' and inhabiting a social or global position of marginality. References to the 'poor, uneducated, and relatively defenceless' are readily found in both genres.[8] Human rights organisations draw a great deal of their rhetorical power from how they represent themselves as campaigning on behalf of weak innocents against powerful and violent governments in the pursuit of justice, truth and the rule of law. This could be one reason why Waldemar Rossi's case was not picked up by human rights agencies, since he was neither weak, poor, uneducated, nor, according to many from his own community, entirely an 'innocent'. As a relatively wealthy politician representing a local elite, Rossi was in the wrong category of self.

There is an acute tension in human rights reporting between recognising the blurred and constructed nature of the category of human rights violation and the desire to assert the veracity of information. On one hand many reports recognise the pitfalls of documentation, as one stated: 'the source of any particular act of violence is not always apparent, and there is often insufficient evidence on which to make a credible allegation'.[9] Yet there is a contrary process whereby cases are documented in a way which drops in 'relevant criteria' about the profile of the victim and the style of the violation. Amnesty International reports usually have only a few

cases which are described in detail, and they are mostly a grisly succession of short case profiles. Usually, these only include several lines, with a standard formula including the date, name, category of victim (for example, student or trade unionist) and manner of murder (for example, with signs of torture) and occasionally a description of the assailants (for example, heavily armed men, wearing plain clothes, in a van with darkened windscreens, etc.). The usual meaningful characteristics are listed without any discussion, which has the effect of making their inclusion seem realistic, natural and unquestionable. Instead of a documentary style which recognises the indeterminacy of a case (which human rights organisations generally recognise at a different level) and the limitations of any media of representation, the facts in the main text of human rights reports simply speak for themselves.

The Murder of an Anthropologist

In this section I consider another case of a political assassination in Guatemala which, unlike the Rossi incident, was actually reported, followed through in the courts and became one of the major tests of judicial reform facing successive civilian regimes – that of Myrna Mack Chang.

Myrna Mack was one of the first Guatemalan social scientists I met on beginning fieldwork in 1987. She had studied social anthropology in the UK at Durham University and had returned to join one of the few independent and critical research institutes, AVANCSO, set up in the mid-1980s. She was helpful in finding a place for me to do fieldwork and after a few months began her own research on the internally displaced in the same locale, Cobán, Alta Verapaz. She would come up to Cobán for a few weeks at a time, carry out her interviews with internal refugees and then return to be with her daughter in the capital. We worked only a few minutes by bus from one another. I lived with a local family near one of the town's main markets and she shared a convent with Catholic nuns on the outskirts of town in a *barrio* made up of refugees who had invaded private lands after the scorched earth policies of the early 1980s. We attended a language course in Q'eqchi' together which was run by the Catholic Church.

Over time we shared ideas but I always felt that our intellectual discussions were restrained, perhaps due to an unstated professional rivalry, or perhaps a resentment of foreign researchers. Yet one area where Myrna was particularly helpful was in negotiating the delicate politics of doing ethnography in a militarised society. I remember clearly her advice when I asked what information I should and should

not publish – how I should begin to define what was sensitive and what was not. She replied that although a writer should be careful about names, all of the 'broad picture' about life in Guatemala could be included in the account. She said: 'There's nothing of any importance that an ethnographer could know that the military doesn't already know. They have their own sources everywhere, so we're not going to tell them anything new.'

After I left fieldwork in Guatemala in 1988, we remained in contact and exchanged research papers, until one morning in September 1990, when I was rung by a member of staff of a London-based human rights organisation and told that Myrna had been killed the day before by an assailant armed with a knife as she left her office at AVANCSO. His account was personalised and highly emotional and subjective. My reaction was one of stunned silence – I think I only managed a few hollow-sounding expletives – but the human rights worker concerned had already moved onto a set of emotions which I would reach later that day – indignation, anger and utter disgust.

The legal investigation into the murder of Myrna Mack became a classic illustration of the struggle over the categorising and representation of human rights violations between the government, elements of the judiciary and police force, the family of a victim and human rights organisations themselves. Within hours of the event, the government's response was that this was a criminal, not a political murder. The official version asserted that Myrna Mack was killed as she was changing money on the black market, in an ideological attempt to divert blame and reduce sympathy for the victim, by portraying her as involved in shady criminal dealings. Local and international human rights organisations countered that Myrna was killed because of the nature of her social science research into the internally displaced population at a time when the government was seeking large amounts of foreign aid for their resettlement.

These immediately contradictory stances were exacerbated by an increasingly bungled and obstructed legal investigation. The forensic evidence at the scene was either ignored or later 'lost' by police. The judicial investigation was characterised by delays, and involved over nine courts and eleven judges. Several judges and key witnesses withdrew after repeated death threats. Almost a year after the event, two police officers filed a report implicating the security forces and identifying a suspect, Noél Jesús Beteta Alvarez, who was a low-ranking member of the Security Directorate of the Presidential Guard at the time of the murder. Shortly after filing the report, one of the investigating police officers was shot dead in the park across from

police headquarters, after having received repeated death threats. The other then fled the country shortly thereafter.

In February 1992, the civilian court referred the case to a military court, but the private prosecutor, Helen Mack (Myrna Mack's sister) was successful in her appeal and the case was returned to the civilian court system.[10] In the end, Beteta was sentenced to 30 years in prison. It was argued that he was a lowly scapegoat, but the appeals court closed the case against Beteta's military superiors. Some time later, the President of the Constitutional Court, Epaminondas Gonzalez Dubón, was assassinated. One likely explanation was that the Court was about to rule on the constitutionality of closing the Mack case without investigating the 'intellectual authors' of the crime.[11]

Decontextualisation in Human Rights Reporting

Meanings exist in a force field of other meanings. You could not talk about the meaning of an action without connecting it to a narrative (including other actions) if you want to interpret its meaning. (Inglis 1993: 144)

If meanings can only be understood in terms of surrounding narratives, then many human rights reports impede the interpretation of meaning by their radical acts of exclusion. Instead of narratives and 'force fields of other meanings', what the reader gets is a pared down and frozen stream of action. The gelatinous thickness of local life, as intimated in my retelling of the Rossi case, is thinned down to a watery consistency. Here, we must make a distinction between reports and narratives. Documenting human rights violations is about reporting evidence, not creating a narrative, since it is incomplete and is abstracted from the motivation and intentionality of actors. Reports begin and usually end within a more narrow time-span than narratives; that is, with the culminating event (the death or attack). Only the evidence from the event can be used to speak about anything before or after. A narrative, on the other hand, starts with actors' intentions, at a point much earlier than the report, which puts the event into a wider context.

This process of delimiting narratives began early on in human rights reporting,[12] as one worker from a major international organisation told me:

When we first arrived in Guatemala in the late 70s, and early 80s, no one even knew who we were, and they started blurting out everything. We had to say to them, 'Just give us the facts.' This probably shaped how people came to talk about the abuses because now they tell us more directly.

This 'just give us the facts' approach inherently implies, among other things, an excising of personal biographies, the filter of memory and the performative dimensions of the speech act. Over time, it appears that private narratives on abuse have themselves transformed according to how human rights workers textualise them. The exclusion of individual interpretations and social context in human rights modes of emplotment has worked its way back through the process whereby life becomes text becomes genre and has transformed survivor's own representations (in public, at least) of human rights abuses.

Turning now to Myrna Mack's case, I increasingly felt while reading reports on her case that, due to their lack of contextualisation of Myrna's circumstances, her case became about an abstract right that had been violated. Like others on the receiving end of violence, Myrna Mack was represented by a monochromatic profile of her age and occupation, rather than as a full social person with a biographical narrative. For instance, very seldom was her daughter mentioned in any reports, which seems to be a general pattern.[13] Human rights accounts often extract 'victims' from their family and class background.[14] Like Waldemar Rossi, Myrna Mack belonged to an elite family. She was of Chinese-Guatemalan descent, and her family has significant economic interests and are large landowners on the Pacific Coast. She moved easily within powerful social networks and counted on connections which reached to the top of national society and government.

Her family's status is also important in fully understanding why this case was subjected to more thorough investigative process than others. The Mack family was able to consult a number of legal advisers and mount its own private prosecution led by Myrna's sister, Helen. Helen Mack was effective in pressuring for the resignation of two judges whom she thought were biased or incompetent. In early 1992, Helen Mack travelled to Geneva to testify before the UN Commission on Human Rights, which generated pressure on the Guatemalan government to prosecute the case with greater vigour. It is much more difficult for the family of a murdered Mayan peasant to respond in a similar fashion. As with property and citizenship rights, the wealthy and educated are more likely to be able to secure and defend the human rights of their members.

The decontextualisation of Myrna Mack's case also operated at another level. Just as there is little to nothing in human rights reports about a wider community's interpretations of events (as I offered for the Rossi case), there was very little about the daily conditions of social researchers in Guatemala. Of course there are lists of how many have

been threatened, disappeared or killed in recent years, but one learns nothing of the climate in which intellectual activity is undertaken. From reading human rights reports, one remains ignorant of what it is like to think and research in a context of violence and impunity.

Before joining the research institute AVANCSO, Myrna worked for the associated press agency INFORPRESS which survived by relying on outside press reports and not sending its own agents into the 'field'. However, after the civilian government of Vinicio Cerezo was installed in 1985, AVANCSO began to tentatively undertake original field research. Myrna was constantly aware of the ambiguity and immanent danger of her situation. She struggled with her own perceptions of the political limits of research, continually pushing at the boundaries of what it seemed possible to research and report. To my knowledge, no human rights report has attempted to portray her situation as a professional social researcher before her murder. Nor is there any follow-up on the institutional response of AVANCSO, which suspended its investigation into the internally displaced, and for a time severely curtailed other projects.

It may be argued, especially by human rights activists themselves, that I have ignored the multiplicity of different organisations and documents produced by them, some of which place a strong emphasis on contextual analysis. It might be obvious that the 1-page AI Urgent Action decontextualises, since it seldom discloses more than the name, age and occupation of the victim, the place and nature of the violation, and a description of the assailants. Other documents such as the AI country reports and special reports, on the other hand, do include more analysis. Yet this is usually little more than a survey of the recent economic and political history which reads like a 'fact file'. The special report on *Guatemala: Extrajudicial Executions and Human Rights Violations Against Street Children* (Amnesty International 1990) has 4 pages of general discussion on street children followed by nearly 30 pages of grim accounts of individual cases. Similarly, AI's 1989 report on Guatemala consisted of 1 page of 'political context', and over 40 pages of individual cases of human rights violations. The most in-depth section of this report was an exploration of the legal system, where it discussed the intricacies of magistrates' investigations under the Napoleonic Code.

Amnesty International is arguably the organisation which puts the greatest emphasis on the limited documentation of individual cases. Other organisations, such as the US-based Watch Committees, offer much more analysis of ongoing conditions. During the 1980s, the reports and photographs of Americas Watch representative, Jean-Marie Simon, were renowned for the degree to which they captured the

prevailing social conditions in Guatemala. So one cannot simply say that all human rights documents are devoid of contextual interpretations. Yet there is a crucial separation between organisations and forms of documentation which detail individual cases and those which explore structural conditions. The importance of this distinction lies in how it separates the individual from the social, facts from interpretations, all in an effort to preserve an unassailable and legalistic regime of truth.

What are the consequences of the tendencies towards decontextualisation found in many human rights reports? First, they can depoliticise human rights violations by drawing attention away from structural processes of class or ethnic power, and reduce violations to a set of technical problems concerning the functioning of the legal system. Second, the gory semiology of human rights abuses, and particularly torture and mutilation, remain incomprehensible except as irrational outbursts devoid of meaning. It is as if the maxim 'To understand is to forgive' has been taken too literally. By underemphasising the structural and transnational dimensions of violence, human rights reports render such acts universal. Yet increasingly, anthropologists have argued that violence, like any other social process, is expressed and interpreted according to sets of metaphors about the nature of power, gender relations and human bodies. This communicative dimension means that violence is never 'meaningless'.[15]

Finally, the removal of victims from their social and family contexts belies an ethnocentric basis to representations of human rights abuses. By disengaging an agent from their socio-historical circumstances, what we are left with is a universal decontextualised individual which is the basic unit of liberal political, economic and legal theory. We could contrast this with the dominant discourse in anthropology on the 'social person' and the view that it is not possible to refer to 'the individual' outside of a concrete historical context. As opposed to a universal maximising individual with a natural set of rights, there are social persons who are engaged in the making and remaking of complex interconnected social processes, and whose rights in those contexts are not natural, but are the result of historical struggles for power between persons and corporate groups.

As this chapter will explore more fully later on, decontextualisation is part of a human rights paradigm which generally tries to maintain as close a likeness as possible with legal texts. The criteria of judgement of human rights organisations are not solely the result of a textual genre for representing violations of rights, but derive from

a radical conception of the nature of rights themselves. As Stan Cohen has commented:

neither decontextualisation nor the exclusion of biographical narratives is a mere artefact of human rights reporting. They are the deliberate results of the human rights credo that no context (circumstances, motives, etc.) can ever justify the violations of universal prohibitions. This exclusion is even more radical than in the case of the criminal law.[16]

The Exclusion of Subjectivity

After hearing the news of Myrna's murder, I was struck by the disjuncture between the language deployed in official human rights reports and the emotionally charged language which human rights workers use to discuss events between themselves. The worker who reported to me personally spoke in a tentative language full of subjectivity, interpretation and uncertainty. He expressed anger and his doubt that it was actually a human rights violation – at the time we did consider the possibilities of it being a 'criminal' murder, given the high levels of street crime in the capital. All of this contrasts with the arid texts produced after the event, which sought to codify the jumbled signs into a clear statement, and one which was devoid of subjectivity. A strange kind of schizophrenia lurks in the space between the emotional lives of those involved in human rights activities and the way human rights texts represent violations.

Once an item is selected for inclusion in the human rights network, it is then conveyed with an aura of authority and legitimacy. Reports engage in an unemotional skeletonising of local narratives which strips subjectivity from the representation of events, in order to construct a version apparently free of distortion. Since perpetrators of abuses do all in their power to efface any record of crimes, there is an obligation both to bear witness and not to distort the record of events. Implicit here is the idea that any departure from a minimalist style is distorting. Correspondingly, human rights reports are written with an unflinching realism which bluntly recounts one fact after another in an unmitigated and relentless barrage of short case summaries. Only a literalist chronicle passes the twin test of authenticity and authority, leading to a suppression of the authorial voice and the deployment of a language purged of all tropes, metaphors and figurative elements.

Few entries are dealt with in the detail that Myrna Mack's case was, and these are generally ones which symbolise a set of violations against a targeted group, or are test cases which demonstrate the limits of the judicial process. Instead, most cases only receive a few short

sentences, which are regular and have a simple subject-predicate-object form. The text makes concise and clean use of the declarative and employs few adjectives. All meaning is on the surface, and the confidence of the assertions is expressed in their lack of elaboration. Local words are seldom deployed, nor are interpretations of translated words particularly in evidence. For example, *'La violencia'* is the term often used by locals to refer to political violence in Guatemala. Yet like the term 'The Troubles' in Northern Ireland, it has a set of political meanings which human rights reports do not delve into or even allude to (cf. Warren 1993). The main categories used in reports are left unexamined, since they are understood to be universal and therefore not in need of interpretation.

At the same time as blunt realism and hard facts are delivered up comes the recognition that:

the data obtained by Amnesty International from human rights workers and others is necessarily fragmented, incomplete and variable. Amnesty International is also aware that the reporting categories used by the various groups collecting such data in Guatemala and elsewhere do not necessarily conform to the organisation's own classifications of 'disappearances' and extra-judicial executions. (Amnesty International 1989: 8)

This recognition of provisionality usually occurs in the preface of a document, yet the style of the main body of the text remains unblemished by contingency apart from the references to 'unknown persons', which the reader must assume are state-directed agents, or why would the account qualify as a 'human rights violation?

This lack of reflexivity makes it impossible to search for answers in the text to pedestrian but vital questions on particular cases, such as: what is the evidence and the counter-evidence and how was it collected (from press reports? key informants? missions of inquiry?). The rough edges of the methods which lead to knowledge in human rights reports are lost in the seamless web of text. Epistemological security is underpinned by transparent facts, not by a self-conscious awareness that knowledge emerges from creative insight, the interpretation of partial connections and in the act of representation itself.

The lack of stated authors in almost all human rights agency reports is characteristic of a desubjectified genre, of a discourse deprived of an author-function. This leads to an extreme polarisation where the de-individualisation of the author clashes with both the highly individualised content of reports and individualistic conception of rights. In contrast, I constructed my accounts of the cases of Myrna Mack and Waldemar Rossi with myself as part of the narrative. My

subjectivity, memories and imputed meanings were inseparable from the events themselves, but in most human rights reports, the only documentors present and named are the photographers. The protection of workers and informants might justify this exclusion, but this cannot explain a blanket policy. Amnesty International reports are likely to have been primarily written by one of a handful of desk officers,[17] whose names are public. Similarly, governments are always aware when they are in the country on a 'mission of inquiry' and they largely know who they talk to.

Evacuating the author serves not only as a protective device, but also creates an aura of objectivity and neutrality by wiping the stain of subjectivity off the surface of the text. The simple recounting of a truthful narrative sets up human rights organisations as honest brokers, who dispassionately dispense disturbing information. Author-evacuated texts, whether human rights reports, scientific texts or legal contracts, are an established literary strategy to convey value-free information devoid of individuality and opinion. The presence or absence of the author has historically defined the binary line between the literary, figurative and expressive from the scientific, literal and realist.

In 'What is an Author?,' Michel Foucault (1979: 149) refers to how:

A reversal occurred in the seventeenth or eighteenth century. Scientific discourses began to be received for themselves, in the anonymity of an established or always redemonstrable truth; their membership in a systematic ensemble, and not their reference to the individual who produced them, stood as their guarantee.

Similarly, the reliability of human rights reports rests not upon a reflexive mode of emplotment, but in the trustworthiness of the genre itself, and the organisations which produce it. The reports are reliable because Amnesty International or Americas Watch are reliable institutions. The validity of the report rests upon reputation and rhetoric, and the reader is forced to choose between either believing or disbelieving. When presented with a seamless style of representation, healthy scepticism has no place to take hold.

The interpreting gaze of the bystander is similarly dissipated. One seldom reads openly recognised eyewitness reports of who saw what and under what conditions. This is partly to protect bystanders from reprisals from security forces, but in many cases the security forces know exactly who is denouncing human rights abuses. For instance, in Latin America, violent actions or threats against trade unionists are regularly denounced by trade union confederations in the national press. Again, in my account of Rossi's murder, the 'bystander effect'

was an important basis of my attempt to persuade you the reader that something did actually happen. Although I did not see the body, I heard the shots, saw the milling crowd, and heard the immediate description of an ashen-faced bystander. The rhetorical power of these statements is both more forceful and more directly questionable than the Olympian view-from-nowhere which characterises human rights reports.

Although the authorial interpretation of often contradictory information is an inevitable aspect of producing human rights documents, this is not acknowledged in order to preserve their status as legal fact. The fact/value distinction is refracted throughout the human rights project, for example, in the already mentioned cleavage between reports and organisations which take a restricted brief to document the bare 'facts' of a case and those which provide more systematic analysis and subjective testimony.

Another example lies in the distinction between desubjectified texts and wholly subjectified public meetings which feature testimony from victims of abuses. Here the audience is exposed to a direct and emotional experience unavailable in reports. Such testimonies do not break down the binary distinction between fact and value, instead they preserve it. Subjectivity belongs only to victims, whereas the organisations hosting them preserve their objectivity. The subjectivity of victims is harnessed in fund-raising letters: one Amnesty International letter of the early 1990s featured a Guatemalan street child with the caption, 'This boy wants to kiss you', accompanied by a testimony as to the effectiveness of Amnesty International's intervention.[18]

It is now commonly accepted that there is no neat distinction between facts and interpretations, where the former is a bedrock of truth and the latter is constructed artifice. Instead, the two are bound up in one another, where every 'fact' is an act of interpretation resulting from the critical judgement of a documentor about what constitutes valuable evidence. Further judgements are then made about the overall development of the narrative in which 'facts' are embedded, and the style and authorial voice to be used. Human rights organisations operate with a false opposition between literal versus figurative speech, since every attempt to represent a human rights violation is a narrative with a plot (however circumscribed), and every emplotment is a kind of figuration. Once it is recognised that all narratives are the result of artifice and design, then rather than hide any reference to this process, it might be preferable to place the interpretative filter in the foreground of the account, to convey

something of the conditions in which knowledge is formulated and represented.

Law and the Language of State Power

The argument thus far has been to understand the genre of human rights reports with reference to their legalistic epistemology: the facts they contain are legal facts which could stand up in a court of law. Their intended aim is not just to assert truth but to demand justice through urging governments to prosecute individuals. Human rights 'missions' go to countries to 'verify and expand the information'[19] which will be instrumentally marshalled to construct a case against a government. That which matters is that which is universal, documentable through reference to 'hard' facts and relevant to rationalist legal inquiry. Subjectivity and information not immediately relevant to the prosecution of the individual case are dismissed.

It could be countered to my line of argument that human rights reporting is not an anthropological study of the local knowledge in which political violence is embedded, nor is it a fictional account of the experiential dimensions of terror. 'Pragmatists' might pose a number of rejoinders; that human rights organisation are not trying to change global systems of inequality, but have had to confine their campaigns to ensuring that international and national laws are upheld; that we have to remember that human rights reports are designed to be a persuasive assertion of truths in order to alter governmental policy or public opinion; and that governments are generally averse to human rights reporting on their own country and seek to undermine the validity of such reports in any way possible.

I recognise the importance of many of these arguments. Without a doubt, the effective deployment of human rights information can and does influence government policy. Further, information presented as legal fact based upon universal criteria of truth in the present global context carries much greater rhetorical power than interpretations made by contextualised individuals relying on a creative subjectivity. Of course, power resides not only in the fact that one genre is more faithful to local truths than another, but in the style of assertion of the same truths.

Returning to Guatemala, it could easily be argued the symbolic capital of human rights, expressed in films and reports had an impact on the legal process in the Myrna Mack case. This was one of the highest profile cases in recent Guatemalan legal history and generated condemnations not only from non-governmental organisations but also from the UN special expert and the US State Department. Helen

Mack's testimony at the UN produced a plethora of international denunciations of the Guatemalan government. Helen Mack's request as prosecutor for records from army files is believed to be the first time that the military have been asked for such evidence. The trial directly led to the disbanding of the Presidential Guard to which the murderer Beteta pertained and to the removal of military advisers from police departments.

The Mack trial contributed to a wider reform of the Guatemalan criminal justice system; a reform which had been foreseen in the 1985 Constitution, but had not been implemented until July 1994, with the advent of the New Criminal Code.[20] In broad terms, this meant a move away from an inquisitorial model where the trial stage consists of a sentencing judge reading a written file during private court proceedings. In this model, the judge sentences or acquits often without listening to the testimony of witnesses. The reformed legal process gives the Public Ministry a role in the initial investigation, and introduces live oral testimony with indigenous interpreters and public hearings at the trial stage. It also makes provision for a special procedure in case habeas corpus is not filed within the allotted time.[21]

Although human rights discourses cannot claim all the credit for the recent changes of the Guatemalan judicial process, it is clear that they have influenced the pace of reforms. The power of human rights is exerted in courts of law, but also through the rhetorical form of human rights documents, and particularly through the legalism of their accounts. The knowledge produced by human rights agencies is part of the exercise of power insofar as it creates subjects and defines a context of injustice which demands to be put right. Since it is opposed to the use of power through control or coercion, the only power of human rights organisations lie in their discourse of denunciation. Since their only resource is the symbolic capital created by the ability to generate certain types of information, then it matters a great deal how that information is constructed.

The language of human rights reports mirrors the language of the modern nation-state, and the texts must engage in that discourse to influence state policy. Thus the effectiveness of human rights agencies' legalistic language lies in the fact that it speaks the language that state agents can understand. Were it to speak outside that discourse, then it presumably would have no effect.[22] Yet there is a tension here in aims, since human rights texts are directed at a heterogeneous audience, made up of other professional campaigners, local groups of non-professional activists, journalists, development workers and the general public, as well as politicians, bureaucrats and official state/UN policy-makers. This variegated community of end users

could conceivably merit a differentiated body of publications of differing styles.

Yet the most powerful argument against the constrained style of human rights reporting concerns the implications it has for the conceptualisation of human rights. By situating social persons in communities and contexts, and furnishing thick descriptions of acts of the violent exercise of power, it can be seen how rights themselves are grounded, transformative and inextricably bound to purposive agents rather than being universal abstractions. The exalting of a legal/technical rationality above history and experience is ironically self-defeating, since despite its dedication to ethical ends, its method itself is denuded of ethics, having displaced value distinctions from its own operation.

Human rights are saturated with what Habermas (1971: 112–13) refers to as a 'technocratic consciousness' which engages in a displacement of values, norms and what he terms 'action-motivating meanings': 'The technocratic consciousness reflects not the sundering of (particular) ethical situations but the repression of ethics as a category of life.' It is this assimilation of ethics into scientific, technological and legal categories, which entails decontextualisation and the eradication of subjectivity. By embracing a technocratic language, human rights reporting lays itself open to the same critique as could be made of the devalued, dehumanised language of abusive forms of governance. Desubjectification, after all, is the chosen *modus operandi* of the torturer, and it hardly seems appropriate to employ a desubjectified narrative in order to represent abusive acts.

Concluding Remarks

What are the implications of the argument so far for the writing of human rights reports? My intention has not been to undermine their effectiveness, but to raise questions about the manner in which they are produced. What I would maintain is that human rights organisations could afford to adopt a greater range of styles of representing human rights abuses. As mentioned in the introduction, Amnesty International is one of many organisations which are engaged in an ongoing internal debate (or rather, struggle) on this issue. While International Council Meetings advocate greater inclusion of contextual material, and Amnesty International workers write reports with more and more social comment, the internal 'Standing Committee on the Mandate', which is made up mostly of lawyers, acts in a vigilant manner to excise what it sees as extraneous information.

As stated in the introduction, the debate about the 'limits of representation' of gross violations of human rights has a long history in writings on the Holocaust. It has been pointed out by Christopher Browning (1992) that the Holocaust was not a legal or philosophical abstraction, instead it was a set of events that actually occurred. A key problem in representing the Jewish 'Shoah' results from an 'experiential gap' and the shortcomings of all forms of representation. Generally historians or social scientists and their readers have nothing in their biographical experience which remotely compares with the Holocaust. Likewise, writers of human rights texts usually know nothing in a personal experiential sense about their subject (for example, torture, mutilation, etc.). It could be concluded that one way of leaping across the experiential gap would be to try to capture the nature of the subject matter through engaging with the existential circumstances of the victims, bystanders, even the perpetrators. What were the choices they faced, the emotions they felt, their coping mechanisms and ensuing changes in personality?

This experiential tack has been preferred over an arid abstract literalism by Jewish writers on the Holocaust. In his latest book, *Operation Shylock*, Philip Roth interviews the writer Aharon Appelfeld, who at the age of 9 survived the Holocaust, by escaping an extermination camp and wandering alone in Ukrainian woods. He has yet to write about the period as a direct experience or as a survivor's tale in as direct a fashion as Primo Levi's depiction of his Auschwitz incarceration. Instead, he writes fiction, and in the novel *Tzili*, retells the events of a young Jewish girl wandering among Ukrainian peasants, and the text is infused with the subjectivity of a sovereign author. In explaining why he used this genre instead of a 'factual' one, Appelfeld replied: 'The reality of the Holocaust surpassed any imagination. If I remained true to the facts, no one would believe me.'

One possible objection to the line my argument has taken could be that it leads towards a soggy relativism where any representation is as good as another. There is a general tendency for debates about modalities of representation and relativism to merge, but this need not necessarily be so. It should be possible to extend the limits of representation to include more modes of emplotment than are conventionally deployed at present in documenting human rights violations without collapsing into absolutist forms of perspectivism. I am not arguing that there exist a multiplicity of equally valid approaches, which could conceivably encourage an ethically dubious lurch into aesthetic fantasy. It could be argued successfully when comparing concrete examples that one mode of emplotment offers a

more plausible rendition of the available evidence than another. As Perry Anderson (1992) has asserted, narratives are bounded both by exterior limits set by the evidence and by interior limits of the genre itself; for instance, it would be inappropriate for the Holocaust to be written about in the genres of comedy or pastoral romanticism.

Yet the main thrust of my argument is directed more towards social researchers, since human rights organisations will probably be committed to a legalistic framework at least for the foreseeable future. I would urge us to think more about the relationship between social research (and particularly anthropology) and human rights reporting, so that the texts of researchers might restore local subjectivities, values and memories as well as analysing the wider global social processes in which violence is embedded. Alex de Waal's (1994) comments are applicable here, insofar as he deliberates on what anthropologists can contribute to human rights and media reports of events like the mass ethnic violence in Rwanda. He concludes that ethnographers can complement other genres with studies that introduce history, local knowledge and an understanding of how identities are constructed, so violence is not only seen as a result of age-old animosities between primordial groups. This contextualisa-tion is needed in order to compensate for the individualised, a-cultural, deracinated and therefore universalistic nature of most human rights accounts.

Notes

1. See especially Saul Friedlander's (1992) edited volume, where there is a discussion of whether aesthetic experimentation is more justified when faced with events which challenge the usual categories of representation. For instance, accounts of the Holocaust by authors such as Ida Fink and David Grossman are both allegories and realistic novels, including enough references to 'real events' to prevent too much distance. Debates on repre-sentations of colonialism have gone in a similar direction; for example, James Clifford (1988) locates the genius of Joseph Conrad in his ability both to penetrate the veil of colonialism and yet to maintain a sense of its hallucinatory quality.
2. The imposing *Banco Imperial* was built in 1991 on the town square in Cobán by a drug-smuggling cartel for the purpose of money laundering and investment, but its function was discovered by law enforcement officials before it ever opened.

3. Christopher Browning (1992) arrives at similar conclusions in his reconstruction of perpetrators' testimonies of a massacre of Jews in the Polish village of Jozefów in 1942.

4. Note the use of legalistic language ('circumstantial evidence') and the equivocal statement which combines a tentative assertion ('appears'), with a confident qualification ('clearly').

5. Since direct state involvement is difficult to ascertain, Amnesty International also uses wider criteria which are not predicated on direct state involvement, by referring to cases 'where Amnesty International believes the available evidence suggests official complicity'. Complicity here means that state officers have not intervened while a crime took place, or they failed to fully pursue an investigation, suggesting official acquiescence.

6. Orin Starn (1992) reports a similar situation in highland Peru, where some community vigilante groups, or *rondas campesinas*, are military-directed counter-insurgency organisations, whereas others were inspired by the Catholic Church in order to facilitate local protection from cattle rustlers.

7. National Academy of Sciences (NAS) (1992: 39).

8. NAS (1992: 29).

9. NAS (1992: 21).

10. At the time, Guatemala's legal system operated under the Napoleonic Code, where magistrates uncovered both exculpatory and incriminatory facts, with no provision for jury trial.

11. As ever, this view competes with other explanations, including the theory that the murder may have been linked to the Court's approval to extradite a Guatemalan army officer to the US for drug smuggling. My thanks to David Stoll for pointing this out.

12. Although it is beyond the scope of this chapter, there is a need for more historical studies of human rights reporting, which look at the emergence and transformation of certain languages of denunciation and the conditions under which such reports are produced. In Latin America, one might start in the early colonial period with Bartolomé de las Casas and Guaman Poma and move into the early twentieth century with Roger Casement's report to the British Foreign Office on the Putumayo rubber atrocities.

13. Children and spouses are only referred to if a person is attacked or abducted in front of them, and it is suggested that this adds to the gravity of the human rights violation, since the bystanders' rights to be free of intimidation are violated as well.

14. Human rights reports did actually include more of Myrna Mack's biography and background than the vast majority of cases due to the importance the case assumed in the legal system.
15. See Kapferer (1988) and Scott (1990) for a heated debate on violence as communication in Sri Lanka.
16. Personal communication.
17. Although they are checked by an internal monitor as well.
18. One Amnesty International desk officer referred to this specific letter as 'maudlin'.
19. NAS (1992: 37).
20. See Costello and Seider (1996).
21. However, the implementation of the new penal code is not widespread and has been hampered by a lack of funds and corruption.
22. See Richard Rorty's (1979) discussion of normal and abnormal discourses in *Philosophy and the Mirror of Nature*.

References

Anderson, Perry. 1992. 'On Emplotment: Two Kinds of Ruin', in S. Friedlander (ed.) *Probing the Limits of Representation: Nazism and the Final Solution*. Cambridge, MA: Harvard University Press.

Amnesty International. 1989. *Guatemala: Human Rights Violations Under the Civilian Government*. London: AMR 34/07/89.

—— 1990. *Guatemala: Extrajudicial Executions and Human Rights Violations Against Street Children*. London: AMR 34/37/90.

Asad, Talal. 1992. 'Conscripts of Western Civilization', in Christine Ward Gailey (ed.) *Civilization in Crisis: Anthropological Perspectives*. Gainesville: University of Florida Press.

Browning, Christopher. 1992. 'German Memory, Judicial Interrogation, and Historical Reconstruction: Writing Perpetrator History from Postwar Testimony', in S. Friedlander (ed.) *Probing the Limits of Representation: Nazism and the Final Solution*. Cambridge, MA: Harvard University Press.

Costello, Patrick and Rachel Seider (1996) 'Judicial Reform in Central America: Prospects for the Rule of Law', in R. Seider (ed.) *Central America: Fragile Transition*. London: Macmillan/ILAS.

Clifford, James. 1988. *The Predicament of Culture: Twentieth-century Ethnography, Literature and Art*. Cambridge, MA: Harvard University Press.

Foucault, Michel. 1979. 'What is an Author?' in J. Harari (ed.) *Textual Strategies: Perspectives in Post-structuralist Criticism*. Ithaca, NY: Cornell University Press.

Friedlander, Saul. (ed.) 1992. *Probing the Limits of Representation: Nazism and the Final Solution.* Cambridge, MA: Harvard University Press.

Geertz, Clifford. 1983. 'Local Knowledge: Fact and Law in Comparative Perspective', in *Local Knowledge,* New York: Basic Books.

Giddens, Anthony. 1985. *The Nation-state and Violence: Volume Two of a Contemporary Critique of Historical Materialism.* Cambridge: Polity Press.

Habermas, Jürgen. 1971. *Towards a Rational Society,* trans. J.J. Shapiro. London: Heinemann.

Inglis, Fred. 1993. *Cultural Studies.* Oxford: Blackwell.

Kapferer, Bruce. 1988. *Legends of People, Myths of State.* Washington: Smithsonian Institute Press.

LaCapra, Dominick. 1992. 'Representing the Holocaust: Reflections on the Historians' Debate', in S. Friedlander (ed.) *Probing the Limits of Representation: Nazism and the Final Solution.* Cambridge, MA: Harvard University Press.

National Academy of Sciences (NAS) Committee on Human Rights and Institute of Medicine Committee on Health and Human Rights. 1992. *Scientists and Human Rights in Guatemala: Report of a Delegation.* Washington, DC: National Academy Press.

Rorty, Richard. 1979. *Philosophy and the Mirror of Nature.* Princeton, NJ: University of Princeton Press.

Scott, David. 1990. 'The Demonology of Nationalism: On the Anthropology of Ethnicity and Violence in Sri Lanka', *Economy and Society* 19(4): 491–510.

Starn, Orin. 1992. '"I Dreamed of Foxes and Hawks": Reflections on Peasant Protest, New Social Movements, and the *Rondas Campesinas* of Northern Peru', in A. Escobar and S. Alvarez (eds) *The Making of Social Movements in Latin America: Identity, Strategy and Democracy.* Boulder, CO: Westview Press.

Waal, Alex de. 1994. 'Editorial: Genocide in Rwanda', *Anthropology Today* 10(3) 1–2.

Warren, Kay. 1993. *The Violence Within.* Boulder, CO: Westview Press.

Wilson, Richard A. 1995. *Maya Resurgence in Guatemala: Q'eqchi' Experiences.* Norman: University of Oklahoma Press.

Zur, Judith. 1994. 'The Psychological Impact of Impunity', *Anthropology Today* 10(3).

7   UNIVERSAL AND SUSTAINABLE HUMAN RIGHTS? SPECIAL TRIBUNALS IN GUATEMALA

Jennifer Schirmer

Author   Once the Special Tribunals were dissolved, what happened to the prisoners?

Ríos Montt   We released 112 from prison. They were later assassinated [by the army] on the street, in their homes, in the countryside, because they were dangerous [and] had done wicked things – PUM! (he mimics shooting a gun against his head). (July 1991, author's interview)

We have a mortgaged justice: we don't own it and we certainly don't control it. ... Yet, the institutionality, the legality, the constitutionality of our society – they are our only hope – and I myself have lost all faith in them. (Guatemalan lawyer for the defence in cases before the Special Tribunals, January 1984, author's interview)[1]

Between September 1982 and February 1983, 15 prisoners, blindfolded, hands tied behind their backs, were positioned in front of prepared graves in the municipal cemetery and executed by firing squad. They had been tried by *Tribunales de Fuero Especial*, Special Tribunals, and sentenced to death for among 18 crimes not considered punishable by death in the Guatemalan Penal Code. Another 14 were sentenced to prison, and two foreigners, due to interventions from their embassies, were released. One year and 11 days later, under intense international human rights pressure by the Inter-American Court and human rights organisations, these *Tribunales* were disbanded.

The cases of 400 individuals were transferred from the *Tribunales* to the Supreme Court where only three to four cases were reviewed while hundreds awaited the verdict in prison. Upon release, 112 were covertly assassinated by army intelligence: the whereabouts of

the other prisoners is still unknown. For international human rights lawyers, this episode is considered a triumph for the rule of law and human rights. For the handful of courageous local Guatemalan lawyers attempting to defend these prisoners, the international support is a mixed blessing: they praise the abolition of the *Tribunales*, yet consider the transfer of the secret cases to the Supreme Court to be an abomination. For the military, who saw the *Tribunales* as forms of 'rapid justice', it is merely an inconvenient delay in ridding Guatemala of corruption and criminal elements.

This chapter traces how this human rights story was understood by three different groups of actors: by the military High Command that created the *Tribunales*, the international human rights community, and those caught in the middle, the lawyers for the defence in cases before the *Tribunales*. The story raises a number of questions about the short-term and long-term consequences of the *Tribunales* and their abolition for rule of law and human rights in Guatemala and about the structural effects of such human rights intervention on the local legal system and its practitioners.

This chapter argues that an over-emphasis on abstract universal standards without the contextualisation and follow-up of rights-in-practice in the end, may hinder what shall be termed a climate for sustainable rights. In fact, minimalist, abstract and formulaic approaches to human rights with purely formal demands made of military regimes, for example the dissolution of the *Tribunales*, may unintentionally give the impression that international demands have been met, that the regime is complying with human rights treaties to protect its citizens, and that repression has diminished even while prisoners remain political/incarcerated and clandestine killings continue. 'This whole nefarious stage of our history has yet to be expunged', one Guatemalan lawyer lamented in 1986 two years after the *Tribunales* were dissolved. 'Nothing at all has changed. The repression continues as before and the court system still has the list of the 400 *Tribunales* cases'(1984 author's interview).

Tribunales de Fuero Especial and the Military View of Law and Crime

Guatemala has suffered a gradual deterioration of its legal and constitutional traditions since 1965. It was during the 1982–83 Ríos Montt regime, with the establishment of the special secret tribunals, however, that this deterioration was codified by those in power. With the March 1982 coup, a National Plan of Security and Development, implemented by the Army General Staff, was designed

to return the country to constitutionality while diligently pursuing scorched-earth campaigns in the highlands.

The Plan was no less than the reorganisation of the State. Congress and the Constitution were suspended while a Council of State[2] was established and a Fundamental Statute of Government 'legislated' (Decree-Law 24-82). This law was promulgated to 'juridically normalise the country' and uphold human rights treaties, while also limiting the right to due process. With this Statute, laws of *'fuero especial'* for the judgement of 'determined crimes' could be enacted by the *junta* when deemed necessary to maintain order, peace and public security (Ministro de Gobernación 1982: 69, 109). They would, however, remain 'within the reach and traditions of the administration of justice' of the ordinary courts (local defence lawyer, 1984 author's interview).

On 1 July 1982, Ríos Montt, who had dissolved the junta of the 23 March 1982 coup and assumed the presidency, issued Decree-Law 45-82 (*Ley de Orden Público*). It established a State of Siege (the first since 1970 and renewed every 30 days until March 1983) that suspended all rights – habeas corpus, union or political activities, inviolability of homes and offices – and granted arrest powers to the armed forces. The news media were forbidden to broadcast or print information concerning 'subversion' other than that provided by the government public relations offices. In a radio speech on 3 July, Ríos Montt defended the state of siege, arguing that 'the 10 years without a state of siege [resulted] ... [in] more than 150,000 people [being] lost' (Nyrop 1983: 189).[3]

Declaring that God had ordered a final battle against the guerrillas, Ríos Montt also promulgated at this time Decree-Law 46-82 (*Ley de Tribunales de Fuero Especial*) to establish special secret courts with the power to impose the death penalty. The law also empowered him to select the judges who were to be, according to Col.-lawyer Girón Tanchez, 'judges of law, men capable of dictating solutions which involve death as the penalty' (1986 author's interview).[4] The decree-law was an ingenious intermingling of counter-insurgency emergency measures (such as the death penalty) with parts of the traditional legal norms of the Penal Code. Born 'out of the inefficiency of the common courts', according to their legal architect Col.-lawyer Girón Tanchez(1986 author's interview), the *Tribunales* were to provide 'rapid justice' and to 'cleanse the courts' of the guerrillas 'even if it means a diminishing of rights'.

They were the personal invention of Ríos Montt: 'He came to me [saying] "Let's have tribunals which really make justice in ... [a] quasi-secret form".' Quasi-secret because 'The names of the judges

were not to be published, although they are in the archives. The military government knew the names' (1986 author's interview). Few of the prisoners were permitted to engage lawyers in contradiction of the decree-law itself. The few lawyers there were, were told to present their papers to an office in the Public or Defence Ministries, and wait for the verdict. Justifications for such secrecy were made by several military officers interviewed who spoke of the weakness of the courts to indict 'terrorists' and stop threats against and kidnappings of judges and government officials during trials in the 1960s.

Rather than follow the example of the previous regime of Lucas Garcia (1978–82) when according to General Gramajo 'if a common criminal entered the jail 20 times, they would place him on a list, and when he re-entered 21 times and the judge was unable to keep him in jail, when he left, they would assassinate him', the 1982 military government created instead Special Tribunals and the legislation for them. The *Tribunales* 'reduced the threats, reduced the scandals in the newspapers' (1990 author's interview). The Under-Secretary of the Public Ministry also argued that 'the other [ordinary] courts cannot judge these [special] cases because the judges are exposed to a series of threats and problems'.[5] He added that secret proceedings are not new to Guatemala, to which one local lawyer responded, 'Does he think we are neophytes of law? We know this is a complete lie. To say so is to be disrespectful of the honour and the destiny of legality in Guatemala' (1984 author's interview).

No mention is made of the threats and assassinations of lawyers and judges by the security forces (80 alone were killed during the Lucas Garcia period). Nor is mention made of the buying of judges' participation in the *Tribunales* (local lawyers wondered aloud about who paid their 'salaries'), of extortion of defendants for their freedom, of the fining of lawyers for filing, and of the threats against these same lawyers forcing them to drop their cases or flee the country. 'Naturally, we were doubtful about this "rapid justice" Ríos Montt spoke about', one of the local lawyers said. 'Especially since the decree-law annulled the Statute's claims of working within the norms of the ordinary courts and abolished the autonomy of the Supreme Court. The secret proceedings of the *Tribunales*, moreover, contradicted its own law's claim to "open and just" courts' (1984 author's interview).

For the military, law represents 'the rational power ... to make [our] force felt'. It is ultimately not about justice but about what one can do with it to carry out operations against opponents who are, by definition, outside the law (cf. Schirmer 1996). Ríos Montt explained the *Tribunales* this way:

We invited the subversion to lay down their arms. We had military encounters, there was a war. ... Later, we legalised a concept of special powers (*fuero especial*) because the violence did not permit us to impart justice. And we gathered up the assassins and criminals, we judged them and we *shot* them, *but in accordance with the law*.[6]

The decree-laws of the Special Tribunals and Public Order served as a reformulation of the penal laws: political crimes could also be judged as common crimes, and vice versa; delinquency not only deserved the same sanction as subversion, but it was one and the same: hence the military's interchangeable terms *delincuentes-subversivos* and *delincuentes-terroristas*. Disrupting public order, such as robbing a store or stealing a taxi, was equivalent to waging war on the nation. Decree-Law 46-82 not only looted the old crimes of the Penal Code and created a generic category of crimes deserving of the death penalty, but legislated new crimes 'in cases not foreseen by this decree' (Article 39). Seeing law as a preventive instrument to control opponents of the state, 'criminals' become:

groups of delinquents, by means of subversive activities, who attempt to violently change the juridical, political, social and economic institutions of the nation. ... Those who perform such activities make use of procedures that disturb public order, gravely alter social tranquillity and destroy lives and property of inhabitants of the Republic. ... In order to protect the order, peace and public security, it is necessary to dictate a law that guarantees a rapid and exemplary administration of justice by passing judgement on crimes attempted against these values.

Those charged with 'arson' (Article 283), for example, would be condemned to death rather than sentenced to 3 years.[7]

The goal of the *Tribunales* was to wage war to prevent war as expeditiously as possible: intimidation and punishment served as forms of 'rapid and exemplary' retribution (Ministro de Gobernación 1982: 68). The effect is a process plagued by contradictions, arbitrariness and what one Guatemalan lawyer would call 'legal lagoons'. The consequence is a violence dressed up as justice, 'assassinations in the name of law' that supersede and neutralise traditional judicial inquiry. According to this inversion of the Penal Code, one lawyer recounted bitterly, 'one is guilty until one cannot prove one's innocence'.

The Operations of the *Tribunales*

With a definition of subversion so expansive that 'anyone could be considered a subverter of the national order',[8] the *Tribunales* by April 1983 had tried 70 persons and convicted 20 while another 250 faced

prosecution. Four men were executed on 17 September 1982; six more were put to death on 3 March 1983 and another five on 21 March after being tried and sentenced by the special courts. The 15 individuals condemned to death had been abducted without arrest warrants, remaining 'disappeared' (that is, authorities did not acknowledge their detention to desperate relatives) for several months before their cases were decided, severely tortured with beatings, electric shock, suffocation and mock execution and forced to sign confessions without being allowed to read the contents of their statements.[9]

As best as can be determined, the accusations did not suggest guerrilla activity, but grew out of personal vendettas and involved poor defendants lacking any political influence. 'The truth is, these tribunals did not in the least combat the guerrilla. They found whatever delinquents they could, denounced them for political revenge, subjected them to these tribunals and *converted these delinquents into guerrillas'*, one of the lawyers who defended *Tribunales* prisoners stated angrily (1984 author's interview). In contrast, some semblance of due process was provided to two foreign tourists. Though the charges against them were not dismissed, they were permitted to leave the country after being held for 28 days 'on parole on their own recognisance (*caución juratoria)'.

Several civilian and military sources, including Ríos Montt, referred to the *Tribunales* as an attempt not only to control the 'subversives' but also to 'clean the house' (*'limpiar la casa'*) of corruption (1991 author's interview). Five 'psychopathic *especialistas'* from the clandestine security forces (two of whom were soldiers) who had preyed on the well-to-do, including commiting rape, were convicted of 'violent immoral abuse' and executed by firing squad on the first anniversary of the coup (21 March) – an execution, one source contends, which members of the security forces were forced to attend (intelligence source, 1991 author's interview). There is a distinct possibility that the *Tribunales* were used to cover up a 'purge' of police and military 'authorities who had not respected the law' during the Lucas years by conjoining them with a group of prisoners initially captured during the coup.[10] Many were released only to be later assassinated 'because they were dangerous' (Ríos Montt, 1991 author's interview).

Most of the *Tribunales* prisoners, though, were not provided with legal aid, but judged by secret military and civilian judges. Family members went from law office to law office desperate for a lawyer to defend their son or daughter. 'Many lawyers didn't want to go against the tide', Lic. Eduardo Fernandez explained in his small, bare office in Guatemala City.

Perhaps they would be threatened, perhaps they wouldn't, but they didn't want to chance it. The parents of the Marroquín brothers approached me, and I felt obliged to offer them my services, to defend their sons until the final motion for constitutional review and stay of execution, if necessary. I'm not speaking here of guilt or innocence, just the right to due process, you see. (1984 author's interview)

Another lawyer, Conrado Alonso, was approached by a relative of a Honduran youth who also had been condemned to death, Marco Antonio Gonzalez. As far as these lawyers knew, none of the six had been defended by lawyers until after the two 'decisions' (first by the Special Tribunal judges and then by the Supreme Court Appeals Review) had been handed down.

If an official public defender had been named and had written a brief, the defendants were never approached by him, never consulted by him, never spoke with him, and the evidence for or against them, they never knew. Lamentably, all 6 were executed: not our requests for stays of execution, not the international petitions, not the pleas of the Pope for clemency made any difference.(1986 author's interview)

None of the lawyers was shown the court records until an appeal in May 1983. Decisions were communicated by anonymous telephone calls. No recourse to appeal was permitted until Decree-Law 111-82 was enacted 5 months later on 14 December. It established special appellate courts and special prosecutors in the ordinary courts to review sentences by the *Tribunales* and appeals from lawyers defending special courts prisoners.[11] The appeal had to be filed immediately upon notification of the sentence or within 24 hours, with only 3 days to offer any new evidence. The special appellate courts, in turn, were granted discretion to limit their inquiries to 'the essentials', but their review had to be completed within 8 days. When the Appeals Court requested materials for its review, however, it received only partial records from the Defence Ministry, causing a confrontation between Supreme Court Justice Sagastume Vidaurre (appointed to the position by Ríos Montt in May 1982) and Defence Minister Mejía Victores. Eventually the Court Justices were permitted to visit the Defence Ministry offices for a limited period of 5 hours to look over the *Tribunales* records. When asked what he thought of the Justices coming to his office to review the documents, Mejía Victores shrugged that 'this would not change either the proceedings or the sentence. The *Tribunales* act in accordance with the law, and thus the execution has to go forward.'[12]

In the end, the appearance of returning to legality was just that; 'because only the decision [guilty and the death sentence] of the

Tribunales judges was allowed to stand'.[13] Apparently, this silence on the part of the Supreme Court in not condemning the *Tribunales* was ordered by the National Palace – either by Ríos Montt or Mejía Victores; the Court had originally intended to decide in favour of requests for stays of execution. 'It had come to that', one lawyer lamented (1984 author's interview).

Supreme Court Justice Sagastume Vidaurre told the press at the time that the Criminal Court 'did not find any fundamental defects alleged by those sentenced [by the *Tribunales*], although there were some small errors in the proceedings which can be attributed to an ignorance of the law'. Although his Court did not scrutinise the statutes under which the death sentences were handed down, he stated that these 'irregularities' did not affect the merits of the case. Sagastume dismissed the claim that the defendants had not been adequately represented by asserting that they had been represented by law students who constituted adequate legal counsel.

For this reason, the Supreme Court rejected the last minute *recursos extraordinarios de amparo* (special constitutional review appeals) filed on behalf of the six defendants to stop the executions – they were delayed for a month, but went forward on 3 March 1983. In desperation, the two lawyers defending three of the six prisoners, Licenciados Conrado Alonso and Eduardo Fernandez, ran to send telegrams to President Ríos Montt begging him to stay the executions, but to no avail.[14] The Supreme Court members, for their part, found the defence claims 'so frivolous' that they fined the two lawyers – a practice repeated in other cases.

Such retribution against lawyers who pressed for stays of execution and clemency on behalf of their clients within the climate of intimidation and death threats had predictable consequences. With five prisoners marked for execution on 21 March, 'no lawyer stepped forward to seek a stay of execution ... although many were asked to do so by distraught families. One said he had been warned not to.'[15] This particular lawyer had been told point-blank he would be assassinated if he did not drop his current case and refuse others of the *Tribunales*.[16] The Guatemalan Bar Association did not back these lawyers, nor condemn the *Tribunales* until 9 months later, once the Special Courts had been discredited internationally.

Sagastume, for his part, explains that there were:

some cases in which the police detained individuals for crimes and sent them to the Special Courts. These courts then decided that 'This is a crime for the ordinary courts'; they were returned to the police who, in turn, sent the cases to the ordinary courts where we sentenced them or set them free.

But there were 2 or 3 cases in which the *fueros especiales* sent the cases over [to us]; someone had complained of the competence of these Special Tribunals courts. But I want to make it clear, these Special Tribunals were not courts of the Judicial Organism. I am not to blame for what they create over there [in the Executive]. (January 1986, author's interview)

He complained that there was constant friction between the Executive and Judiciary during his 2-year tenure from May 1982 to May 1984.

The largest legal 'error', one of the fined lawyers complained, was the a priori definition of subversion, and the belief that one could publicly proclaim those sentenced as guilty, even before the trials. And to prove his point, he referred to the statement made by Defence Minister Mejía 9 days before the execution of five '*delincuentes*' on 22 March 1983, saying that the executions 'must continue because one can't combat delinquency with speeches. I think they will be shot; they deserve to be.'[17] Ríos Montt believed 'his' tribunals were a chance to restore confidence in the rule of law: 'If [justice] is not rapid, then it loses its effectiveness, and confidence in the law is lost. Normally, the legal process just goes on and on and on ...' (1991 author's interview). In announcing the execution of six 'terrorists', the army's paid advertisement in *Prensa Libre* proclaimed, '*Tribunales de Fuero Especial. A Social, Juridical and Moral Necessity. The Law is Tough, But it is the Law!*' (4 March 1983: 79).

It was the execution of six prisoners just three days before Pope John Paul II arrived in Guatemala that was possibly the gravest political error made by the Ríos Montt regime. International response to the executions was 'explosive'. The Vatican had appealed to the Government of Guatemala for clemency. Vatican Radio characterised the Guatemalan military regime as 'arrogant and drunk with power in trying to kill in the name of God'.[18] Despite this furore, five more men were executed 2 weeks later. With the European Parliament demanding that the *Tribunales* be dissolved for economic aid be granted to Guatemala, one of the first things General Mejía did when he came to power in an internal coup against Ríos Montt on 8 August 1983, was to ask Col.-lawyer Girón Tanchez, the Special Tribunals' proud author, 'Look, do me a big favour, repeal the law of those Special Tribunals' (1986 author's interview).

Four days later they were dissolved with Decree-Law 93-83. International criticism had become 'too ugly'[19] and too damaging to maintain them. The decision to dissolve the Tribunals did not come about, though, because of any change in the political circumstances used to justify the need for creating them in the first place – there was still subversion – but from a 'personal' decision that they were no longer

necessary.[20] 'But, it wasn't so easy because many objects [*muchos objectos*] had already been condemned to death [and shot]. There was no repairing that. Others sentenced to prison had their sentences commuted. The Special Tribunals were born dead', stated Girón-Tanchez sadly (1986 author's interview).

For many Guatemalan politicians at this time, it was not the legal irregularities of the Special Courts that was the problem. They focused, instead, on the international criticism Guatemala was receiving. 'The *Tribunales* give the government a repressive and unjust character to outsiders', complained the UCN candidate Roberto Carpio Nicolle in a January 1984 interview in Guatemala City. Similarly, newspaper editor Jorge Carpio Nicolle stated that:

There is hardly anyone in Congress or the State Department who doesn't criticise us. They continually point to the secrecy of the proceedings. They [in Washington] say they know that [the executed] were guilty, but they reproach us for the method used to judge them, as well as the poor political judgement of executing them just before the arrival of the Pope.[21]

Mejía Victores's Ambassador to the United Nations, Lic. Andrade Díaz-Durán, who had denounced the *Tribunales* as a 'juridical aberration' at the UN and OAS, too, thought it 'truly painful to listen to the comments abroad about their functioning, which were no more, no less, secret tribunals'(1991 author's interview). In one speech in 1988, Andrade refers to the Special Tribunals as 'returning to past stages in juridical evolution ... that [were] totally unacceptable in a modern democracy'. But as the speech proceeds, he reminds the audience of the need to 'simplify things ... in order to facilitate the [democratic] process' (1988: 7–9).

Yet, while the 'legal monstrosity of the Tribunals' was being recognised albeit reluctantly by Guatemalan government officials, the estimated 400 pending cases were being transferred to the Court of Appeal of the Supreme Court and those sentenced by the *Tribunales* still remained in prison. One of the handful of defence lawyers for the Tribunal prisoners, Lic. Conrado Alonso, laments that 'an initial aberration continues to add to [other] juridical aberrations by giving validity to sentences carried out under legal pretexts'.[22]

The Inter-American Commission and Court

On 18 September 1982, three days before the Inter-American Commission's arrival for an on-site human rights investigation, four *Tribunales* prisoners were executed by firing squad despite last minute efforts to save the men's lives.[23] By cable, the IACHR urged the

government to suspend further executions and reform its criminal procedures 'to meet recognised standards of due process', including the rights to legal counsel and to present evidence at the trial level. It beseeched the President to commute the death penalty. The Guatemalan Foreign Minister responded by temporarily suspending the executions and allowing for a hand-picked appellate court to consider the case, although the verdict was final. Citing Guatemala's reservations to the American Convention on Human Rights and claiming due process standards had been met, the executions proceeded.

In February 1983, the IACHR Chair sent another cable to Ríos Montt advising him that the executions would constitute a violation not only of the Convention by legislating the death penalty for crimes not subject to capital punishment, [24] but also of the new Fundamental Statute of Government itself. In response, as noted earlier, on 3 March at 6a.m., the Guatemalan government executed six more men, notwithstanding the Pope's plea and impending visit. Later that day, the Foreign Minister cabled the IACHR justifying the executions by the gravity of the men's crimes, by the longevity of Guatemala's death penalty and by the fact that the six sentences had been reviewed by the Supreme Court. He noted in a later cable that 'in its fight against subversion, the Government had the right to defend itself'. To allow the Commission's 'rigid and restrictive' interpretation of the Convention, he contended, 'would be to deprive a state of the right to alter its internal legislation in accordance with the political requirements and social conditions of the times'.[25]

By its reservation to Article 4(4) regarding political offences related to common crimes and notwithstanding the Convention, Guatemala reserves the right to apply capital punishment to other crimes should the need arise. In seeking an advisory opinion from the Inter-American Court of Human Rights and by extension all member states of the OAS in April, the IACHR argued both procedurally and substantively. Reservations to human rights treaties and the issue of right to life in particular, they argued, must be subject to a 'restrictive' interpretation given the stated purpose of the Convention.

The nexus between political offences and related common crimes had not been properly defined in the Guatemalan legislation that subjected these crimes to capital punishment, indicating a violation of Guatemala's international human rights obligations. Moreover, the death sentences of the *Tribunales* were inherently flawed by virtue of the secret proceedings. At the public hearing before the Inter-American Court in Costa Rica on 26 July 1983, the Foreign Affairs Deputy Minister announced that the Guatemalan government 'has considered

the possibility of re-examining and suspending, for the time being, the carrying out of the sentences handed down by the Special Tribunals in which those who have been tried have been sentenced to death' (Moyer and Padilla 1984: 515).

The conclusion drawn by Moyer and Padilla (1984: 520) to this chain of events is the successful demonstration of:

the potential for the Inter-American system for the protection of human rights. ... The responsiveness of the system and the seriousness and celerity with which the case was handled constitute a triumph for the rule of law and the human values at issue ... [and] has helped to set a high standard for future international litigation in the Americas on questions of human rights.

Yet if Moyer and Padilla had looked beyond this momentary 'success', followed up on the consequences of transferring the cases to the Supreme Court with regard to the fate of the *Tribunales* prisoners, and spoken with the local defence lawyers and Bar Association about their experiences with the *Tribunales* and later decree-laws, they might have been more modest.

The Local Lawyers

If such international recognition of the 'barbarity' of the Special Tribunals was gratifying for the handful of courageous Guatemalan lawyers who attempted to defend *Tribunales* prisoners, both lawyers and prisoners experienced a 'total deterioration of justice' after the dissolution of the *Tribunales*.

Instead of creating juridical security, what was achieved was a major distrust of justice. First of all, no one could understand why there had been military justice in the Special Tribunals; all we got were political assassinations. Second, the image of the Supreme Court itself deteriorated because it had acceded to the whims of the Defence Minister. (1984 author's interview)

The small circle of defence lawyers involved in these cases saw themselves 'as puppets in the hands of the military regime, of the secret *"señores"* of the *Tribunales*', raising for them the moral dilemma as to what extent their 'collaboration with these *militares* in this parody of justice' legitimated the repressive regime (1984 author's interview). Nevertheless, these legal practitioners, ideals tattered but still intact, felt obligated to defend their clients as best they could. As Alonso explained in 1984 (author's interview):

We never knew nor could we approach the judges, we couldn't discuss a particular Article (of the law), a position, a piece of evidence, *nothing*. We handed in our briefs at a small window in the Public Ministry or at a desk at the Defence Ministry. ... They told us nothing: what they did with our briefs,

what evidence was or was not presented and to whom it was offered. In the case of the two foreigners, the prisoners and embassies were informed of their release; we lawyers were told nothing. ... Despite there being a president, a Supreme Court with appeals courts, etc., these tribunals existed on the margin of the judicial organism and solely on the basis of a 'juridical-executive order'.

Bitter that the Guatemalan Bar Association 'didn't have the dignity, the morality, virtue or honour to protest [against these tribunals]' until March 1983 (lawyer, 1984 author's interview), these lawyers had to write individual telegrams and letters directly to Ríos Montt and Supreme Court Justice Sagastume Vidaurre pleading for pardons and stays of execution, to which they never received a response. This 'lack of solidarity' of the Bar Association and the 'complicity and lack of authority on the part of the Supreme Court' were viewed as obstacles to providing as much protection to their clients as they could.

Upon hearing of the execution of their clients, the defence lawyers were devastated, angry that these judgements were nothing more than 'death sentences ... more political than judicial' (Alonso 1986: 138). At the trial of the six prisoners, one lawyer related with horror, one of the civilian Public Minister officials protested the writ of habeas corpus (*exhibición personal*) that had been submitted with the lawyer's brief: 'It is an injustice to maintain these people without shooting them' ('*Es una injusticia mantener a esa gente sin fusilarlos*'). The *Tribunales* for them were 'the consummation of injustice. ... The *fuero* – the medieval Spanish exemption of ecclesiastics from the courts – has been turned into its opposite, or *desafuero*: the deprivation of citizens of their rights' (1984 author's interview).

All the lawyers interviewed concurred that they represented political assassinations in the name of law with no due process. Conrado Alonso Perez has since written in his book *Fusilados al Alba* that 'none of the 15 [executed] was authentically proven to be terrorist as set forth in the Penal Code. And if you think I lie, then let the proceedings of every one of those executed be revealed [to the public]!'[26] As to the secrecy of the judges, the lawyers scoffed that 'X's had been filled in as signatures after the death sentences had been carried out':

in a cowardly act so as not to reveal their identities; that is a grave juridical error because (ordinarily) a lawyer can protest that a certain judge doesn't know the case or that he has a conflict of interest. We couldn't ask for anything because we didn't know who they were. (lawyer, 1984 author's interview)

As for the justification that the judges needed to be protected from threats, the lawyers responded that they, too, then should have been able to 'hide our identities with *capuchas* so we couldn't become

victims of the military!' They complained of people accusing them of being 'lawyers who defend not just impossible causes, but [even] as defenders of subversives'. 'For me', said one in response, 'I don't care which path my defendant follows because I am defending principles of law' (1984 author's interview). As Alonso summed up the situation:

Alonso Violence here is not only physical, it is also a violence of the law. The military violates statutes, laws, everything. If they complied with their own statutes, there would at least be a minimum of guarantees, but there are no guarantees here of any kind.
Author Not even of life?
Alonso Ha, of life? That is even less certain. Violence and law have been directed toward an all-out physical violence. (1984 author's interview)

The local lawyers were in agreement with the Inter-American Commission lawyers regarding the travesty of procedures and the tragic loss of life in the Special Tribunals. Once the tribunals were dissolved on 1 September 1983 and the estimated 400 cases were transferred to the Supreme Court with Decree-Law 93-83 and the traditional forms of law became even more immersed with those born of counter-insurgency, they became disillusioned in seeking to maintain the 'majesty' of the traditional rule of law apart from the 'law in the shadows'. One of the lawyers explains:

I want to say one thing: when the Secret Tribunals were created, the Law we believed in was never appropriated because the Secret Tribunals were indeed that – clandestine: there was no oral debate or defence, there was no meeting with one's client. ... The executive and legislative functions had been subsumed under the executive. When I submitted the habeas corpus, I saw the differences: on one side, the Supreme Court in all its majesty, all the organisms of justice, and on the other side, the Secret Tribunals which were not part of the Supreme Court. Thus, we were in the presence of two judicial organisms: one which acts publicly and the other which acts in the shade, clandestinely. Different, you see? *Two* different powers. With the transfer of 400 cases of the Secret Tribunals to the Supreme Court, the juridical barbarity becomes synonymous with the Supreme Court – creating an even graver situation because they are viewing the cases *as though they were [ordinary] law*. (January 1984 interview)

Although the decree-law cancelling the *Tribunales* gave the Supreme Court the right to apply 'the most benign law' for sentencing, in a 1983 letter written to the President of the Bar Association, this lawyer and another lawyer ask, 'Will the Supreme Court be able to [merely] reduce the sentence ... if they find, upon making an analysis, that the

fuero especial proceedings are a flagrant violation of the most element of human rights?'[27] Many of the lawyers felt that as 'the process continues day after day, it only gets worse because now it is the Supreme Court handing down these sentences, albeit reduced, but based on *la ficcion juridica*', explains Lic. Alonso. He refers to the situation as working in a landscape of 'legal lagoons', not knowing which law was operating.

Although formally dissolved, the political reality for *Tribunales* prisoners was to hope for a reduced sentence, or to obtain enough money to pay mysterious contacts in exchange for their freedom (Alonso 1986: 204). The Supreme Court treated them as cases of ordinary (and not *fuero especial*) law, reducing the sentences but seldom reviewing the proceedings. Lic. Fernandez, for example, had three clients condemned to 20 years each, and with a *revisión de proceso*, these sentences were dropped to 11 years.

One particular case in January 1984 illustrates the corrupting and distorting legacies of the Special Tribunals and its decree-laws on the system of law and the experience of injustice in Guatemala once these cases were transferred to the ordinary courts. Lic. Alfonso Ordóñez Fetzer, appointed the task of reviewing for the Supreme Court the *Tribunales* proceedings of the young married couple Mario Alberto Tejada Bouscayrol and Maria Concepción Saenz Ortega de Tejada, sentenced to 21 and 19 years respectively, took his investigation too far and too seriously 'bringing upon himself the persecution of power' writes Alonso (1986: 206). His petition before the Appeals Court states that the President of the Republic, by arresting the couple through the police, charging them by way of the district attorney and judging and sentencing them in Special Tribunals, acted as police, prosecutor and judge, demonstrating the lack of the necessary impartiality to impart justice to this couple.

Ordóñez referred to the fact that all the briefs seem to have been directed to the Ministry of Defence which 'has nothing to do with matters of justice', and were contrary to the tenor of the Fundamental Statute of Government itself. But where one sees the meddling of the executive most evidently is in the stamp that appears on the pages of the Special Tribunal proceedings, which reads *'Presidencia de la republica, secretaria de fuero especial No. 1, Guatemala, C.A.'*. The denial of defence counsel to be provided by Lic. Conrado Alonso Perez to the couple illustrated even further, the need to annul all proceedings in this case Lic. Ordóñez argued, and to grant them amnesty. In his response to the petition, Supreme Court Justice Sagastume felt obliged to state in his brief that while he 'accepts and recognises the excesses

of the *fuero especial* judgements and that it would be imperative to annul them' (Alonso 1986: 206), a new law was needed in order to do so.

In terms of the Tejada couple, however, because there had been no review of *segunda instancia* by the Supreme Court a new law was not necessary to enter an argument regarding annulment. The lawyer petitioned the Court for amnesty on the grounds of Decree-Law 89-93, a law intended for the politico-military purpose of drawing guerrillas in the counter-insurgency war in the highlands to the side of the army. The use of this decree-law to gain amnesty for his clients must have suggested to the military a 'political abuse of the law' for Lic. Alfonso Ordóñez Fetzer was forced, under threat of death, to leave the country under diplomatic protection.

Earlier, in November 1983, the Guatemalan Bar Association, not previously noted for speaking out on human rights abuses, had requested under a new president that another decree-law be promulgated that would allow traditional courts 'to correct or revise what had occurred in the proceedings of the *Tribunales* and to make certain the judgements conformed with the norms of the law and due process. In this way, the sentences handed down would be fair judgements.'[28] The statement makes clear that: 'the administration of justice here in Guatemala has become extremely formalistic to the point of sacrificing the foundation and essence of matters submitted to the courts'.

As far as is known, the Bar Association has never received a response either from the government or the Supreme Court. But the local lawyers who had faced the Special Tribunals alone thought 'the entire farce should be ended, and if there is even a little reasonable doubt that the accused are innocent, they should all be set free' (1984 author's interview). They also thought the Bar Association's statement was long overdue: 'These lawyers should have made this pronouncement during the time of the Special Tribunals, during the regime of Ríos Montt' (1984 author's interview).

Finally, while the international community was celebrating the demise of the Special Tribunals, the human rights that were purportedly assured by the Fundamental Statute were only a few months later quietly modified and further undermined. The new Decree-Law 91-83 stated: (a) it would not be necessary to obtain a judge's warrant 'in cases of flagrant crime or [in arresting] fugitives of justice. The detained must be presented immediately to judicial authorities' and kept in prison; and (b) 'Defence of the person and his rights is inviolable. Nevertheless, in cases of fraud and injury to the well-being of the Nation, he will be "processed" for the immediate recuperation of said damages ...' (revision of Article 23 1983: 330–1).

This secondary decree-law's newly formulated but not so-named *fuero especial* emergency measures of arrest, detention and trial were to replace the assurances of inviolability of the defence of an individual's human rights within the existing 'species of constitution' of the nation, according to Col.-lawyer Girón-Tanchez (1986 author's interview). These modifications did not escape the notice of two of the local defence lawyers:

Those principally responsible for the degradation of human rights in the country for the last 17 months are now trying to change their image and that of the country. ... It is not a secret for anyone, even less for a legal professional, that many matters are resolved before public security authorities without going through the courts, preferring the ill-treatment of an unjust detention under conditions in which the victims cannot complain against abuse and arbitrary treatment ... which undercuts the prestige and authority of an administration of justice.

In the end, finding themselves in 'legal lagoons', the lawyers ask:

In what juridical condition is the right and guarantee to due process left? Where does it leave the Statute if once again a secondary law such as the one that dissolved the special tribunals dares to leave the sentences prevailing while the proceedings are annulled – in violation of the new right and guarantee to an open trial and due process, and clearly on the margins of the instituted courts of justice?[29]

Those local lawyers who had the experience of defending *fuero especial* prisoners were unwilling legally and unable politically to separate out the political context within which law is practised. As a result, they found themselves in the untenable and ironic position of being against the very decree-laws that abolished the *Tribunales* and modified the Statute because of the deteriorating effect they believed these decree-laws would have on the Supreme Court, due process, justice and human rights. It is not that these lawyers had given up their universal ideals for a culturally relative position; it is that the decontextualised formalities of the universal did not provide them with the necessary instruments with which to defend themselves and their clients in a sustainable manner.

Of the estimated 200 individuals sentenced by the *Tribunales*, their cases were reviewed by the Supreme Court and either confirmed, reduced or released for lack of evidence. Many more remain disappeared. *Denuncias* by relatives appeared daily in the newspapers during this period asking about the whereabouts of family members who were known to have been abducted and detained by security forces, and who were said to have been sentenced by the *Tribunales*, but could not be found (possibly being held at the numerous

clandestine torture centres, including the major military base in Guatemala City). With the promulgation of Decree-Law 74-84 on 18 July 1984, the Chief of Staff pardoned all those sentenced by the *Tribunales*. In a 1986 interview, one of the lawyers states that 'Nothing has changed much in 2 years, it is still a negation of juridicality.'

What was Accomplished by Human Rights Pressure?

The two foreigners, Maria Magdalena Monteverde Ascanio (Spanish citizen), 27 years old, niece of the Chief of Staff of the Spanish Army and Michael Glenn Ernest (US citizen), 26 years old, son of a Colorado corporate executive, who were abducted by security forces on 11 January 1983 were 'saved from execution in time by the intervention of the US Embassy. From then on, they [the Guatemalan government] had to act in a different manner' with regard to this particular Special Tribunal case. The prisoners were released in less than a month on 9 February 1983, 'escaping from these juridical ends' (Alonso, 1986 author's interview).

The other 15 were executed before the *Tribunales* were dissolved. Hence, human rights protections were differentially meted out, allowing *el fuero especial* to provide, as the Bar Association states, 'privileges or rights to a given group as may be required by its social conditions', while discriminating against others who were executed despite pleas for stays of execution by several lawyers (1983: 3).

As for the military, they accomplished what they set out to do with or without the Special Tribunals: to regain a degree of international legitimacy by using the electoral and judicial apparatuses for their own purposes, while continuing to 'cleanse the house' of *delincuentes subversivos* by quietly assassinating their former prisoners. Their only complaints are that it took so long, and that the international community does not understand their difficulties of maintaining the stability of the nation against 'opponents of the state'. The politico-military project, established in 1982, went on to create a co-governance system in which the civilian presidencies 'handle foreign affairs' while army and presidential intelligence remain in charge of 'security' issues. The number of killings remains high with ten bodies a week arriving at the morgue in the year of the 1995 presidential campaign, most with signs of torture by army intelligence.

The military has established its own Human Rights Commission within the Presidential Security Office staffed by both civilians and military officers who write the human rights reports of the civilian government for the Human Rights Commission in Geneva, lobby the US Congress for military and economic aid and 'liaison' with the US

embassy. This decade-old project has also infiltrated the Human Rights Ombudsman and Archbishop's Human Rights offices, looting the vocabulary of human rights and democracy to suit their political and military purposes. They have succeeded in creating what I have termed 'a violence called democracy' (see Schirmer forthcoming).

Finding themselves working in legal lagoons created by the cannibalising tendencies of the Secret Tribunals and the lack of resoluteness on the part of the Supreme Court and the Guatemalan Bar Association, on the one hand, and finding international human rights organisations touting the abolishment of the *Tribunales* as a triumph of the rule of law on the other, many of the local defence lawyers became frustrated and disillusioned. For them, contrary to the IACHR's perspective, it was better to keep the cases of the *Tribunales* separate from the Supreme Court because at least then 'the juridical barbarity' did not become 'synonymous with the Supreme Court'. International human rights standards at this critical moment had become anathema to and destructive of local faith in the rule of law, with lawyers growing cynical about the long-term effectiveness of human rights pressures in the name of international law.

Universalism and the Decontextualising of Human Rights

Local translations of and experiences with domestic and international legal and human rights practices remind us that when sites of law (military courts, Special Tribunals) are condemned for human rights violations without understanding the political culture within which law is practised and experienced, this may further complicate and even undermine rather than enhance and guarantee human rights. Put simply, intervening in the name of the universal good without recognising the political and legal realities of local life may not just backfire but may even worsen human rights violations.

The case of the Special Tribunals in Guatemala exemplifies how international human rights law and language may initially help support and strengthen a critical local response to military-style tribunals; this position is, however, turned on its head when the logic of the Special Tribunals first cannibalises the Penal Code and then physically inhabits the traditional judicial system with its pending cases and defenceless prisoners to counter these very same international human rights discourse and pressures.

Both the international and local lawyers agree on the need for rule of law and human rights standards. Local lawyers, though, because of the power of the military and their understanding of the local legal practices, which includes being forced to operate within illegal

structures to defend prisoners as best they can, have an entirely different relation to that law, and thus recognise that shifting legal procedures to another institution (the Supreme Court) does not mean guaranteed rights, as it might in the US and elsewhere. These local lawyers are caught in the legal lagoons of post-interventionism: by asking that the cases of the Special Tribunals be kept separate from the Supreme Court, they are going against the international community's solution in order to be able to save some semblance of ideals in local traditional civilian law.

While debates of human rights in anthropology today still tend to revolve around the issues of universals versus cultural relativism, I would argue that this debate is rendered insignificant when confronted by such a case in which repressive regimes loot a human rights discourse and recognise the political potential in merging cultural relativism with universalism to solve their international relations problems. They relativise the universal by saying 'we recognise and respect the covenant of human rights, but we must at the same time understand the reality of *"delincuentes terroristas"* in Guatemala'.

The Guatemalan story also counters the mistaken pluralistic assumption of a universal standard of equivalency found in much of the human rights literature: for example, all societies, and all those citizens within these societies, are all equally vulnerable and all equally powerful within the international political and economic order. But as we have seen, the differential abilities to protect Special Tribunals prisoners condemned to death reveals the social positions and political realities that count *in relation to the politics of international pressures*. While distinctions are clearly drawn between the powerful and the powerless, between those 'outside the law' (that is, *delincuentes-terroristas*) and those within it, the lives of some are deemed more important than those of others.

The most salient example here of such differentiation is the release of the abducted foreigners, while the 15 Guatemalans and one Honduran were executed by firing squad. Similarly, in the recent case of the cashiering of two colonels believed to be involved in two murder cases involving US citizens[30] by the new President Arzu, which is a more contemporary case of a purge being touted in the cause for democratic ideals and rule of law, the sanctity of Americans who have been killed in Guatemala has created a degree of resentment among some Guatemalans whose demands over the last decade for information about the disappearance and killing of their relatives fall on deaf ears in the government. To say that human rights standards are universally applied is not the political reality for most poor and middle-class Guatemalans.

Finally, rule of law and the administration of justice are too often seen by the legal community as timeless, decontextualised ideals, rather than specific, social forms of regulation at certain historical and political moments. They are both instrumental and constitutive in the formulation of human rights regulations and doctrine. In the Guatemalan case, there remained a gap between the traditional ideals of liberal, just legal structures and the executive use of law, as the Guatemalan lawyer lamented. The human rights community must learn to contextualise not only the perceptions and practices of 'rights', but to understand how the legal structures and constitutional orders themselves are part of the social and political realities in each situation.

Thus, as important as the universalism-vs.-cultural-relativism debate may be, it needs to be connected to the way global discourses of rights are reproduced and translated within local political realities. More ethnographies of human rights based on grounded actions and intentions of actors within the framework of daily local and institutional life can be of enormous importance in creating a dialogue about how to expand beyond the minimum requirements to make international standards more culturally viable (An-Na'im 1992). This is not to say that international standards, human rights theories or even cultural relativism are not relevant; they are only part of the story. Nor should this chapter be seen as an argument against human rights intervention; it is but a plea to more fully understand the long-term ramifications of changes for local legal and human rights practitioners resulting from both domestic and international pressures. Continued reliance on a decontextualised, formulaic language that allows the meaning of rights to be obscured and open to looting by repressive states calls into question how sustainable concessions obtained by the international human rights community actually are (cf. Schirmer 1996).

Conclusion

As we know, human rights are not acted out in a vacuum: it is the social position and political realities in which people find themselves and their specific relation to international standards that give human rights their substance and meaning. If human rights are to play a sustaining role in protecting individuals from particularly dangerous kinds of harm and injustices, the human rights and legal communities must learn not only to contextualise the perceptions and practices of rights but also to understand that momentary actions may not be lasting victories.

They must also recognise how legal structures and constitutional orders may be appropriated and redefined as instruments for repressive purposes. Otherwise, we may find, as in this human rights story of the Special Tribunals in Guatemala, that human rights intervention can first empower local actors and then, once particularly egregious forms of public execution are dissolved and international attention wanes, such 'rapid justice' reasoning quietly inhabits traditional institutional forms of justice to not only undermine legal practices and ideals, but to also allow extra-judicial assassinations to continue *sub rosa*.

One could in fact argue that human rights pressures have been effective to the extent that the Guatemalan military learned to eliminate 'terrorists' in secret, to bury their tortured victims in clandestine graves and to cloak their security needs in constitutional garb. An ethnographically informed approach for sustainable human rights calls for taking cues from local legal and human rights practitioners with political experience who are in the habit of asking under what juridical conditions is the right and guarantee to due process left in? Where does it leave the Statute if once again a secondary law such as the one that dissolved the Special Tribunals dares to leave the sentences prevailing while the proceedings are annulled – in violation of the new right and guarantee to an open trial and due process, and clearly on the margins of the instituted courts of justice?

Unless the international legal and human rights communities take these cues and reach beyond sanctioning the easy targets of ill-devised and illegal methods of law, then no amount of positive will to make human dignity and life of international public concern, or innumerable humanitarian enunciations and denunciations often 'inspired more by sympathy than by realism', as Guatemalan social scientist Edelberto Torres-Rivas writes (1986: 470, 478), can expose and counter the more insidious, brutal structures of repression that have haunted Guatemalans for 40 years.

Appendix

Those individuals whom we know were condemned to death by the Special Tribunals:

17 September 1982 (date of execution)
Julio Cesar Vasquez Juarez
Jaime de la Rosa Rodríguez
Julio Hernandez Pérdomo
Marcelino Marroquín

11 January 1983 (detained)/9 February 1983 (released)
Maria Magdalena Monteverde Ascanio (Spanish citizen), 27 years old, niece of the Chief of Staff of the Spanish Army
Michael Glenn Ernest (US citizen), 26 years old, son of a corporate executive

3 March 1983 (date of execution)
Pedro Raxon Tepet, 45 years old, *comisionado militar*
Carlos Subuyuj Cuc, 30 years old, day labourer
Walter Vinicio Marroquín Gonzalez, 24 years old, insurance salesman
Sergio Roberto Marroquín Gonzalez, 19 years old, student (2 brothers)
Hector Armoldo Morales Lopez, 21 years old, student
Marco Antonio Gonzalez (Honduran citizen)

These four were originally sentenced to death for 3 March 1983 for the crime of 'terrorism' but were released for 'lack of sufficient evidence':
Edgar Daniel Aldana Escobar
Alfonso Barrillas Chacón
Fernando Contreras y Contreras
Leonardo Álvarez García

21 March 1983 (date of execution)
Mario Ramiro Martinez Gonzalez
Rony Alfredo Martinez Gonzalez
Otto Hugo Virula Ayala
Jesus Enrique Velasquez Gutierrez, soldier
Julio Cesar Herrera Cardona, soldier

26 May 1983
Mario Alberto Tejada Bouscayrol and Maria Concepción Saenz Ortega de Tejada, sentenced to 19 and 21 years respectively; January 1984 their case was argued before the ordinary Court of Appeals

400 other individuals had their 'legal cases' consigned to the *Tribunales*, and are believed to have been released later, but this has not been confirmed.[31]

Notes

1. The author wishes to thank the handful of Guatemalan lawyers willing to speak with her about the Special Tribunals between

1984 and 1986. Names are provided only where previously published in newspapers or books. This article is dedicated to their courage and stubborn idealism.

2. The 34-member Council of State was organised in an advisory role to the President to replace the defunct Congress thereby 'creating the impression that there existed powers autonomous from the State and that they were functioning practically in a state of legality, while the truth is, the governments before and after August 8 [the 1983 coup] were military governments ...' (Lic. Andrade Díaz-Durán, Foreign Minister under Mejía Victores, 1991 author's interview).

3. 'Loss of life during three decades had been terrible, but even the highest estimate pale beside [his] figure; analysts were at a loss to explain the highly exaggerated figure or the reasons why the president used it' (Nyrop 1983: 189).

4. General Ríos Montt said they were both civilian and military (1991 author's interview), while General Gramajo claimed they were all civilian.

5. *Diario de Centro America* (21 de marzo 1983: 1a, quoted in Alonso (1986: 180)).

6. 1989 television interview, emphasis in transcript.

7. Article 4 of Decree-Law 46-82 lists the crimes for the death penalty as: abduction, arson, the manufacture or possession of explosives, railroad disasters, attacks against the security of shipping and air transport, attacks against public utilities, air piracy, poisoning of waters, foods or medicines, treason, attacks against the security and independence of the State, traitorous behaviour, genocide, terrorism, arms or munitions caches, traffic in explosives.

8. Alonso (1986: 181).

9. In an interview with Walter Vinicio Marroquín, one of those executed on 3 March, said he had been 'disappeared' for 52 days, and that he, along with the five others executed, had all been tortured, one so severely that he lost sight in one eye (*Impacto* 20 March 1983).

10. Intelligence source, 1991 author's interview. General Gramajo has since confirmed this: 'Five assailant-rapists, members of a band of *policias militares*, were shot in March 1983' as part of the Special Tribunal executions (1995: 204).

11. All lower court judges, appellate court members and all special prosecutors were to be appointed by the President. The only stipulation was that they had to be lawyers in active practice, or

army officers. Both tribunal and appellate court members' names
were undisclosed, even to the defendants.

12. Quoted in Alonso (1986: 117); 1990 author's interview with
    retired General Mejía confirmed this attitude.
13. Alonso (1986: 183).
14. Alonso (1986: 123–4).
15. *Central America Report* 8 April 1983; Alonso (1986: 188).
16. Jean-Marie Simon, personal communication (1983).
17. *El Grafico* (12 de marzo 1983: 4); quoted in Alonso (1986: 195). One
    year after the *Tribunales* were dissolved, one of the cases was
    thrown out of the Appeals Court precisely on the grounds that
    imputed crime was too generic a category proffered without
    any evidence.
18. *Excelsior*, Mexico (11 de marzo 1983: 1a, 12), quoted in Alonso
    (1986: 132).
19. 'El término de tribunales de fuero especial suena muy feo en
    Guatemala y en el mundo', *El Grafico* (24 de julio 1983: 8).
20. August 1990 author's interview with Mejía Victores.
21. Quoted in Alonso (1986: 130).
22. Quoted in Alonso (1986: 238); January 1986 author's interview.
23. This section is mostly based on Moyer and Padilla (1984).
24. Article 4(2) of the Convention states, '[t]he application of such
    punishment [the death penalty] shall not be extended to crimes
    to which it does not apply'.
25. Quoted in Moyer and Padilla (1984: 509).
26. Quoted in Alonso (1986: 12).
27. *Excelsior*, Mexico (11 de marzo 1983: 1a, 12), quoted in Alonso
    (1986: 132).
28. Alonso (1986: 233); President Lic. Luis Arturo Archila (January
    1984 and 1986 author's interviews).
29. 25 de agosto 1983 letter to the Bar Association, pp. 5–6.
30. Col. Roberto Alpirez is accused of complicity in the torture and
    slaying of guerrilla prisoner, Efrain Bámaca, the husband of
    American lawyer, Jennifer Harbury. Col. Mario Roberto Garcia
    Catalán along with Col. Alpirez helped to cover up the killing
    of another US citizen, Michael Devine.
31. See *Justicia y Paz* (agosto 1983: 58–9).

References

An-Na'im, Abdullahi Ahmed. 1992. *Human Rights in Cross-cultural
Perspectives. A Quest for Consensus.* Philadelphia: University of
Pennsylvania Press.

186 *Human Rights, Culture and Context*

Alonso, Conrado. 1986. *Fusilados al Alba. Repaso Histórico Jurídico sobre los Tribunales de Fuero Especial.* Guatemala, C.A.: Serviprensa Centroamericana.

Andrade Díaz-Durán, Fernando. 1988. 'Transición Política en Guatemala, Naturaleza, Alcances y Perspectivas', Speech given to IV Seminario Sobre la Realidad Nacional 'Transición Politica, Dialogo Nacional y Pacto social en Guatemala' organised by ASIES (Asociación de Investigación y Estudios Sociales), 23–25 de mayo.

Bar Association. 1983. See Presidente del Colegio de Abogados.

Gramajo, Gen. Hector Alejandro. 1995. *De la Guerra ... A La Guerra.* Guatemala: Fondo de Cultura Editorial.

Justicia y Paz. 1983. *Los Tribunales de Fuero Especial en Guatemala.* Mexico, D.F.: Comité Pro Justicia y Paz de Guatemala, con la colaboración del Consejo Mundial de Iglesias.

Ministro de Gobernación. 1982. *Decretos-Leyes.* Tomo I. Guatemala, C.A.: Departamento de Recopilación de Leyes.

Moyer, Charles and David Padilla. 1984. 'Executions in Guatemala as Decreed by the Courts of Special Jurisdiction in 1982–83: A Case Study', *Human Rights Quarterly* 6(4): 507–20.

Nyrop, Richard (ed.). 1984. *Guatemala. A Country Study.* Washington, DC: US Government.

Presidente del Colegio. 1983. *Colegio de Abogados carta a Mejía Víctores de Abogados.* Guatemala (21 de noviembre).

Schirmer, Jennifer, 1996. 'The Looting of Democratic Discourse by the Guatemalan Military: Implications for Human Rights', in E. Jelín and E. Hershberg (eds.) *Constructing Democracy, Human Rights,Citizenship and Society.* Boulder, CO: Westview Press.

——Forthcoming. *A Violence Called Democracy: The Guatemalan Military Project 1982–1992.* Philadelphia: University of Pennsylvania Press.

Torres-Rivas, Edelberto. 1986. 'Comment: Constraints on Policies Regarding Human Rights and Democracy', in Kevin Middlebrook and Carlos Rico (eds) *The US and Latin America in the 1980s.* Pittsburgh: University of Pittsburgh Press.

8 TO WHOM SHOULD WE LISTEN? HUMAN RIGHTS ACTIVISM IN TWO GUATEMALAN LAND DISPUTES[1]

David Stoll

In 1993, human rights activists undertook a 10-day march to the Communities of Population in Resistance of the Sierra (CPRs) in northwestern Guatemala. This is one of three concentrations of internal refugees – the others are in the Ixcán and the Petén – that remain beyond government control after more than a decade of offensives by the Guatemalan army. The marchers were a cross-section of the human rights community, including Catholic and Protestant clergy, foreign solidarity activists, journalists and militants of the Guatemalan left.

'The land where you are going is holy land, watered with the blood of innumerable martyrs', a Catholic bishop told the marchers:

You are going to meet the crucified Christs of the Population in Resistance. You are going to see them with your own eyes, you are going to hear them, you are going to touch them. You are going to help them come down from the cross ...[2]

The marchers forgave the bishop his hyperbole. This was part of his diocese, the Department of El Quiché, where the Guatemalan army murdered hundreds of Catholic leaders during a counter-insurgency drive against the Guerrilla Army of the Poor in the early 1980s. Many CPR leaders were Catholic catechists before the army burned their villages and corralled most of the population into closely watched 'model villages'. As the bishop made contact with the CPRs in the early 1990s, death squads tried to dissuade him by murdering one of his layworkers. They also killed Myrna Mack Chang, a Guatemalan anthropologist knifed to death outside her office; her offence was serving as a liaison with the CPRs. Led by her sister Helen,

187

Mack's colleagues pressed the case, until it led to the army intelligence units that surround Guatemala's weak civilian presidency.

When I began interviewing the population under army control in this region in 1987, human rights was hardly in the vocabulary. I tried to be circumspect by blending in with other foreigners, aid workers who concentrated on ameliorating the situation. Treading gingerly, we did not consider it our responsibility to challenge the dominant position of the Guatemalan army. Now we were being followed by a new generation of foreign activists recruited by human rights and solidarity networks in North America and western Europe. They called themselves *internacionalistas*, like the foreigners who joined the Sandinista Revolution in Nicaragua. They arrived in large numbers; and they were determined to open up the territory for human rights. Not inclined to accept the compromises that I did in the late 1980s, they aimed instead to challenge the Guatemalan army. They did so by publicising human rights cases, exhuming clandestine cemeteries and using their cachet as foreigners to practice 'accompaniment' – serving as human shields to protect dissidents from the security forces.

Internationalists are significant players in the struggle to democratise Guatemalan society, but their work is being complicated by conflicts between peasants that cannot be reduced to the moral dichotomies that so often move foreigners to become involved in the Third World. What has made Guatemala such a popular destination for activists is the terrible human rights record of the army, a Praetorian institution that has dominated the country since the early 1960s. Because the military's lack of accountability puts it squarely in the way of a more democratic society, human rights activism in Guatemala – to pressure the state to respect international law – has been difficult to distinguish from solidarity activism – to support the left against state repression. Whether internationalists refer to themselves as solidarity activists or human rights monitors, their main task has been to bring international pressure to bear on the military.

As a result, many newly arrived activists have assumed that any conflict involving human rights can be reduced to the army versus 'the people', with the latter represented by the dissident organisations with which they happen to work. Since the left's popular organisations need all the international support they can get, they have been all too happy to agree, by assuring foreign supporters that hostile peasants are manipulated by the army. That peasants might have their own reasons for distrusting the left, or quarrelling among themselves, is something that has been slow to enter the picture, with the result that human rights activists can find themselves in a more partisan position than they anticipated.

Now that the army–guerrilla fighting is dying down, and will hopefully end in a United Nations-brokered peace agreement in 1996, many of the conflicts coming to the surface involve land. Even though such disputes have been complicated by the war, they also reflect a long history of competition for land, not just between *ladinos*[3] and the Maya-speaking *indígenas* who make up half the country's population, but among Mayas. Because of the obvious challenges posed by the Guatemalan army, until recently internationalists tended to consider peasant competition over land a secondary problem. Typically, the refugees they accompanied were coming home to dispute property with peasants who were still organised into the army's civil patrols. This made it easy to attribute problems to army manipulation. Then in 1994–95, in the Ixcán region, returning refugees organised by the left and accompanied by foreigners found themselves in conflict with other groups organised by the left.

In other parts of Guatemala, the army vs. the people paradigm can still guide how internationalists insert themselves into disputes between peasants. Such is the case in northern Quiché, around the three Ixil Maya towns of Nebaj, Cotzal and Chajul, which the Guerrilla Army of the Poor (EGP) used to claim as a bastion of support. (See map on p. 216) The Ixils of Chajul have a long record of defending their land against usurpers. This is where, in 1975, the EGP launched its armed struggle by assassinating a well-known *ladino* plantation owner. Chajul is also the town where the Guatemalan army killed Petrocinio Menchú, an event memorialised by his sister, the winner of the 1992 Nobel Peace Prize, in the most dramatic passage of *I, Rigoberta Menchú*.

Since the early 1990s, and thanks in part to the arrival of foreign activists, human rights has come out of the closet in northern Quiché. Most Ixils seem pleased by this. But those of Chajul have divided feelings, because internationalists are supporting their antagonists in land disputes. One conflict is with the CPRs of the Sierra. To escape army offensives, this Mayan peasant population settled on Chajul land which is so fertile that now they do not want to leave. Chajul's other dispute is with the K'iche' Maya village of Los Cimientos, which has a national-level title to land which the Chajules believe to be part of their own municipal grant. In each case, internationalists operating on the army vs. the people paradigm have decided to support the other party against the Chajules.

These are very particular conflicts, but the kind of challenge that Chajul poses to the human rights movement is increasingly common. No longer must human rights activists in Europe and the United States confine themselves to writing letters to far-off heads of state, or pressuring their own government to take action. Now they can take

action themselves. Thanks to jet travel and the growing influence of human rights activism, outsiders can be at the scene of a crisis within days. Prior to arrival, they have decided to get involved on the basis of information that has been filtered and simplified by long-distance reporting.[4] At the scene, they must attend to a wider and more contradictory range of voices, including those of presumed victimisers who claim to be victims too. If the victimisation starts looking mutual, whose grievances are to be given priority?

Another issue cuts to the very definition of a human rights abuse, in terms of state involvement. By definition, a violation revolves around a failure by agents of the state to respect due process, whether by directly misusing their authority or by failing to use it to protect citizens' rights. This also holds where state authority is weak, as is often the case among subordinate groups like peasants, and part of the population is pitted against another, for reasons that extend beyond the state's authority, to competition over land or other long-standing enmities. Yet human rights agencies can invoke their mandate only by attributing responsibility for violations to the state.

In theory, this does not have to mean reducing one of the local factions to the status of state-supported victimisers, while ennobling the other as state-oppressed victims. But this has been the tendency in Guatemala, because of the obvious power of the military. If underlying conflicts are factored out as a human rights agency translates a situation into the state-centred terms it requires to report the case, the result may be to ignore other sources of legitimacy in popular consciousness, such as local customary law. In other words, what makes sense in terms of international human rights discourse can have the unintended effect of marginalising local actors with their own conception of what is right. In the case of Chajul, to put this in more concrete terms, human rights activists are supporting national titling laws against a more indigenous conception of land rights.[5]

To illustrate these issues, this chapter looks at human rights images of the Communities of Population in Resistance and the Los Cimientos K'iche's, the land conflicts in which they are involved, and how they are perceived by their Mayan neighbours.

Attacked by Soldiers and Administered by Guerrillas

The army just kept coming. Where smoke was rising, the soldiers would call in an attack plane, also helicopters with machine-guns. Some people managed to flee, others were killed. So we had to hide ourselves somewhere else. ... Little by little more people were showing up, among us were some who had

ideas, who had studied so among the youth we organised a watch system to defend ourselves. When edible greens gave out, we had to come up here to look for more, because all the maize had been burned. Many died from hunger, there were entire families who died, I know of a family of 18, none of whom survived. (CPR member recalling the early 1980s)

Since seeking ties with the outside world in 1990, the Communities of Population in Resistance have become a pilgrimage site for human rights activists from Europe and the United States. Currently several dozen internationalists, especially from the Basque country, Catalonia and Spain, reside in the CPRs of the Sierra to protect them from a resumption of army offensives. From 1982 to 1991, army attacks in this region took an uncounted number of lives and reduced the majority of survivors to living in 'model villages'. The CPRs were the only internal refugees to remain beyond army control. Given the long record of bombardments and raids, the international presence is an important deterrent to their resumption.

For the human rights movement, the CPRs are above all victims of the army's counter-insurgency campaigns. How they are perceived by their Ixil neighbours is more complicated. Many Ixils in government-controlled towns and villages have relatives and old neighbours in the CPRs, and many express sympathy with them as fellow victims of the war. At the same time, they suspect that, just as they must live under the control of the Guatemalan army, the CPRs continue to be dominated by the Guerrilla Army of the Poor.[6] Their feelings about the EGP are also complicated but tend toward strong rejection: while many acknowledge sympathising with it in the early 1980s, they also say that the army's *castigos* (punishments, that is, systematic terror) convinced them that the EGP's promises of victory were an *engaño* (a deception).

Visiting internationalists tend to discount Ixil complaints against the CPRs, on grounds that government-controlled villagers have been organised into the army's civil patrols, hence are subject to strong ideological controls. Yet much of the Ixil population shared the CPR experience of refugee life in the *montaña* or mountains, some for more than a decade, and many former refugees are willing to provide detailed accounts of how disillusioned they became.

'They get us into problems', complained a man of the EGP, in whose auxiliary forces he served, 'like they did before':

All of us [hiding from the army in this area] were pure CPR. But not any more. Lots of obligations. They made us practice ambushing the army, a pile of work they made us do, then agricultural labour. Every month they took twenty-pound quotas of maize and tortillas. Here [in the town of Nebaj, under army

control] no one prevents us from going where we want. There, it's not possible
to leave.

They say that the CPRs don't have anything to do with the guerrillas, but
in practice we see that they do. 'Now we don't know anything about the
guerrillas', they say. 'We don't know where they are', they say. But when we
go out through Las Canoas, there they are. Moreover, they come to buy
things [dressed as civilians] and a week later there they are, with all their
[military] equipment. ... How the guerrillas talk is how the CPRs talk.

'How the CPRs talk' is to demand that the army unilaterally
withdraw from the region, while refraining from criticism of the
guerrilla activities that brought the army into Ixil country.[7] Yet CPR
representatives deny that they continue to work with the guerrillas,
and that they ever did. Their version of events begins with the same
narratives of persecution that army-controlled Ixils express, of how
the army offensives of the early 1980s forced them to flee their villages
for the *montaña* or surrounding mountains. CPR members describe
how, with their villages burned and cut off from towns controlled by
government killers, they adopted an autonomous collective existence
on the mountain ridges above army-controlled territory. The guerrillas
figure in these accounts only as an excuse for the army to repress
civilians.[8]

CPR representatives deny having much knowledge of the Guerrilla
Army of the Poor, saying only that it comes and goes unbidden by
them. Yet Ixils living in government villages are often willing to
describe how the guerrillas organised them in the early 1980s, and
at the time the EGP claimed considerable success in this respect. 'In
your question you artificially separate something which is intimately
linked: the guerrillas and the population', insisted a spokesman in
nearby Huehuetenango Department.

The people have become the guerrillas. ... This does not mean that all the people
are guerrillas in the military sense of the term, but that they are organised
basically in function of support for the revolutionary armed struggle. A local
military force is organised in each location.[9]

'It is very hard for me to distinguish between the people and the
guerrillas,' agreed Silvia Solórzano Foppa, a medical doctor who
operated in Ixil country and, like her two brothers, gave her life
fighting for the EGP. 'When a family member decides to join one of
the four guerrilla organisations', Solórzano explained, 'he knows
that his siblings, in-laws and parents will participate in different
tasks for the war. The army knows it too. Hence the [army's] massacres
of the civilian population ...'[10]

Judging from such statements, the EGP insurgency was a popular struggle, growing out of deeply felt local needs and representing popular aspirations. This is the prevailing assumption among internationalists, but what is expressed by Ixils who lived through more than a decade of violence and dislocation is, again, more complicated. Many admit that they were attracted by the EGP's promise of a more equitable society, but they also describe organising tactics which became coercive. The EGP's first step was to build a clandestine network of contacts. Then guerrilla columns would show up to hold rallies, warn the population to organise itself against the army, and promise an easy victory. As the EGP's local clandestine committee surfaced and asserted authority, local leaders voicing the most opposition to the new agenda would die mysteriously, with the committee later explaining that the dead men had been 'ears' for the army.

The assassination of village opponents does not disprove that the insurgency was a popular movement, but it makes it harder to demonstrate that it was. Since the Ixil region was not occupied by the army before the guerrillas appeared, the first armed groups that many Ixil villagers saw were guerrillas. The inhibitions on free speech created by strangers showing up with guns dated to the arrival of the EGP, not the army. Any space for choosing whether or not to align with the EGP was further constrained by the army's arrival and its indiscriminate reprisals. Any sample of peasant testimony will show that army kidnappings, massacres and scorched-earth tactics played a large role in building support for the guerrillas. What is harder to find in testimony are pre-war grievances – such as conflicts with labour contractors and plantation owners – motivating Ixils to welcome the guerrillas as a drastic but necessary solution to their own problems. This is why I believe that the guerrilla movement in the Ixil area did not grow out of pre-existing social struggles in the way that the EGP claimed.

From ex-combatants living under amnesty in Nebaj, I learned how the EGP's Ho Chi Minh Front administered Ixil villagers through cadre-staffed regional and district committees appointed from above. A parallel structure of village and area committees may have been elected by the civilian population, but while some ex-refugees describe these committees as autonomous, others say they were part of the same vertical structure of authority. Except for a brief period in 1982 when the EGP became unhinged by the army's success in organising civil patrols, guerrillas did not kill villagers on the scale of the soldiers. But into the mid-1980s, according to peasants who used to live under EGP administration, its cadre executed civilians who wanted to

surrender to the army. The reason was the security risk they posed, as a possible source of information for the army's next offensive.

The army's human rights violations have been so severe, and the resistance to them so courageous, that dissent against guerrilla strategies has been far less visible. But after a few years in the densely forested *montaña*, former refugees told me, more and more of them were blaming the guerrillas for leading them into a debacle. They felt trapped, not just by fear of what would happen if they fell into the army's hands, but the deceptions of the EGP – its failure to win the war as promised.

Army offensives and growing despair are why, in 1990, refugees still eluding the army suddenly began to publicise themselves as the Communities of Population in Resistance, with their own civilian leadership and demands, the most fundamental of which was to be recognised as a non-combatant civil population. Now the area committees came to the fore – one each in the three CPR-Sierra zones of Santa Clara, Cabá and Xeputul – subject to annual assemblies and elections by the people themselves. While one of my sources claims that the new CPR structure came out of a grassroots rebellion against the guerrillas, others say that it was the EGP that planned the reformation, as a response to growing disillusion.

Eventually the decision to distance the CPRs from the guerrillas may be clarified by insiders. What is clear is that more than one tendency was asserting itself in these communities, with some leaders – particularly older men with experience as Catholic catechists – less enthusiastic about the EGP's demands than others who owed their formation to it. Henceforth the guerrillas stayed away from CPR settlements except for occasional choreographed visits, occasional displays of force to protect CPR territory and quietly delivered 'orientations' to CPR leaders. Away from watchful committee members, some CPR members voiced the same neutralist sentiments as government-controlled Ixils. 'Apart the army, apart the guerrilla, apart the population', a member visiting Nebaj told me, 'because we are civilians and want them to retire from our area'.

Again, the EGP's killing of non-combatants (usually selectively) does not mean that it lacked popular support in the early 1980s. But the use of such drastic coercion should warn us against concluding that the guerrilla movement represented an apogee of popular self-determination – still the assumption of internationalists who dismiss anti-guerrilla sentiment among Ixils. Once we stop denying the parallels between army and guerrilla treatment of peasants – such as restricting their freedom of movement and repressing dissidents – it can be argued that the zones of refuge were the 'model villages' of

the EGP.[11] Like the notorious resettlements which the army called by this name, the EGP's zones of refuge became a reorganisation of peasant society for a political strategy that had been decided upon elsewhere.

The Feud with Amajchel

Everyone here was CPR before, for ten years we struggled at their side. ... They always talk about the Triumph, but we couldn't bear it. It's true that there is peace, but I don't go out of the village, I don't leave, I always used to go out, but not any more. There's always uncertainty, there's always worry, because we're very isolated here, and the guerrilla is always bad with us, they don't want to listen, if one talks back, they might misinterpret. (Elder from the village of Amajchel, Chajul, 1994)

Conflict between CPR and government settlements was especially obvious in the village of Amajchel. Although an extreme case, Amajchel dramatises how people trapped in a civil war can become simultaneously victims and victimisers. Remote in the mountains of northern Chajul, Amajchel used to be the centre of an EGP-administered zone of refuge. Then in 1987–88 the army set up a garrison, ravaged the surrounding settlements, captured some refugees and pressured others into surrendering. To show other refugees hiding nearby that they could surrender without losing their lives, the army also set up a resettlement in 1989. Perched on a knoll next to the army's hill-fort, the tightly clustered village of 150 households consists of Ixils of Nebaj. Before the war, some of these families were hacking farms out of the surrounding cloud forest, and many became active in the guerrilla movement.

Amajchel is isolated from other government villages – the nearest is a 5-hour walk away – and it is surrounded by the CPRs, whose fields adjoin its own. Guerrillas have often haunted the long, lonely trail into the settlement, and army officers have not fully trusted their new subjects, most of whom used to work for the guerrillas in one capacity or another. Hence, the new Amajchel civil patrol was not given rifles at first, until after the EGP penetrated the village to shoot at the garrison.

Owing to their exposed geographical position, the Amajchel patrollers were forced to join the army's periodic forays against their relatives and neighbours in the CPRs. Aside from shoot-outs with guerrillas, this meant helping soldiers burn huts, carry away livestock, slash maize fields and capture 300–400 refugees. Sometimes it also included killing non-combatants who were trying to run away. The body count was nothing like the slaughters of the early 1980s, but I

heard of two deaths, and there could be more. 'The army forced us', one patroller admitted:

We had to obey, if we didn't there was punishment – they send us out to cut firewood with a dull axe. If the lieutenant says we have to burn a house, we just say, *está bien*. It's true that we went out to capture people, we went out to burn huts, we went out to cut down maize, but it's not true that we went out to kill people. It wasn't our fault.

Having defected from the guerrilla movement, then participated in army offensives, the Amajchel patrollers earned the enmity of their CPR neighbours, and of the guerrillas too. While the guerrillas usually pay for the supplies they requisition, they simply robbed travellers from Amajchel. In early 1992, some Amajchel families moved out of their overcrowded settlement to a new one at a place called El Pino. Ignoring EGP warnings, the group had just put up huts when the guerrillas arrived to burn them out. Because the new village would have sat astride the trail between CPR zones to north and south, it could have become a base for civil patrol interdiction of people travelling between the two.

When I visited Amajchel in May 1994, the patrollers had not gone out on any expeditions for two years. They learned their lesson after five were killed and seven wounded in April and May 1992 – most on a single day when the guerrillas lured them into an ambush. 'Many orphans were left behind. That was a sad day in the village', one survivor told me. 'That was the end of the sweeps', said another. 'Not any more', the villagers told the army, 'it's not that we're guerrillas, it's that we have families'. Thereafter, serving in the civil patrol meant keeping a rifle in one's house and mobilising for emergencies.

Another sign of the EGP's enmity was its assassination of four men from Amajchel in non-combat situations.[12] The last was that of a respected elder named Pedro Brito. He disappeared on 23 May 1993, a year after the Amajchel civil patrol stopped helping the army raid the CPRs, and as guerrilla leaders insisted on human rights guarantees in national peace negotiations. During his years in the *montaña*, Pedro Brito spent 4 years as a *responsable* for the guerrillas, a job which involved collecting food for them from 30 families. Fed up with the privations of life with the EGP, he was one of the first refugees around Amajchel – and perhaps the first leader – to change sides, in November 1987. He also helped lead the army-sponsored resettlement of Amajchel. When encountering CPR members on trails, he would invite them to come live there too.

Since the late 1980s the EGP has not had a reputation for punishing civilians who change sides. Yet in the case of Pedro Brito and other former comrades at Amajchel, the guerrillas were said to be looking for them, interrogating passers-by on trails and writing down names in notebooks. Shortly before Pedro disappeared, the guerrillas showed up at the village cemetery and issued a challenge. Referring to him as commander of the civil patrol – a function he never performed, being exempt from service as a 48-year-old village leader – they dared him to come out with his men for a fight.

About 20 days later, on an afternoon when the guerrillas opened fire on the army garrison, he failed to return from his chilli patch. His wife found numerous boot prints, which a search party followed to a place where someone had been tied to a tree. Months later, a story began to circulate, of Pedro Brito's calvary. Attributed to a source who I was able to identify but not interview, the story is that Pedro Brito was paraded through CPR villages and presented as a traitor. He is also said to have been kept without food for weeks, then forced to dig his own grave before being shot.

Life at Amajchel continued to be anxious in mid-1994, partly because the army had evacuated its hill-fort as part of a wider pullback. To avoid falling into the EGP's hands, men continued to travel in and out of the village only at night. They were not just afraid of the guerrillas. They were also afraid of CPR civilians who they had a hard time distinguishing from guerrillas. Such individuals are *semi-alzados* (part-time combatants), I was told, and they are organised into the Local Irregular Forces (FILs). The EGP stopped referring to its FILs long ago. CPR leaders deny any knowledge of them. As far as I know, they have never been mentioned in human rights reports. But serving in the FILs comes up regularly in testimony of peasants who lived under EGP administration.

'We had to patrol for them [the guerrillas] when we were down there', an ex-EGP auxiliary turned army civil patroller told me bitterly. 'We had to patrol for them [the army] when we came here. It's just the same.' Interestingly, the FILs pre-dated the army's civil patrols, and it can be argued that they provided a model for the army's far wider militarisation of civilian life.[13] According to the EGP in 1981, the FILs:

[are] made up of young men and women who undergo military training in their home village, and whose role is self-defence of the population: guard duty to detect enemy presence, laying ambushes ... with 'popular arms' and explosives, capturing unknown persons suspected of being enemy agents. They also act as messengers to guarantee communication between villages and with guerrilla units, and they carry supplies for the guerrillas.[14]

As the FILs functioned in the CPRs of the Sierras into the early 1990s, according to an ex-CPR member, volunteers served for a month at a time, for perhaps three times a year, in squads of eight to ten, and carried Galil or M-16 assault rifles. Their tasks included hauling supplies from the Ixcán; carrying wounded guerrillas; and defending settlements from the army, a task which evidently included keeping the Amajchel civil patrol intimidated. Amajchel villagers told me about experiences with FILs who included their own estranged relatives. How do you know that CPR members are still active with the guerrillas? I asked a man from Amajchel. On four occasions he had seen men from the civilian population with guerrillas. What happens when they stop you? I asked. 'We're kept for an hour, or an hour and a half. Of course we're afraid. Someone could say, "This one has patrolled, that one has patrolled."'

It should be emphasised that these are the only complaints I received about the FILs, the most recent of which dated to early 1994. Any problems posed by FILs are dwarfed by the far more widespread problems posed by the army's civil patrols, so the two should not be equated as commensurate, at least beyond this locality. But I would like to draw several implications. First, like the army's civil patrol, the FILs make it harder to define a civilian population that is off-limits to military action. Second, just as the army is held responsible for civil patrollers exceeding their authority, the EGP and the CPRs could be held accountable for abuses committed by armed auxiliaries, even if these are pursuing private vendettas. Third, the Amajchel complaints against the FILs underline the importance of not automatically reserving victim status and legitimacy to one side of a conflict.

Surviving the End of the Army Blockade

The land problem was, is and will be a huge problem. We have to open our eyes to this fact. We have to open up our conception of human rights. We can't continue denouncing the army as the only problem ... (Ricardo Falla, author of *Massacres in the Jungle*, 1994)[15]

The army dissembled its offensives against CPR villages, but these continued until a United Nations representative, Christian Tomuschat, witnessed a helicopter attack on one in April 1991. Since then, the army's response to human rights pressure has been sophisticated. While continuing to identify the CPRs as a guerrilla logistical base, it relaxed its commercial blockade against them, making it easier for members to go home if they wished.

Until this point, the army had killed anyone it caught engaged in trade between the CPRs and the villages it controlled. By the army's

definition, anyone who lived outside the villages it controlled was a guerrilla. The army's blockade was second only to its scorched-earth offensives in making life in the *montaña* miserable. Food was usually not a problem, but commodities that had to be purchased – including tools, clothes and boots, medicine and salt – became too costly for most people in the CPRs. Yet the blockade also worked against the army's interest, by reinforcing EGP warnings that a terrible fate awaited refugees who gave themselves up.

As the army relaxed its blockade, in June 1993, a lieutenant-colonel welcomed CPR traders to Chajul. Although occasional harassment continued, it did not take lives, and commodity prices in the CPRs dropped to more reasonable levels, alleviating a serious source of discontent among members. The guerrillas reduced their unpopular practice of requisitioning supplies from buses and trucks, apparently because they could now buy what they needed from the CPRs. The Catholic Church sent a priest, the French-based organisation Médecins sans Frontières set up a clinic, and the flow of human rights activists increased through an office which the CPRs set up in Guatemala City.

Yet even after the army gave CPR members and internationalists safe passage through government towns, the CPRs continued to impose their own restrictions on movement, through *permisos* similar to the permit system that human rights pressure has forced the army and its civil patrols to abandon. The controls on outsiders, leaders explained, were a necessary form of protection from army spies. As CPR members became an everyday presence in government towns, townspeople resented that they still had to apply for permission in order to reciprocate.

CPR committees also applied the permit system to their own members. The stated reason was to make sure that members returned safely from visits to army-controlled towns, but another was to discourage them from going home permanently. Up to early 1994 (but not after that), I talked to four different men who used deception to make good their departure from the CPRs. None feared for their lives, but they wished to avoid an overpowering display of moral and political persuasion from a CPR committee.

One reason for discouraging members from going home was to protect the cohesion of the group against a paradoxical effect of the new era. If ending the blockade removed a major source of discontent with life in the *montaña*, it also undermined the rationale for being there. As CPR members began to visit government-controlled towns, what they saw contradicted years of political education revolving around the theme that conditions had not changed since the early 1980s.

Once assured that soldiers would not murder or rape them, more wished to return to their old villages.

Lurking behind the reluctance of CPR leaders to allow members to return home was another sensitive issue, that of how many people actually lived under their authority. When I interviewed a delegate in 1992, he gave me the widely published figure of 6,000 people in the CPRs of the Ixcán and 17,000 in those of the Sierra. Strangely, even after the 1994 national census obtained a *permiso* from the CPR office in the capital to count its population, the leadership in northern Quiché refused to honour it. No census was allowed, nor was this the first time that the CPRs suddenly backed out of a head count.[16] When I visited the CPRs in August 1994, not a single person would admit knowing the number of families in his village – information on the tongue of anyone in a government settlement. What appeared to be separate villages on the CPR map proved, on inspection, to be different neighbourhoods in what amounted to the same village. Judging from various sources, the CPRs of the Sierra contain no more than half the 17,000 people they used to claim, and possibly only a third.[17] Yet this may prove to be good news for everyone concerned, for reasons to which we will now turn.

The Underlying Conflict, Over Land

We've already been here for years. The government should replace the land the Chajules had. They should be paid for it. They have to recognise our land here because we've been defending it for more than thirteen years. We've paid for it with our blood, our children have been born here, we have our crops here, and the government has not arranged other land for us. So where we are going to go? If they kick us out of here, we don't have anywhere else. (CPR member refuting Chajul's claim to CPR land, 1994)

What refugees are supposed to want, above all, is to return to their homes. But what the CPRs of the Sierra wanted, above all, was to stay where they were, on land in the Ixil town of Chajul. Because Chajul is a large jurisdiction, until recently its native Ixil population was willing to accommodate other smallholders who respected the authority of the Ixil-dominated local government. But the Chajules also have a reputation for defending their land from usurpers, whether *ladino* plantation owners or Mayan peasants, who fail to go through proper channels. For the Chajules, who understand little of the national land-titling system and care for it less, the proper way to homestead land in their *municipio* is through their own town hall.[18]

Just before the internationalists passed through Chajul on their February 1993 march to the CPRs, the Ixil mayor warned his

constituents that the foreigners were about to give away their land. 'Rise up people of San Gaspar Chajul!' he shouted through a loudspeaker on another occasion. 'Because today arrives a commission to take away our lands!' To the internationalists, the accusation was sheer demagoguery: they had come to Ixil country to protect refugees from the army, not to become involved in land disputes. Yet the fears of the Chajules were well-founded.

Prior to the war, hundreds of families hacked out clearings in the cloud-forested mountains north of town. Most left during the violence, to be replaced by refugees fleeing the violence in Nebaj and other municipalities. As if to compensate their suffering, the newcomers found themselves on land that was lower, warmer and more fertile than the worn-out elevations they had fled – the best land in the area still open to peasants, where they could grow coffee, fruit and two maize crops a year.

Unfortunately for the CPRs, their rights as wartime squatters were not recognised in the 1994 refugee agreement signed by the government and the guerrilla movement, as a step in the peace talks that continue as this book goes to press. Instead, the negotiators assumed that peasants forced off their land by the violence would want to return to their former holdings. Judging from the agreement, just as CPR members have the right to return to their villages before the war, the previous Chajul owners have the right to return to properties currently occupied by the CPRs.

With the two populations cut off by the war, the issue of ownership remained dormant until 1992–93, when the arrival of foreign delegations provided an unmistakable sign that hostilities were ending. The steady stream of internationalists through Chajul seemed to legitimise the appropriation of a treasured agricultural frontier. Chajules also resented the crown of martyrdom that the foreigners suddenly bestowed upon the CPRs. The opportunity for offence was high because there is a certain amount of boasting and resentment between villagers on the two sides – who lives in more miserable conditions, who gets the most aid, who has to waste the most time working for the army or the guerrillas. From the Guatemalan left, meanwhile, internationalists picked up the condescending vocabulary of 'controlled' government villagers who failed to match the heroically resistant CPRs.

The CPRs tried to blame their conflict with the Chajules on army manipulation. It is true that the army, the civil patrol and various Chajul politicians did their best to agitate around the issue. But the CPRs of the Ixcán north of Ixil country faced similar problems, not only with army-organised civil patrollers but also with returning refugees from Mexico organised by the Guatemalan left.[19] In Chajul, the CPRs

contributed to the anxiety by giving off only vague and contradictory signals on the critical question of when, if ever, they would vacate the properties they occupied during the war.

Even local human rights activists – Ixils who welcomed contacts with the CPRs and appreciated the presence of the internationalists – were preoccupied by the uncooperative attitude. 'They expect to have three years more, but our people will not wait for three years', one Chajul activist warned. He also said that the CPRs were boycotting his organisation – the local branch of the archbishop's human rights office – because it had asked for talks on the land issue. Stung by the Chajul mayor's Red-baiting, the CPRs refused, not just to recognise the authority of the municipal government, but to discuss the land issue with it, arguing instead that the problem would have to be resolved in the national-level peace process.

The CPRs versus Civil Patrollers at Amajchel

The CPRs have no business on our land. That international commission ... watching out for the CPRs is to blame for encouraging them to commit these misdeeds, because several of its members asked if we could sell our lands to the CPRs. ... We're poor and they want to leave us poorer. (Letter of protest against CPR land claims, Amajchel, 1994)

One of the villages in the *municipio* of Chajul where the land issue was surfacing was Amajchel. Two kin groups from before the war – one numbering 17 families and the other eleven – were preoccupied that CPR members were settling permanently on their land, in a place called Santa Clara. According to one of the groups, when three of its men went out to inspect their property in December 1992, they were run off by a mob threatening them with machetes. Later the CPR authorities of Santa Clara tried to resolve the dispute peacefully, by inviting the pre-war owners to 'join our struggle' – that is, to come live under CPR authority. 'But we don't want to any more', one of the Amajchel owners told me, 'now we've seen their lies'.

The disagreement dated back to the first army offensives, in which pre-war owners viewed the settlement of refugees on their land with mixed emotions. According to a CPR leader, the pre-war settlers of Santa Clara were fighting each other over land before the refugees even showed up – a possible motive for some of the threats, robberies and killings attributed to the EGP or its FILs. 'From our arrival we found families very divided over land', the CPR leader recalled. 'The families were very isolated, and when they got drunk at times they would fight. This kind of disagreement goes back forever, they always were fighting and moving their boundary markers.'

Shortly before I visited in May 1994, the Amajchel villagers wrote a letter with the help of a government schoolteacher: it was addressed to the 'person in charge of human rights' in Chajul and signed with 98 thumb prints. Some excerpts include:

We have made countless requests [to the CPRs], but they do not understand, perhaps they have lost their reason, telling us that although we have our documents they're not worth anything, that they're in charge and no law will stop them. ... The CPRs have made life impossible in our village, they talk so much about human rights, but they themselves are the worst violators. ... In what head could fit everything they do to us? Taking away land from *campesinos*; eating and destroying our crops ... building their houses on our properties; and wanting us to join their struggle again ...

Until this point, CPR leaders had always maintained that, once peace returned, their members would return to their homes or seek land elsewhere. What their members said, however, is that they wanted to stay – in possession of some of the most coveted real estate in Ixil country. While a minority of CPR members went home to their pre-war holdings around the Ixil towns, others had little to go back to, typically because it had been pre-empted by siblings, not to mention the problem of where to situate their own children. Still others wished to re-establish themselves in their old villages and hold onto their new claim in warm country, fulfilling the *campesino* dream of cultivating across ecozones.

Soon after the villagers of Amajchel poured out their complaints, the CPRs ratified a new position at their 1994 annual assembly. As victims of army offensives and as a displaced population, the CPRs now claimed the right to stay where they were. The following year, the CPR annual assembly discussed how to persuade international agencies to build a road into what they now considered their own property. At least a few CPR members were also inviting relatives living elsewhere to come join them.

As for the pre-war Chajul owners, the CPRs said they were welcome as long as they submitted to the new form of authority. But most of the old owners were not willing to do that, because the CPRs were not simply peasant communities: they were also a popular organisation of the left with political commitments which many of the old owners rejected. Because of their bitter experiences with the guerrillas as well as the army, these Chajules did not want anything more to do with the left, at least in its present form. Recognising the chasm, the CPR assembly demanded that the government buy out the Chajules.

But even if an international agency could be found to put up the money, what of the old owners who insisted on their right to go back

to their homes? Of the latter there would probably be many. 'The people here don't want to sell', a Catholic catechist trying to mediate between the two sides told me. '"We have children and grandchildren, and where are we going to put them?" they say. Here the culture has everything to do with the land. The only thing a father can give his son is land.' Moreover, because a new Catholic association was having great success selling smallholder coffee in Europe, many now wanted coffee-growing land of their own.

Organised in a protest committee, hundreds of Chajules were soon claiming to have occupied every square metre of CPR territory before the war. The mayor of Chajul obliged by handing out documents attesting to prior possession, to any constituent who asked for one. These writs had little legal standing above the municipal level, but the ones that were phoney would complicate any settlement, and if the worst came to the worst they would strengthen the rationale for confrontation.

Angry Chajules were not just claiming what they had cleared and cultivated before the war, which by local custom clearly belonged to them. They also were claiming the surrounding forest, which meant disrespecting the right of newcomers to clear land for themselves. Some Chajules talked about using violence to extract the CPRs from their land. 'They have to be chased out with bullets', a Chajul student told me. 'Even the children?' I asked. 'Yes, all of them, because otherwise they hide. ... They're guerrillas because they're outside the *pueblo* and that's where the guerrillas are, they're guerrillas.'

Ixils versus K'iche's at Los Cimientos

'We are supported by the international,' they say, and this is why they don't want to move. I'm not against them [the internationalists] providing help, but they shouldn't take the side of the Chiules [the K'iche' Mayas of Los Cimientos]. What are they doing there? It's like taking a plate of food from one child to give it to another. Now we don't like *gringos* much here. That they put themselves in between, fine. But that they take one side, no. (Mayor of Chajul, 1995)

Because land is distributed so unequally in Guatemala, between an export-oriented plantation sector and peasant smallholdings, human rights activists tend to assume that most land conflicts are between Mayan peasants and *ladino* plantation owners. This certainly occurs, and it could be argued that the most important land disputes are of this nature, but confrontations between Mayas are far more frequent, including those between Ixils and *ula'* ('those who come from afar'), an uncomplimentary term for the K'iche' Maya colonists who have

moved into northern Quiché over the last century. Quarrels between Ixils and *ula'* fester up and down the valley of the Río Copón, along the eastern border of Ixil country.

If we look at a map from the national registry, the land to the south and east of Ixil country is covered with a grid of nationally registered private titles. They date to the country's liberal (capitalist) reform in the late nineteenth century, which gave outsiders the right to claim land in Mayan towns. Most of the titles were obtained first by *ladinos*, but many have passed into K'iche' hands. In contrast, the registry map for Chajul is mainly blank, reflecting the municipal land grants under which Ixils continue to hold and transfer title among themselves. It is along the frontier between these two cultures of land titling that conflict has bubbled.

The most volatile is at Los Cimientos, along the river that divides Chajul's municipal grant from the private titles to the east in Uspantán. At the surprisingly early date of 1901 – a time when Mayas were still subject to forced labour – K'iche' colonists from the south managed to set in motion the legal machinery to title 1,350 hectares on the Chajul side of the river. As warm-country ridge and valley bottom, it could be used to grow coffee for the booming export economy.

As far as the Ixils of Chajul were concerned, this was their land because it was their *municipio* – an ideology of ownership dating to the colony under Spain.[20] Because the K'iche's had not purchased the land from Chajules, this was another invasion to be resisted, by machete if necessary, leading to several killings in the 1970s. On at least two occasions, the K'iche's obtained court orders to expel Ixil families living within their boundaries. Even though justices of the peace showed up with national police, the Ixils refused to leave or were soon back again.

What forced the K'iche's to abandon their property was the army–guerrilla confrontation, in 1981. The army ordered them to leave and destroyed their village, like everyone else's. For the next decade they subsisted with relatives in Chiul, a village in Cunén just south of Ixil country through which their grandparents had passed. Meanwhile, Los Cimientos became a strategic location on the southern edge of the CPRs. In 1988 the army asked the displaced K'iche' owners, by now organised into a civil patrol, to help it resettle the place. Escorted by soldiers, K'iche' civil patrollers began to clear away brush for a garrison and a new village. Just as they were to return with their families, unfortunately, hostile Ixils showed the army their own municipal title. Choosing the path of least resistance, the army decided to alienate hundreds of K'iche's rather than thousands of Ixils, by authorising the latter to resettle Los Cimientos.

Over the next several years, the hapless K'iche's pursued legal remedies, at great cost and with no result. Even if they went to the expense of obtaining an expulsion order, the police would not be able to enforce it any more than they had before the war. The K'iche's even offered to donate land to the Ixils, but their overtures were rejected. Disgusted with the army, the K'iche's stopped patrolling for it and turned to the Guatemalan left. Coming to their aid was the 'Runujel Junam Council of Ethnic Communities' (CERJ) and its founder Amilcar Méndez, who have won international honours (including the Robert F. Kennedy Human Rights Award) for opposing compulsory service in the army's civil patrols.

To present the situation in terms of human rights, the K'iche's minimised their long-standing feud with the Ixils. Instead, they set up a more familiar target for human rights activists, by blaming the entire problem on the army garrison. The Ixils, said the K'iche's, were just civil patrollers sent out by the army. Unfortunately, the anti-military argument began to unravel in March 1994 when the army suddenly evacuated its post. Soon the army began telling the K'iche's that it had nothing against their return, to the point of discouraging its Ixil civil patrollers from mobilising against them. What remained was the problem from before the war: if the K'iche's tried to come back, the Chajules threatened, blood would flow.

In August 1994 the first of several K'iche' contingents returned to Los Cimientos. Instead of trying to dislodge the Chajules from the village, they avoided physical confrontation by camping on a nearby ridge. Unfortunately, that meant settling into coffee groves claimed by another Ixil village, this one in the municipality of Cotzal, with whom the K'iche's had a similar land dispute. As soon as the Cotzaleños of San Marcos Cumlá recovered from their surprise, they became even more agitated than the Chajules of Los Cimientos.

The K'iche's were accompanied by activists from the international human rights network, which has continued to rotate *acompañantes* through the encampment ever since. Before the return, internationalists debated the wisdom of whether to accompany it, with at least one group deciding against. Those on the scene try to serve only as observers, without taking sides. But this is not how they are perceived by the Ixils, one reason being that the internationalists have not offered to accompany them as well, even though they express fear of the K'iche's just as the K'iche's do of them.

As the two sides awaited the arrival of the next official commission, a careful report explained 85 years of confusion over who owns Los Cimientos. The problem is not that the K'iche's obtained a fraudulent title for already-titled land – a common occurrence.[21] Instead, two surveys misled both sides about the location of their boundaries.

The first survey, in 1896, provided the Chajules with a map indicating that their eastern boundary followed the curving line of the Rio Copón – just as the Chajules thought it should. But according to the written description, which the illiterate Chajules failed to comprehend, the boundary of their municipal land grant never actually reached the river. Instead, it went no farther than the ridge above the river, leaving a strip of low, warm land that remained open for private titling – a typical manoeuvre to set aside Mayan land for *ladino* planters. In this case, however, the property was snatched up by K'iche' smallholders.

The second erroneous survey occurred in 1967. A surveyor hired by the K'iche's mislocated a boundary marker, sending their property line south into the Ixil town of Cotzal, where they may be claiming land that does not belong to them.[22] If so, the Ixils of San Marcos Cumlá, Cotzal, should benefit from a rectification of boundaries, along with the K'iche's, leaving the Ixils of Chajul as the losers. Yet when a government surveyor showed up in June 1995, to correct the property lines, the Ixils of Cotzal joined those of Chajul to chase him off.

Meanwhile, human rights lawyers have taken the K'iche' case all the way to the Inter-American Commission on Human Rights in Washington, DC. There the Guatemalan government has agreed, not just to support the K'iche's right to their land, but to compensate them for their wartime losses – an unheard-of concession that could conceivably become a precedent for other cases. What remains is the problem from before the war: how to coax bewildered but defiant Chajules into moving off land they regard as their own.

As the most monolingual, self-sufficient and openly distrustful of the Ixils, the Chajules have the least experience presenting themselves in a favourable light to outsiders. They have minimal legal help, they have been abandoned by the army on Los Cimientos (although not on the CPRs), and sometimes they have issued threats. Since most Chajules are convinced that Los Cimientos as well as CPR territory belongs to them, any town mayor who loses either case will be regarded as a traitor. After one meeting at which national functionaries explained that Los Cimientos belonged to the K'iche's, the mayor of Chajul was distraught. 'What's going to happen to me?' he wept. 'I'm afraid for my life, I have to win for my town, the people demand it, I won't sign anything.'

The Limitations of Victim/Victimiser Dichotomies

If it weren't for the delegations, if there were no internationalists, who knows where it would end, whether we would be alive or dead? The bombing and

shelling has stopped, thanks to the national and international delegations. (Elder from the CPRs, on his first visit to Nebaj in 14 years)

A few years ago, it was impossible to imagine that CPR members would be visiting their families in the Ixil towns, passing back and forth between two political regimes while the war went on. It was also hard to imagine that the K'iche's would be able to return to their land at Los Cimientos. To be thanked is human rights pressure from abroad, channelled through the Catholic Church, the United Nations, and activist networks in Guatemala, the United States and Europe. As a result, the army has virtually ceased military operations against the CPRs.[23] Pastoral workers, UN functionaries and internationalists have become valuable allies, who may be able to help the CPRs find new ways forward that are not defined by the political needs of the army and the EGP.

For internationalists, the CPRs are a model of political education, social organisation and autonomy which they hope will inspire the army-controlled population to reorganise under the left's leadership for a more democratic Guatemala. Despite the current enmities, this is not necessarily far-fetched. CPR members have many kin in government villages, invitations to soccer matches and fiestas are on the rise, and hostility to the CPRs is not pervasive. Instead, it focuses on their perceived connections with the guerrillas and on the land conflict. The first issue will be allayed once the government and the guerrilla organisations can be persuaded to sign a long-delayed peace agreement that requires both sides to demilitarise northern Quiché. But that will hardly resolve the second issue, the land, upon which the CPRs' survival as a social organisation and a political bloc ultimately hinges.

What brought the CPRs to the mountains of northern Chajul was fear of the army. Now that the fear is dwindling, the most evident source of cohesion is the attractive land they occupy. Yet the very headquarters of the CPRs, the village of Cabá, was once a settlement of Chajules who now want their land back. If pre-war owners are allowed to repossess their claims, it will pose many problems for the tight CPR social organisation, in which peasant settlements are also ideologically defined popular organisations.

At the time of writing, the best hope for resolving the land issue is mediation by the Catholic Church. A year ago, in February 1995, the parish priest of Chajul and local human rights activists were able to launch talks between the Chajules and the CPRs. When their efforts stalled, negotiations resumed under the considerable moral authority of the bishop of Quiché. In January 1996, the two sides issued a joint

declaration recognising that 'our roots are one', blaming their conflict on the war, and calling on the government to resolve it – exactly how is not specified.[24] One possibility is finding international donors to buy property for the CPRs elsewhere – if land of acceptable quality can be found, which will be difficult.

Should the CPRs have nowhere to go, the task will remain of persuading, not just the CPRs to allow the Chajules to return to their pre-war holdings, but the Chajules to acknowledge the right of the CPRs to forest they have cleared. If the Catholic Church could talk the CPRs into making painful territorial concessions, that might also help convince the Chajules to recognise the rights of the Los Cimientos K'iche's, who might then be persuaded to donate a modest share of their land grant to Chajules who were there before the war.

The Catholic Church is trying to rebuild common ground between peasants who were divided by the war. Its success in maintaining credibility with both sides, by not dismissing the position of either, suggests that the appropriate role for *acompañantes* is also as mediators rather than advocates. To clarify the non-advocacy role they already claim, the accompaniers at Los Cimientos could mitigate their support for the K'iche' return by offering to post half of their teams in the two affected Ixil villages. In the CPRs, accompaniers could distinguish between supporting the CPRs as a civilian population and backing their claim to pre-war Chajul property. Making accompaniment more bipartisan could contribute to the negotiating climate, by showing each group that international support is not unconditional.

The larger lesson of the Chajul experience is that exalting certain groups of peasants as victims, while reducing the claims of others to army manipulation, overlooks the complexities of a civil war and can alienate peasants from the human rights movement. Foreign activists in Guatemala include people with considerable experience and insight, but two assumptions derived from solidarity presentations in the United States and Europe were still common in 1993–95. One is that social conflicts can be reduced to the Guatemalan army vs. the people, which does not leave room for understanding contradictions between peasants. The other assumption is that the Guatemalan left has already adopted the most legitimate position on an issue, allowing contrary points of view to be dismissed as the result of army manipulation. Not all internationalists share these assumptions as Guatemala struggles toward a peace agreement, but I suspect that they still provide a lowest common denominator for achieving consensus.

In the case of Los Cimientos, what results is a simplistic portrait of Chajul civil patrollers victimising uprooted K'iche's, when both groups were uprooted by the war and both groups were forced to

patrol by the army.[25] In the case of the CPRs, what results is disdain for Chajules who are still displaced from their pre-war properties. 'They don't want to talk with people in government villages', one internationalist observed of some of his colleagues in the CPRs in 1994, 'because they think they're all "sold out". If the people are outside the CPRs, they are "under control" and there's no need to talk with them, no need to pay attention to them.'

Hopefully this kind of paternalism is disappearing. What encouraged it is the left's attribution of the violence exclusively to the army, without reference to the guerrilla contribution, an omission that many human rights activists have taken at face value. For activists, downplaying the guerrilla contribution to the violence has had the virtue of focusing attention on the state and its army, whose involvement is necessary to define an internationally recognised human rights violation. What has dropped out of the picture, unfortunately, is how the disastrous results of guerrilla strategy alienated much of the population that human rights activists want to support.

The cost of not attending to the diversity of peasant opinion is high. I think it is important to pay attention to the Chajul case because it illustrates the danger of dichotomous thinking when foreign activists intervene in complicated local situations. The particular problem in this case is that of reducing conflicts among subordinate groups to state human rights violations, permitting an over-simple classification of the opposed parties into victims and victimisers. The case of the CPRs, Los Cimientos and the Chajules also suggests other issues that need to be attended to, by scholars as well as activists. Can land disputes be publicised without editing out the complexities of mutual victimisation? Is it possible to focus on state involvement in human rights cases without implying that the situation is entirely of the state's making? Are there ways to take into account the conflict between state and international law and local customary law? Surely there are, and dealing with these issues will strengthen the human rights movement.

Notes

1. I would like to thank Barbara Bocek, Richard Wilson, members of the Guatemalan Scholars Network, various human rights activists, and members of the K'iche' community of Los Cimientos for their critical comments on earlier versions of this paper. I would also like to thank the Harry Frank Guggenheim Foundation

and the Woodrow Wilson International Center for Scholars for their generous support of my research.

2. Quoted in 'La "Caravana de la Paz" Visita las CPR', pp. 56–7, *Voces del Tiempo* (Guatemala), no. 6, April–June 1993.

3. Or those who claim to be of Hispanic descent.

4. Cf. Richard A. Wilson, 'Representing Human Rights Violations: Social Contexts and Subjectivities', in this volume.

5. This is a familiar problem for indigenous rights activists and anthropologists. See Ellen Messer (1995: 75–6).

6. 'What are the CPRs?' a former EGP cadre pondered. 'Are they under the control of the guerrillas? Here we no longer patrol [for the army], but we continue under the control of the army. And I believe that it is the same there: they're no longer guerrillas but continue under the control of the guerrillas.'

7. The CPRs of the Ixcán express themselves differently on this point, perhaps because the fighting continues to be heavier and more threatening in their vicinity: 'This is the reason we had to have the army posts moved', a CPR-Ixcán delegate explained, 'because we knew there would be attacks on them'.

   After an attack the guerrillas disperse into the forest and the army can't find them. So the soldiers come after the civilian population instead, and the population has to pay for what the guerrillas have done. The army treats both the guerrillas and the civil population as their enemy; they come into our areas and commit all kinds of violations. ... So if the guerrillas want to fight the army, we ask that they fight over there and not in our area. 'Interview with CPR Leader Vicente Ramírez Calmo: "The People Will Always Be in Resistance"', *Report on Guatemala* 16(1): 10–13, Spring 1995.

8. 'It was during this period that the guerrillas appeared and the army began to capture the people, saying "you work with the guerrillas"', a Catholic catechist told me.

   Many catechists disappeared, and the people began to flee. When the army saw that the people fled, it began to burn the houses. And when it found the people in church, meeting together to pray, it killed everyone. So we all decided to defend ourselves in the forest. But if we worked alone, the army could kill us. This is how collective work began. ... In the beginning there were just local committees, in Salquil and Sumal. When we relocated around Amajchel, we found ourselves with people who arrived together from other places like Aguacatán. So the idea developed of forming area committees, around 1985.

9. 'Guatemala: Talk with rebel leader', *Noticias de Guatemala*, 9 December 1981: 13 (interview with leader of the Frente Guerrillero

Comandante Ernesto Che Guevara); see also 'El pueblo se hace guerrilla', *Noticias de Guatemala*, 20 October 1981: 4–7.

10. Simon Mejía Puc, 'Silvia Solórzano Foppa: En Guatemala, guerrilla y pueblo somos lo mismo', *Uno Mas Uno* (Mexico, D.F.), 27 June 1982: 6–7.

11. Henrik Hovland, personal communication.

12. The first three were men in their late teens or early 20s:

> *Tomás de la Cruz* was going out to his old house site to recover a grinding stone on 27 March 1989, about the time Amajchel was re-established, when he was taken prisoner by the guerrillas and later killed.
> *Nicolas Cobo Jacinto* was working in a field when the guerrillas took his watch. He reacted with his machete and was shot through the head and the heart, on 9 August 1989. Like Tomás de la Cruz, he was an adolescent who had spent about half his life in the *montaña* under EGP administration. He was not a member of the civil patrol, having been on a visit with his mother.
> *José Brito Raimundo* had recently left the CPRs, presented himself to the army, and lived in Amajchel for about two months when he was captured by guerrillas, on 27 May 1991. According to a cousin who was released after being robbed of 700 quetzals, the guerrillas accused them of burning CPR houses and destroying maize fields.

13. Yvon Le Bot (1992: 201).

14. 'Guatemala: Talk with rebel leader', *Noticias de Guatemala*, 9 December 1981: 13.

15. Falla's (1992) book about the Ixcán region north of Chajul, provides the most detailed description of army massacres during the early 1980s.

16. Following lengthy negotiations, in 1992 a medical team from the International Red Cross arrived to vaccinate children. The CPR leadership had agreed to the participation of a single representative of the Guatemalan government. Yet this condition became the rationale for a stormy demonstration at the team's arrival, on grounds that the vaccinations could be poisoned. As a result, the vaccination campaign was not carried out. One possible explanation is that the campaign would have revealed the true population level, which could have reached the national Red Cross, which is typically headed by a retired army officer.

17. By way of comparison, the CPRs of the Ixcán now claim only half as many members as they used to.

18. Most Ixils hold, inherit and sell family land through a municipal land grant administered by their town hall. The only paperwork is rustic, such as an old document of sale with vaguely specified boundaries. Neighbourhood consensus on the boundaries of family holdings is necessary to avoid conflict. Other properties have been carved out of the municipal land grant by registering them with the national government. Although these properties are supposed to be surveyed, on the ground there is often considerable disagreement over where the boundaries lie. If a claimant within the municipal grant becomes dissatisfied with how he is faring at the local level, he can escalate his claim (along with the legal costs for himself and his adversary) by registering it at the national level, removing the case from the town hall's jurisdiction. This two-tier system grew out of the Liberal Reform of the late nineteenth century, which opened up Mayan-controlled *municipios* to *ladino* plantation owners without destroying the earlier system inherited from the colonial regime under Spain. As for how conflicts between the two systems are resolved, the results are perhaps better described in terms of conflict magnification. In Chajul the older, municipal system has been challenged by outsiders – first *ladinos*, then the K'iche's of Los Cimientos (see below), and now the CPRs – who do not trust in the ethnic authority of an Ixil-dominated town hall and appeal to the superior legal standing of the national system.

    The most thorough study of traditional land ownership in the region is Shelton Davis (1970), while the most vivid portrait of how land ownership has evolved nationally is David McCreery's (1994) *Rural Guatemala 1760–1940*.

19. The refugees in question settled in the Ixcán rainforest in the 1970s, only to be driven over the border into Mexico in the early 1980s when the army reacted to EGP activity by massacring villagers. After more than a decade in refugee camps, thousands of these former Ixcán colonists are returning from Mexico to find that the army has resettled other peasants on their land. Because the CPRs of the Ixcán have also settled on some of the pre-war holdings of refugees returning from Mexico, the local popular movement has divided over how to deal with the problem, to the point that one faction may accuse another of being manipulated by the guerrillas. ('Internal Conflicts Surface in Ixcán Grande Cooperative', *NCOORD Newsletter* 3(6): 8–11, October 1995, Chicago: National Coordinating Office on Refugees and Displaced of Guatemala.) Another problem that the CPRs of the Ixcán face is how to hold together as an organisation now

that trade has reopened with government villages, enabling members to resume their separate interests in a capitalist economy (Perillo 1995: 8–9, 13).

20. As the town's mayor told me in 1995:

    they are not of the Chajul race, they're from Cunén, which does not border Chajul. ... How is it that they can jump from Cunén to here? They showed up to borrow land, and the people lent it to them. More people showed up and they grabbed land. There was a government from which they solicited vacant land, but it was not vacant, it was occupied by my people, and the government did not check with the town hall. The Chiules [the local term for the K'iche's, by their village of origin] just told the government that it was vacant, but they should have investigated.

    The disputed area was only thinly settled when the K'iche's arrived, if that, but they claimed a lot of it, including what became two Ixil villages.

21. As suggested inaccurately in my earlier report on Los Cimientos, 'Guatemala Solidarity Activists Head for Trouble', *Christian Century*, 4 January 1995: 17–21.

22. Comisión Técnica Jurídica, 'Documento Final, Los Cimientos, Quiché', February 1995, Guatemala.

23. The most recent incursion was on 21 April 1994, when soldiers occupied the CPR community of Pal and accused the population of being guerrillas. In contrast to the assaults of several years before, the army did not burn houses, destroy crops or take prisoners. It did point guns at various people and appropriate sugar cane (CPR press release, 29 April 1994).

24. 'Joint Declaration on Chajul/CPR-Sierra Conflict', *NCOORD Newsletter* 4(1): 15–16, January/February 1996.

25. In the 1980s, when the civil patrols accompanied the army on counter-insurgency sweeps, some of the Ixils who now live in San Marcos Cumlá were still in the *montaña* under EGP administration, while the civil patrollers hunting them included the K'iche's of Los Cimientos.

References

Davis, Shelton. 1970. 'Land of Our Ancestors: A Study of Land Tenure and Inheritance in the Highlands of Guatemala', PhD dissertation, Harvard University.

Falla, Ricardo. 1992. *Massacres in the Jungle*. Boulder, CO: Westview Press.

Le Bot, Yvon. 1992. *La Guerre en terre Maya*. Paris: Editorial Karthala.

McCreery, David. 1994. *Rural Guatemala 1760–1940*. Palo Alto, CA: Stanford University Press.

Mejía Puc, Simon. 1982. 'Silvia Solórzano Foppa: En Guatemala, guerrilla y pueblo somos lo mismo', *Uno Mas Uno* (Mexico, D.F.), 27 June 1982: 6–7.

Messer, Ellen. 1995. 'Anthropology and Human Rights in Latin America', *Journal of Latin American Anthropology* 1(1): 48–97.

Perillo, Robert. 1995. 'CPRs of the Ixcán: New Challenges to a Collective Way of Life', *Report on Guatemala* 16(l): 8–13.

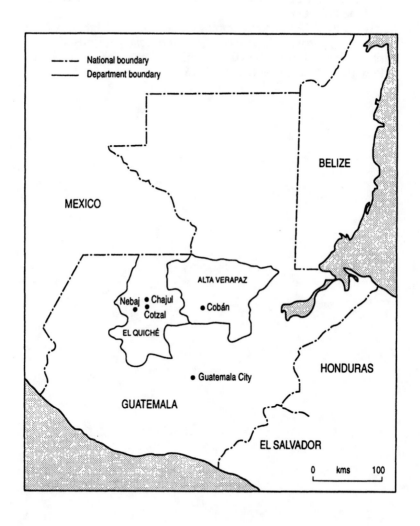

National boundary
Department boundary

BELIZE

MEXICO

ALTA VERAPAZ

Nebaj • Chajul
Cotzal • Cobán

EL QUICHÉ

• Guatemala City

HONDURAS

GUATEMALA

EL SALVADOR

0   kms   100

INDEX

Africa societies, concept of human
    rights in, 13
agency, in legal process, 14–15
Algiers Declaration on Rights and
    Duties of Peoples (1976), 42
Alonso Perez, Conrado,
    Guatemalan lawyer, 167, 170,
    172–3, 174–5
Amajchel village (Guatemala)
    EGP murders in, 196–7, 212n
    local feuds, 195–8, 202–4
American Anthropological
    Association (AAA), 1, 2, 5
    and basic rights, 74
American Convention on Human
    Rights, Guatemala and, 171
American Indians, concept of
    human-ness, 6
Americas Watch Committees,
    human rights reporting by,
    147–8
Amnesty International
    on common or state crime in
        Guatemala, 141, 158n
    form of reports, 142–3, 147, 150
    increased context in reports,
        135, 155
    reliability of, 151
    Rossi murder unreported by,
        139
    use of subjectivity, 152
anthropology, 15
    cultural relativism of, 28
    and culture, 1–3
    philosophical, 24n, 89

role in human rights reporting,
    135, 157
army see military regime
    (Guatemala)
Arzu, President, of Guatemala, 180
Australia
    Aboriginal land claims, 96
    Aboriginal management of
        Ayres Rock, 95
authorship, of human rights
    reports, 150–1, 152
AVANCSO research institute
    (Guatemala), 147

Bangkok Declaration of Asian
    States (1993), 15
Barth, Fredrik, on holistic model of
    society, 10
basic needs, theory of, 102
Bengal, famine in, 76
Bentham, Jeremy
    on natural rights, 4
    on pain and suffering, 116–17,
        130–1n
    utilitarianism, 83
Berlin, Isaiah, on freedom, 90
Beteta Alvarez, Noél Jésus, Mack
    murder suspect, 144, 145, 154
black civil rights
    South Africa, 71
    United States, 88–9
Blaisdell, Kekuni, Hawaiian
    Sovereignty Movement, 37
Boas, Franz, cultural relativism of,
    50
Bosnia, ethnic identity in, 101

217

Printed in the United States
109705LV00002B/70/A

9 780745 311425